Judgment Calls

Judgment Calls

Principle and Politics
in Constitutional Law

DANIEL A. FARBER
AND SUZANNA SHERRY

OXFORD
UNIVERSITY PRESS

2009

OXFORD
UNIVERSITY PRESS

Oxford University Press, Inc., publishes works that further
Oxford University's objective of excellence
in research, scholarship, and education.

Oxford   New York
Auckland   Cape Town   Dar es Salaam   Hong Kong   Karachi
Kuala Lumpur   Madrid   Melbourne   Mexico City   Nairobi
New Delhi   Shanghai   Taipei   Toronto

With offices in
Argentina   Austria   Brazil   Chile   Czech Republic   France   Greece
Guatemala   Hungary   Italy   Japan   Poland   Portugal   Singapore
South Korea   Switzerland   Thailand   Turkey   Ukraine   Vietnam

Copyright © 2009 Daniel A. Farber and Suzanna Sherry

Published by Oxford University Press, Inc.
198 Madison Avenue, New York, New York 10016

www.oup.com

Oxford is a registered trademark of Oxford University Press.

Library of Congress Cataloging-in-Publication Data
Farber, Daniel A., 1950–
Judgment calls : principle and politics in constitutional law /
Daniel A. Farber and Suzanna Sherry.
   p.   cm.
Includes bibliographical references and index.
ISBN 978-0-19-537120-8
1. Judicial discretion—United States.   2. Judicial process—United States.
3. Law—United States—Interpretation and construction.
I. Sherry, Suzanna.   II. Title.
KF8840.F37 2008
347.73'12—dc22   2008012374

This one is for Nora

—D.A.F

For Paul, again and always

—S.S.

Life is painting a picture, not doing a sum.

—Oliver Wendell Holmes

Preface

This is a short book, but it took a long time to write. In two previous books, *Beyond All Reason* and *Desperately Seeking Certainty*, we criticized some currently popular theories like originalism, the view (held by many conservative constitutional scholars) that the Constitution's meaning is fixed by the history of its creation. We also criticized theories of leading scholars at the other end of the ideological spectrum. Having taken shots at the views of so many of our academic colleagues, it seemed only fair that we lay out our own views of how law, and constitutional law in particular, should operate. Easier said than done! It took us longer than we would like to admit to crystallize our own views, let alone write them up in a comprehensible fashion.

Our thesis begins with the assumption that many key constitutional cases leave judges with leeway because the results are not clearly dictated by any source of constitutional authority, whether the language of the Constitution, its history, or precedent. We believe, however, that this leeway does not preclude reasoned decision making. Our major aim is to explain and defend the thesis that even in hard cases, reasoned legal decisions are possible. We also want to show how judges can make such decisions, what kinds of judges are likely to be best at doing so, and which institutional structures are most conducive to reasoned decision making.

One goal of this book is to defend the role of the judiciary, particularly the Supreme Court's role in shaping constitutional law. American constitutional law has developed as a series of Supreme Court decisions erected on a foundation of constitutional text and history. Critics sometimes argue that as currently practiced, constitutional law is just a charade whereby judges conceal their political views and pretend that decisions are based on something beyond personal preferences. Although these critics agree on the diagnosis, they disagree about the cure. Some want judges to play a smaller role, leaving constitutional decisions to the political process; others want judges to follow some methodology that will supposedly lead to objective, nonpolitical results. As to the latter, it is well to recall the words of Justice Cardozo, one of the giants of twentieth century jurisprudence: "[W]e all need to utter [a prayer] at times when the demon of formalism tempts the intellect with the lure of the scientific order."[1]

If judges must attain perfection in order to be legitimate, the critics are clearly correct in their disdain for our current body of constitutional law. But this demand for perfection is a guarantee of failure. We view the judiciary as a human institution, and so we ask only whether the judiciary can do its job well enough to make the enterprise worthwhile. We believe the answer is clearly yes: Judges collectively can do a reasonably good job of deciding constitutional issues, guided by text, precedent, history, and contemporary values. As a great Chief Justice of the Israeli Supreme Court put it, "[t]he life of the law is complex. It is not mere logic. It is not mere experience. It is both logic and experience together."[2]

The materials with which judges work do leave room for leeway, but we think judges can operate within this leeway in a responsible, reasoned way. We think judges do fairly well on the whole; they might do a little better with some changes in legal culture and institutional processes. In short, we think judges can be *both* guided by "the law" *and also* active participants in molding the law.

The biggest barrier to accepting this view is the common assumption that law equates with logic and is therefore the opposite of discretion. We believe, however, that the reasoned exercise of discretion is not an oxymoron. In this, we follow in the footsteps of the old "legal process" theorists of the 1950s, but we reject their assumption that reason will necessarily produce "right answers" if judges are sufficiently smart and sufficiently principled. Decisions inevitably involve judgment calls, and reasonable people will sometimes disagree about the best answers.

We should make a brief comment on references. We provide sources for direct quotations and other key materials in the notes. All of the sources for each paragraph are combined in a single note. For readers who are interested in exploring topics in more depth, we also have a lengthy discussion of the literature at the end of the book.

For readers who have not followed the debates on constitutional theory, it may be helpful to explain some basic terminology at the outset. Here are some key terms:

- *Originalism* is the view that, at least where an issue is not irrevocably settled by precedent, cases should be decided on the basis of the original meaning at the time a constitutional provision was adopted. Sometimes this approach is phrased in terms of the original intent of the framers or the original understanding of those who ratified a constitutional provision. More recently, originalists have tended to refer to the original "meaning" of the constitutional provision. The key element is that constitutional meaning is fixed, at least where it can be ascertained, in the late eighteenth century when the original Constitution and the Bill of Rights were adopted, or in the mid-nineteenth century when the Fourteenth Amendment was adopted. Those holding the opposing view are more apt to refer to the "living Constitution."

- *Textualism* is closely related to originalism, especially in its "original meaning" form, but emphasizes the importance of the specific words used in the Constitution.

- *Foundationalism* is the view that constitutional law should rest on a single value (such as majoritarianism or protection of individual rights) or a single interpretive strategy (such as originalism or textualism) rather than involving a pluralist constellation of values and methods of interpretation.

- *Pragmatism* is a word that seems to mean many things to many people. In the constitutional setting, we view it as entailing the pursuit of multiple goals (such as legal stability, majoritarianism, and protection of minority rights). More generally, it is the view that judicial decisions, at least in hard cases, inevitably require a consideration of values and not merely an "objective" application of authoritative texts (whether constitutional, statutory, or judicial). Constitutional provisions and precedents thus are incapable of generating answers to hard cases on their own—which does not mean they are irrelevant.

- The *countermajoritarian difficulty* refers to the supposedly anti-democratic nature of judicial review, since it allows courts to overturn the handiwork of elected officials. Much of constitutional theory seems to view this as the central problem of constitutional law, although we will argue otherwise.

As with all our books, we could not have done it alone. We thank Stephen Jordan, Andy Lewis, and Hannah Edelman for providing a variety of research assistance, and Dianne Farber and Paul Edelman for carefully reviewing the final text. Janelle Steele took a pile of individual chapters—in two different word processing formats—and turned them into a manuscript suitable for further mix-and-match editing. Over the years during which we worked on this book, four different deans have offered us support, financial and otherwise: Bob Berring, Christopher Edley, Edward Rubin, and Kent Syverud. Finally, we thank the friends and colleagues who have helped us develop and hone our approach to constitutional adjudication. Because this book is an outgrowth of such a long gestation, it is difficult to list all of the individuals who contributed to our thinking. We are, however, deeply grateful to all of those with whom we have discussed these issues, including friends who vehemently disagree with us.

Dan Farber
Berkeley, California

Suzanna Sherry
Nashville, Tennessee

Contents

1 Introduction, 3

I The "Problem" of Judicial Review

2 The Inevitability of American Judicial Review, 11
    The origins of judicial review, 12
    The unsatisfactory alternatives to judicial review, 13
    The Supreme Court and the states, 16

3 The Democracy Worry, 21
    Worries about judicial review, 22
    The countermajoritarian difficulty, 23
    Misguided efforts to escape the countermajoritarian difficulty, 26

II Discretion and Judgment

4 How to Think About Discretion, 35
    Decision making without recipes, 36
    Discretion, legislative and otherwise, 38
    The administrative analogy, 40

5 Reason and Relevance, 43
    The importance of reasoned elaboration, 44
    What arguments are relevant? 46
    How judges should make value judgments, 48
    The risk of overreaching, 50

6 The Anatomy of Judgment, 53
    Judicial reasoning and the common law, 54
    Improving judicial decision making, 56

III Precedent as a Safeguard

7 Respect for Precedent, 63
     Precedent and the rule of law, 64
     The value of precedent, 70
     Precedent and the modern constitutional order, 72

8 Explaining Precedent, 75
     What kinds of precedents? 75
     What does it mean to follow precedent? 78
     Does precedent really matter? 81

IV Process Safeguards

9 Deliberation and Multiple Decision Makers, 87
     Tiered, multimember courts, 88
     Judicial deliberation, 90
     Other structural supports, 93
     Public scrutiny of judicial opinions, 94

10 Transparency, 97
     Failures in transparency, 99
     Arguments against transparency, 102

11 Incrementalism, 105
     Incrementalism and school desegregation, 106
     Incrementalism and the First Amendment, 108
     When process fails, 110

V Internalized Safeguards

12 Professionalism and the Selection Process, 113
     Professional norms, 113
     Judicial selection and politicization, 116
     Some institutional changes, 119

13 The Role of the Legal Academy, 123
     Scholarship and popular perception of the courts, 124
     The traces of postmodernism, 125
     The turn toward novelty, 126
     Suggestions for improvement, 129

VI Case Studies

14 Terrorism, 133

15 Abortion, 141

16 Affirmative Action, 157

Closing Words, 167

Notes, 169

Bibliographic Essay, 181

Index, 197

Judgment Calls

1

Introduction

T HIS IS A book defending judicial review: the power of courts to strike down laws that violate the Constitution. Judicial review was an American invention, but it has spread to most democracies around the world. Courts in countries as diverse as Canada, India, Israel, Germany, and South Africa now exercise the power to enforce their constitutions.

Ironically, American judicial review has seemingly suffered a kind of crisis of legitimacy at home just when it has attained acceptance abroad. Some critics denounce judicial rulings as politics disguised in legal jargon. Other critics seemingly believe that judicial review can be salvaged, but only by adopting some rigid method for deciding cases, such as strict adherence to the original understanding of the Constitution at the time of its adoption. Both sets of critics agree that constitutional law, as it has actually been practiced, allows a few justices to impose their political preferences on the population at large. Their solutions may vary, then, but their diagnosis of the problem is the same: When it comes to judicial discretion, it is either the heavens or the abyss. The rhetoric adopted by critics suggests that constitutional decision making comes in only two flavors: either pure politics or pure formalism. Unless judges in constitutional cases can be tightly constrained by "strict constructionist" approaches such as originalism or textualism—and some do not think this is possible—the only alternative seems to be the unfettered discretion of politicians masquerading as judges. For these scholars, there is no middle ground.[1]

We disagree, and in this book we describe and defend this middle ground. Constitutional decisions can be judicial and principled (and thus firmly rooted in the rule of law rather than in politics), as well as judicious and pragmatic (and thus range beyond the narrow confines of text and original intent). Good constitutional adjudication should be neither the mechanical application of formal rules nor the freewheeling exercise of pure politics.

Lawyers know that some arguments are "rational"—they do not violate any of the rules of logic—but not reasonable; others fail to qualify as legal arguments because they involve extraneous considerations. Our thesis is that judicial decisions can be judged on the basis of this standard of reasonableness—whether their readings of texts are plausible, whether they consider all of the relevant factors (but not others), whether they acknowledge and adequately account for competing considerations, whether they articulate plausible distinctions and intelligible standards—in short, on the basis of the strength of their legal reasoning. This may seem like an uncontroversial thesis—and it should be—but in fact we have received remarkably sharp rejoinders from skeptics.

To be clear, we do not mean that legal reasoning is a purely objective exercise that has no connection to the varying perspectives and values of judges. Judges do not operate in a vacuum, and their worldviews inevitably—and properly—shape their rulings in hard cases. But judges operate in a different world than do legislators. There are both internal and external constraints on their decisions. These constraints do not provide definitive answers to every case. Especially in important cases, reasonable judges may differ about the correct outcome. How judges resolve these hard cases is inevitably connected with their views of the world and their political leanings. But there is a space between ironclad logic and unrestrained discretion, a space in which judges as well as administrative officials often operate. Trying to eliminate this middle ground is fruitless. Instead, we need to consider how judges can responsibly exercise their leeway in deciding hard cases—or in other words, what makes it possible for the rule of law, rather than lawless fiat, to operate in a world that lacks the comforting certainty of mathematical reasoning.

This book seeks to present a new picture of judicial review—new in the way it combines elements, though not in the individual elements. We seek to reconcile the democratic rule of law with the recognition that judges have discretion. That discretion sometimes requires judges to make controversial value judgments. Our argument is directed in part against those who see a stark choice between a formalistic conception of law and raw politics as the basis for judicial decisions. Our approach to constitutional adjudication, then, cannot be captured in a catchword or a set of instructions. We must instead describe in detail the processes by which judges should—and largely do—decide constitutional cases, and the built-in constraints that filter the effect of politics or personal values.

Implicit in this vision of judicial reasoning is an understanding of the role of the Supreme Court in American society. We do not see the Court as either the keeper of ancient wisdom (as some originalists seem to) or a crusader for social reform (as some progressives would like). Rather, we view the Court's role as evolutionary, fostering change and also maintaining stability. Sometimes the Court's role requires it to frustrate the efforts of elected officials or ignore some indications of public opinion. This is not surprising given that a key role of constitutions is to protect political minorities. But constitutions are also meant to empower governments and democratize the political process, and it is not surprising that these too are functions of the Court.

In order to understand how judges should implement this role, we will address a broader range of questions than one might expect to find in a book on constitutional adjudication. Indeed, we will not talk much about the text of the Constitution, because—as we suggest in the next chapter—it usually does not offer much in the way of either guidance or constraint. Instead, we will focus on both positive and negative influences on judicial decision making. So we include a lengthy discussion of the role of precedent as well as comments on seemingly unrelated topics such as legal education, the structure of the American judiciary, and the judicial selection process. Focusing on how all of these influences work together to shape judicial behavior will give a much more realistic picture of judges and judging. It will help us evaluate the current state of constitutional adjudication as well as enable us to suggest improvements.

In the chapters that follow, we try to describe the judicial role from both a positive and negative perspective, to explain both what judges should aspire to and what keeps them from straying too far from those aspirations. The former turns out to be the briefer discussion. Much of our emphasis in this book is on the forces that help channel judicial decision making and prevent it from degenerating into simple fiat. This emphasis is a response to current tendencies to view constitutional decisions as an exercise in ideology or to go to the other extreme by trying to shackle judges to a rigid theoretical framework.

In emphasizing the restraints on judges, we do not mean to ignore the degree of creative statesmanship involved in the judicial role. Good judges do not feel free to make constitutional law into whatever shape they desire, but they do feel the responsibility to advance the basic goals of our constitutional democracy in a changing world. They do not think of themselves as legislators or as having a free-wheeling mandate to improve the world, but they take seriously the impact of their decisions on society.

Taking judging seriously requires us first to place judicial review in context. We begin, therefore, by "normalizing" judicial review. In the next two chapters, we argue that rather than being an antidemocratic aberration, judicial review is an integral part of our constitutional system.

Having rehabilitated judicial review as an American institution, we turn our attention to how good judges make decisions. In chapters 4 through 6, we analyze the concepts of discretion and judgment, showing how to distinguish between arbitrary decision making and responsible legal judgments. These three chapters—part II of the book—form the core of what might be called our positive description of judging. They offer both guidelines for judges who honor the rule of law and criteria for evaluating judicial decision making.

But readers concerned about judicial discretion will want more reassurance. We therefore turn in parts III, IV, and V to the pressures that keep judges from either freely imposing their own values or deciding cases on a purely ad hoc basis. We describe and defend three key safeguards against judicial lawlessness: (1) adherence to precedent, (2) process constraints, including reasoned deliberation, transparency, and incrementalism, and (3) internalized norms. Although these might not seem like powerful restraints on judges' political impulses, we will demonstrate that they do have real effects. We rely not only on our intuitions as students of the legal system, but on rigorous empirical studies. And even where these safeguards do not serve to constrain, they nevertheless provide tools with which to evaluate and critique less than stellar judicial behavior.

Justice Holmes famously said that the life of the law is experience rather than logic. With this injunction in mind, we turn away from abstractions in the final portion of the book to provide some critical examples of how the Court has sometimes succeeded and sometimes failed in its exercises of judgment. As case studies, we have picked three of the most important and sensitive issues that the Court has confronted in the recent past: terrorism, abortion, and affirmative action. None of the judicial opinions in these areas comes close to being perfect. They fail in various ways, and with varying degrees of seriousness, to meet the ideal of reasoned decision making that we have advocated. Nevertheless, they show that judicial decision making is not just a matter of ideology. Precedent, history, and values do matter, and the result is something that cannot be readily dismissed as judicial fiat.

Our purpose is not to place judges on pedestals. They are generally responsible, hard-working individuals, but as prone to error as the rest of us. Nor are they moral prophets or social reformers who can rescue society from its follies. What judges can do, however, through the evolving fabric of constitutional doctrine, is to provide a framework for democratic governance—one that respects the authority of the majority while providing basic protection for minorities. That is not everything, but it is a lot—and it is worth celebrating and protecting.

PART I

The "Problem" of Judicial Review

2

The Inevitability of American Judicial Review

MUCH OF THE discussion about judicial review is distorted by an almost superstitious sense that it is a suspect practice. This attitude leads either to an overwrought fear of undemocratic rule by unelected federal judges, or to an effort to tame this fear by making the judges mere puppets of the framers of the Constitution. This suspicion of judicial review seems increasingly anachronistic in a world in which judicial review is the rule rather than the exception for democracies.

The reason for this spread is simple: Much of the rest of the world has come to share the traditional American view that some basic values are too important to be left entirely to the protection of politicians. Majority rule by itself cannot be trusted to protect religious, political, racial, and geographic minorities from oppression, nor to protect fundamental human rights when they are needed by the powerless or the unpopular. Nor do elections offer a complete check against the desire of politicians to aggrandize their power and enrich their friends. These are lessons Americans learned early, in the years before the Constitution was drafted. Others have learned the lesson more recently in the post–World War II wave of protections for human rights—or even more recently in the post-9/11 world.

In this chapter, we will trace the history of judicial review, showing just how deeply rooted it is in the American tradition. The alternatives simply proved unacceptable. One alternative would have been to abandon the idea of the Constitution as setting enforceable limits on government. Americans, however, have never been willing to give up this idea in favor of treating the Constitution as merely a set of political aspirations. The other alternative was to give other governmental entities, either singly or in combination, the power to make binding interpretations of the Constitution. As we will see, the only serious effort to implement that approach was by the South before the Civil War, where constitutional theorists argued that the states were the ultimate arbiters of constitutional issues. The Civil War demonstrated just how dangerous that idea was. In the end, judicial review emerged as the solution to resolving constitutional disputes and checking political officials.

The origins of judicial review

A casual reader of op-ed columns might come away with the idea that judicial review was invented by Earl Warren in the 1960s. Nothing could be further from the truth. Judicial review has a much deeper history. American courts were exercising the power of judicial review—that is, the power to invalidate statutes inconsistent with a constitution—even before the adoption of the United States Constitution. They have done so ever since.

Chief Justice John Marshall famously defended the practice in the 1803 case of *Marbury v. Madison*, and students are often left with the impression that he invented it out of whole cloth. But judicial review was in fact a common practice long before then. Since that time, courts have used the same power to shape the contours of American federalism, to define the scope of legislative, executive, and judicial authority, and to set the balance between individual rights and governmental power.[1]

In cases whose names are household words and cases that are long forgotten, courts have measured the constitutionality of state and federal statutes, presidential and agency actions, and all manner of state and local governmental conduct. It is judicial review that gives our Constitution its practical bite and makes it more than mere rhetoric. Without it, government officials would be free to evaluate the constitutionality of their own conduct—and it is unlikely that they would find it wanting. States could segregate schools, police officers could coerce confessions, municipalities could ban peaceful protest demonstrations, the president could seize private property, and legislatures could prohibit speech critical of the government. Lest the reader think we are exaggerating: Each of these governmental actions has occurred, and each has been invalidated by a federal court.

The critics we discuss in the next chapter contend that judicial review is flawed in theory because it is undemocratic and flawed in practice because it does at least as much harm as good. These criticisms are weak in their own right, but they also fail to compare judicial review in a realistic way with its alternatives. We cannot ask whether judicial review is desirable without asking "compared to what?" And it turns out that in the American context, the alternatives were all historically untenable, and they remain so today.

Unlike many American legal traditions, which are largely derived from English law, judicial review was an American invention with only a few precursors in English legal thought. But historical circumstances virtually guaranteed that Americans would turn to the judiciary to enforce the limits of their written constitutions. In the American constitutional regime, there are in theory four potential institutional contenders for the title of final constitutional arbiter: the Congress, the president, the states, and the courts. As a historical matter, however, each of the first three possibilities was rejected, leaving only the courts as authoritative interpreters of the Constitution.

The unsatisfactory alternatives to judicial review

The first alternative to judicial review is the traditional (but now changing) English system in which complete power resides in the legislature. Under conventional English constitutional theory, the word of Parliament is the final authority, and no power can limit its autonomy. But in the American context, a similar variety of congressional supremacy was never really in the cards.

Having experienced the excesses of Parliament—in which the American colonies were not represented—the founding generation was determined not to leave Congress as the sole judge of the constitutionality of its own actions. In particular, American revolutionaries preferred Coke's constitutionalism to Blackstone's parliamentary supremacy. In a case that was virtually ignored in England but lionized in the colonies, Lord Coke wrote that "when an Act of Parliament is against common right and reason, or repugnant, or impossible to be performed, the common law will controul it, and adjudge such Act to be void." William Blackstone, on the other hand, opined in his influential *Commentaries* that if Parliament enacts an unreasonable law,

"I know of no power that can control it." American colonists learned to their detriment that Blackstone more accurately portrayed English jurisprudence, and they therefore turned to Coke for inspiration for their own constitutional scheme.[2]

If the colonial experience inclined Americans away from congressional supremacy, so too did constitutional theory. The existence of a *written* constitution, with procedures for amendment, may not be utterly incompatible with legislative supremacy, but it did make it hard to maintain that Congress was the ultimate sovereign in the same sense that Parliament was sovereign in England. Indeed, the quintessentially American faith in the power of legal texts—reflected in a long-standing tradition of written compacts and constitutions going back to the *Mayflower* (literally)—further distanced Congress from Parliament and made legislative supremacy all the more unlikely. And the American fear that republican governments exhibited a universal tendency toward eventual corruption and tyranny led to a need for some check on legislative excesses.

Nor could congressional supremacy rest on a notion of popular sovereignty, since it was hard to identify Congress as the sole embodiment of that sovereignty. With senators allocated on the basis of states rather than population and originally selected by state legislatures (until the adoption of the Seventeenth Amendment in 1913), the Senate could not be considered an incarnation of the popular will. Moreover, the president had at least as good a claim to represent the entire American population as did Congress, and the state governments also had a collective claim to represent the people. As just one of several institutions with a claim to represent the popular will, then, Congress enjoyed no special status as constitutional arbiter and no special right to judge the constitutionality of its own actions.

Thus, by the early decades of the nineteenth century, American commentators saw the courts as guardians of the rights of the people against legislative excess. One described the judiciary as "the bulwark of the Constitution to guard it against legislative encroachments." Another noted that "much reliance was placed on the security, which the due exercise of the judicial power would accord, to the rights of states, as well as of individuals, when infringed or invaded by the encroaching spirit of legislative bodies."[3]

Congressional supremacy is, if anything, even less appealing today. Congress is one of the least popular of all governmental institutions, and there is no chance that the public would entrust it with final authority over all of our liberties.

Presidential supremacy over constitutional interpretation was also more of a theoretical possibility than a real one. The colonists were no happier with the king than they were with Parliament, and indeed a number of early state constitutions provided for a very weak executive. New Hampshire's 1776 constitution had no executive at all.

Later experience—especially during the Revolutionary War—convinced American constitution writers that a somewhat stronger executive would be better able to conduct wars and other foreign affairs, and might also serve as a counterbalance to the legislature. But the mistrust of an overly strong executive lingered. A president who is the final judge of the constitutionality of his own actions—at least in the domestic context—comes close to what one commentator has called "elective Caesarism," and is certainly incompatible with our constitutional traditions. In fact, our system of law has generally evolved in the opposite direction, bringing executive action squarely under judicial oversight. Recent experience, at least in our view, does not inspire confidence in the likelihood that the executive will provide a reliable safeguard for liberty.[4]

In theory, all three branches of the federal government might have shared authority to interpret and enforce the Constitution. Known as "departmentalism," this view has always had some adherents. Under a departmentalist regime, each branch would be supreme within its own sphere: Congress would determine whether its enactments were constitutional, the president would judge his own actions, and the Court would decide which laws it would enforce.

Ultimately we did adopt a form of departmentalism, but in only one direction. Modern judicial review gives the Supreme Court the last word only if it holds an enactment *un*constitutional. If it decides instead that a particular course of action is *consistent* with the Constitution, other governmental actors may still decline to follow the course of action if they believe that it is unconstitutional (or even simply unwise). For example, even if the Court holds that a particular federal law is valid under the First Amendment, members of Congress who think otherwise are still free to vote to repeal that law. Similarly, if the president thinks a proposed law would be unconstitutional, he is free to veto it, even if he believes that the courts would uphold the law. Thus a proposed law can be blocked if Congress thinks it is unconstitutional and refuses to adopt it, if the president thinks it is unconstitutional and refuses to sign it, or if the courts think it is unconstitutional and refuse to enforce it.

Departmentalism thus reigns to the extent that no action can be taken, no law enacted and enforced, unless all three branches of government agree that it is constitutional. This one-way departmentalism provides a particular benefit in a democratic regime. When no single branch can enact its preferences into law, one form of majority tyranny is less likely: Minorities can prevent the enactment of detrimental policies by prevailing in any branch.

A stronger form of departmentalism, however, would give the judiciary the power to check the will of the president or the legislature only when those branches ask for judicial help. That is, the courts could not—as they do now—reach out and declare an act of Congress or the president to be unconstitutional, but could only decline to enforce it when asked to do so. Thus, where the legislature or the executive (or both acting together) could accomplish their goals without involving the courts, the courts could not step in at the behest of an individual to declare the proposed action unconstitutional. In criminal cases, the courts might still refuse to enforce an unconstitutional law, but no individual (or state) could ask the court to strike down or enjoin an unconstitutional act by Congress or the president. Our constitutional history, of course, is rife with examples of the courts issuing just such orders: In *Bolling v. Sharpe*, parents successfully asked the courts to declare segregated schools in the District of Columbia unconstitutional; in the *Steel Seizure* case, steel companies successfully asked the courts to invalidate the president's sei- zure of private property; in *Clinton v. New York*, the state of New York persuaded the courts to strike down the federal Line Item Veto Act; in various Establishment Clause cases, individuals asked the courts—sometimes successfully and sometimes not—to invalidate Congress's allocation of federal funds to religious institutions. There are many other cases like these, and even more in which the courts exer- cised jurisdiction to decide on the constitutionality of federal action but ultimately concluded that the action was constitutional.[5]

The strong form of departmentalism has the same problems as legislative or executive supremacy: It leaves these branches as the sole judges of the constitu- tionality of their own actions, providing no remedy for the founding generation's mistrust of legislative and executive power. Historically, even the few adherents of departmentalism tended to emphasize it mostly in the context of foreign affairs, especially as conducted by the president. To some extent, this is the system we have in foreign affairs: The courts are usually quite deferential to executive decisions— unless those decisions conflict with congressional determinations, in which case the courts must serve as umpires. But a broader form of departmentalism never took hold, largely because of the mistrust of concentrated power. This mistrust is not unfounded: As events since September 11 have shown, presidents are not prone to see the Constitution as a barrier to their favored policies. Moreover, multiple federal interpretations of the Constitution create a potential for uncertainty and instability, a problem that we turn to shortly.

The Supreme Court and the states

History thus left the federal courts and the states as the primary competitors for the role of constitutional arbiter. In this context, however, the most viable prop- osition was not state supremacy, but state autonomy. In other words, federalism offered the possibility of a kind of departmentalism, with the states and the federal government each supreme in their own spheres. This possibility lingered until definitively rejected by the Civil War and its aftermath.

Although the Constitution established the basic structures of federalism—dividing sovereignty between the state and federal governments—defining the exact contours was a source of conflict in the early republic. The dispute over the contours of federalism stemmed from an even more basic disagreement about the nature of American statehood. Was the United States a nation or merely a confederation of states?

Great nationalists like John Marshall and James Madison represented one position and powerful advocates of states' rights, such as John Calhoun, represented the other. The nationalist position prevailed early, at least temporarily. Between 1815 and 1825, Chief Justice Marshall's Supreme Court found itself embroiled in a series of disputes about whether states—especially state courts—had independent authority to interpret the Constitution contrary to the interpretations of the Supreme Court. The issue, as described by Marshall, was whether the states (especially Virginia) were correct to assert that "the constitution of the United States has provided no tribunal for the final construction of itself, or of the laws or treaties of the nation; but that this power may be exercised in the last resort by the Courts of every State in the Union." Marshall described the states' rights position as contending that "the constitution, laws, and treaties, may receive as many constructions as there are States; and that this is not a mischief, or, if it is a mischief, is irremediable." In all of these early federalism cases, the Court rejected the state position and unequivocally affirmed its own authority to oversee and overrule decisions of state courts (as well as state legislatures and executives).[6]

In reaching this conclusion, the justices sketched out the nationalist view of what the Constitution had wrought. In *Martin v. Hunter's Lessee*, Justice Story wrote that "[t]he Constitution was an act of the people of the United States to supersede" the prior confederation of states. Similarly, in *Cohens v. Virginia*, Marshall emphasized: "That the United States form, for many, and for most important purposes, a single nation, has not yet been denied. In war, we are one people. In making peace, we are one people. In all commercial regulations, we are one and the same people." In terms of these and other aspects of national unity, the federal government "alone [is] capable of controlling and managing their interests in all these respects." In short, Marshall said, "America has chosen to be, in many respects, and to many purposes, a nation; and for all these purposes, her government is complete; to all these objects, it is competent. The people have declared, that in the exercise of all powers given for these objects, it is supreme." Rather than being sovereign entities in the fullest sense, Marshall said, the states "are constituent parts of the United States. They are members of one great empire...." In *Cohens*, Marshall, like Story, concluded that the Supreme Court had power to impose its own interpretation of the Constitution and federal law on defiant or mistaken state courts.[7]

But the nationalist view that the United States was a nation rather than a confederation—and therefore that the Supreme Court was the ultimate arbiter of the Constitution, to the exclusion of the states—was not without its challengers during this time. A number of amendments to the Constitution were unsuccessfully proposed to limit federal judicial power and make either the states or the Senate (whose members were then chosen by state legislatures) the final judge of constitutional issues. Some members of Congress attempted to repeal the federal statute that gave the Supreme Court jurisdiction to review state court decisions.

The extreme antinationalist strategy was John Calhoun's theory of interposition and nullification. States, he argued, had the right as independent sovereigns to interpose themselves against abuses of federal power, including federal judicial power. This was so because the Constitution was a compact between states, not a charter that created a single national community. According to Calhoun's *Discourse on the Constitution and Government of the United States*, the federal government "is the government of a community of States, and not the government of a single State or nation." The states "established [the Constitution] as a compact *between* them, and not as a constitution *over* them," and thus "these States, in ratifying the constitution, did not lose the confederated character which they possessed when they ratified it,... but on the contrary, still retained it to the full." For Calhoun and his followers, state interpretations of the Constitution stood on an equal footing with federal court interpretations, since states were coequal sovereigns.[8]

James Madison, the driving force behind the Constitution, is sometimes mistakenly described as an antinationalist. But like John Marshall, Madison was unequivocal and consistent in his belief that the Supreme Court should have the final word on constitutional questions. In response to *Cohens'* rebuke of the Virginia state court, Virginia judge Spencer Roane sought to persuade Madison to write a rebuttal. Madison refused, responding that the "sounder policy" was that federal decisions should prevail when in collision with state courts. As he wrote to Thomas Jefferson a few years later, he believed that the Constitution "intended the Authority vested in the Judicial Department as a final resort in relation to the States," and that such had always been his opinion. In 1830, he denounced Calhoun's nullification theory: "Those who have denied or doubted the supremacy of the judicial power of the U.S.... seem not to have sufficiently adverted to the utter inefficiency of a supremacy in a law of the land, without a supremacy in the exposition & execution of the law." And although Madison had always described the constitutional regime as a "compact" (and would continue to do so), his definition of the compact had more in common with Marshall than with Calhoun. The constitutional compact was among the *people* of the *all* the states rather than among the states themselves, and thus could not be nullified by an individual state or its people.[9]

By the middle of the nineteenth century, then, Americans could draw on at least two competing theories of American nationhood, with very different implications for the power of judicial review. If the United States was a confederation or compact among the states, then polycentric constitutional interpretation—with interpretive authority shared between the states and the federal courts—was a possibility. If, on the other hand, the United States was a unified nation, the Supreme Court was the ultimate constitutional arbiter. The ultimate resolution of this conflict came not in a courthouse, but on the courthouse steps at Appomattox.

The Civil War illustrated in the most graphic way possible the dangers of polycentric constitutional interpretation. While multiple interpretations with no authoritative final arbiter are theoretically possible, they carry an unacceptably high risk of instability. The escalating tensions between the states and the federal government during the first half of the nineteenth century illustrate this instability; the denouement of the Civil War was all but inevitable. And it was the Civil War itself—cemented by the Reconstruction Amendments added to the Constitution after the war—that finally resolved the dispute, definitively rejecting the compact theory (with its implication of nullification and secession) and allocating ultimate interpretive authority to the federal courts. With the exception of a brief and unsuccessful attempt by southern states to revive the interposition doctrine in the wake of the Court's decision in *Brown v. Board of Education*, the Supreme Court's authority vis-à-vis the states has not been seriously questioned since. But, as the next chapter shows, a different challenge to the Supreme Court's authority has recently arisen.[10]

We should emphasize that when we say that the Court is the "final" arbiter of constitutional disputes, we do not believe that the Court operates in a vacuum. The justices partake of the public culture around them. In the long run, the Court can never get too far out of touch with the views of society as a whole, if only because of the influence of new appointments. In the end, the body of constitutional doctrine must be acceptable to the people of the United States and their democratic representatives—not in every single respect, but as an overall fabric. If the Court were not basically acceptable to American society, its rulings would get little credence. But this is a long way from the kind of role that some of the Court's critics envision for the public, as we discuss in the next chapter.

3

The Democracy Worry

WHILE THE EARLY struggles over judicial power involved questions of federalism and nationhood, the modern attacks on the courts stem from concerns about popular sovereignty and separation of powers. Why should unelected, politically unaccountable federal judges be permitted to second-guess legislation enacted by representatives of the people? In this chapter we examine the sources of this discomfort with judicial review, rebut its most exaggerated form, and show how an overdrawn version of the democracy worry has warped much of modern constitutional theory.

At the outset, we should make clear the scope of our argument. We do not mean to argue that the courts are as responsive to shifts in majority opinion, or even to sustained majority opinion on specific issues, as the president and Congress. But we think that there is too frequently a tendency to view judges as if they were self-appointed, all-powerful Platonic guardians, while viewing the democratic qualities of the other branches through rose-tinted spectacles. The difference is one of degree, and even the degree is often exaggerated. It is also easy to forget that majority rule is not our only social value: The Constitution also aims to protect the rights of political, geographic, religious, and racial minorities, among others. An institution that was perfectly responsive to majority sentiment would be unlikely to play such a role effectively.

Worries about judicial review

The modern discomfort with judicial review derives from a number of well-known factors. The unavoidable ambiguity of language guarantees both that the "meaning" of the Constitution is uncertain and that any interpreter will have some amount of discretion. The uncertainty and discretion vary with each clause. It is harder (although not impossible) to disagree on the meaning of a requirement that the president be thirty-five years old than it is to disagree on the meaning of "the equal protection of the laws." The vaguer the clause, the more likely it is to spawn litigation. Constitutional interpretation is thus more art than science, and, in any heterogeneous society, cannot help but create disagreements on all but the most trivial matters. Moreover, the very nature of a constitution, as John Marshall recognized, creates additional interpretive difficulties: Unlike statutes, constitutions tend to be written in general and abstract language, although they must nevertheless be applied to particular situations.

This universal fuzziness of all language is exacerbated, in the case of the United States Constitution, by the age of the language and the multiple authorship—over different time periods—of the document. First, because of this multiple authorship, it is often almost impossible for a reader to reconstruct a single intended "meaning" of any given bit of language. As anyone who has served on a document drafting committee knows, the final product represents various compromises, often deliberately evading particularly sensitive questions or adopting positions that command no support but also spark no opposition. When this group drafting exercise is layered over time, as the Constitution was, the interpretive task becomes even more fluid.

Moreover, the age of the document (the most recently adopted litigation-engendering portions are now almost 140 years old) creates its own difficulties. As we can see from recalling the founding generation's belief in natural law and its inability to predict the almost-immediate rise of political parties, the founders inhabited a world quite different from ours. While the English language—at least the portion of it relevant to the Constitution—probably has changed only moderately since 1787, the context in which the words are used has changed considerably.

Thus, even if we could accurately capture the 1787 (or 1868) "meaning" of the language in its own time—unlikely for the reasons described above—that meaning might well be anachronistic when transplanted to our own century.

In addition to these essentially objective problems arising from the age of the document, there are also normative questions. The original Constitution was drafted by fifty-five white patrician men and ratified, sometimes by narrow margins, by other groups of white patrician men elected by a small and comparatively elite segment of the population. All of these people lived in a bygone age; even their great-grandchildren are long dead. As the franchise gradually broadened, the subsequent amendments reflected the majority will of an increasingly larger portion of the population. Nevertheless, the amendment process filters rather than directly reflects the will of the populace; moreover, until at least the 1960s, a variety of legal and extralegal barriers ensured that the franchise was not fully extended to all adult citizens. In interpreting the ambiguous language of the Constitution, then, modern interpreters must decide whether to take into account its decidedly undemocratic pedigree.

Thus, in interpreting the Constitution, we must navigate between fidelity to the past and the needs of the present, between the general and the particular, and between the abstract and the concrete. And those are only the problems common to almost any aging constitution—we have not yet turned to the specifics.

Those specifics only increase the discretion and uncertainty. It does not help that *our* Constitution contains internal tensions that must be resolved by any interpreter. The most significant, of course, is that it provides for both majority rule and minority rights. Where do we draw the line between majority rule and majority tyranny? Pure libertarianism or pure majoritarianism may be a poor foundation for a constitutional regime, but either would certainly make constitutional interpretation easier. Other tensions are found within or between individual clauses of the Constitution: What is the optimum balance between liberty and equality, between religious exercise and religious establishment, between governmental powers and accountability?

The countermajoritarian difficulty

The questions discussed so far would exist regardless of the identity of the constitutional interpreter. A largely American concern arises from the fact that we assign interpretive authority to unelected judges. This gives rise to what Alexander Bickel called the countermajoritarian dilemma: the "Lincolnian tension" between principle and consent. To what extent does the legitimacy of a democratic government rest on the consent of the people, and to what extent does it rest on the rightness of its core principles? If a majority agrees that torture is an acceptable practice, is it therefore legitimate? Or think about the Court's 1954 declaration that racial segregation was unconstitutional: In asking about its legitimacy, do we really care what a majority of the population believed about the principles of nondiscrimination?[1]

Bickel himself viewed judicial review as a valuable tool in navigating the tension between principle and consent, and his work was designed more to defend the practice than to criticize it. But modern scholars have used the idea of a counter-majoritarian judiciary as a springboard to undermine the legitimacy of judicial review and to urge taking decision-making power from an "activist" court and returning it to the people and their representatives. As one contemporary scholar notes, the countermajoritarian dilemma has become an academic obsession. That development is unfortunate, however, because, unlike the uncertainty inherent in the process of constitutional interpretation—which is unavoidable and quite real—the countermajoritarian dilemma is largely a fallacy.[2]

The countermajoritarian dilemma rests on three core premises, each of which is either false or greatly exaggerated. The premises are: (1) In a constitutional democracy, all final policymaking authority reposes in the majority of the citizens, and therefore must be assigned to popularly accountable bodies; (2) The United States Congress is a popularly accountable body; and (3) The United States Supreme Court is not a popularly accountable body. These premises provide a treacherous foundation for the argument against judicial review. The first premise is simply false, and the second and third are much weaker than they may seem.

The first premise equates democracy with the electoral accountability of decision makers. It fails to recognize that our constitutional democracy—and, indeed, any legitimate constitutional democracy—contains limits on majoritarian authority; furthermore, it mistakenly evaluates the democratic legitimacy of the whole by looking to whether individual parts are sufficiently democratically accountable. Both points warrant additional discussion.

Majority rule is a key part of our constitutional fabric and of our vision of democracy, but it is not the be-all-and-end-all of the Constitution. That the American Constitution is not wholly based on majority rule seems obvious. Indeed, as one political scientist notes in making the same point, "I must admit that advancing such an obvious point feels rather silly. However, the persistence of the countermajoritarian paradigm in constitutional scholarship—a straw-man argument if there ever was one—makes such silliness necessary." Numerous provisions in the Constitution protect against majority tyranny by limiting the damage that consenting majorities can do to the rights of dissenting minorities. The question then becomes one of decisional authority, not majoritarianism: If individual rights limit the power of majorities, who gets to draw the lines? As an initial matter, it is counterintuitive to let the majority routinely determine the limits of its own authority. Doing so, as one wag pointed out, is like letting a sheep and two wolves vote on what's for dinner. Moreover, in the context of U.S. history, as suggested in the previous chapter, the judiciary was the natural choice for interpreting and enforcing limits on the desires of the majority as reflected in the legislature.[3]

The countermajoritarian difficulty also assumes that every policymaking part of a democratic government must be majoritarian to be legitimate. That simply cannot be true in the American system: Few question the legitimacy of the Senate, for example, which cannot by any stretch of the imagination be called majoritarian since it allocates equal votes to decidedly unequal populations. California has no more senators than Wyoming, which has about half the population of the city of San Jose. (The population of Wyoming is a bit over 500,000, while San Jose has around 900,000.) It is purely a historical accident that Wyoming gets its own senators while San Jose does not. Proportionality would require that California have about fourteen senators instead of two.

The electoral college is also tied rather loosely to majority rule: Four times in our history—most recently in 2000—the loser of the popular vote for president nevertheless occupied the Oval Office. The countermajoritarian aspect of the electoral college is exacerbated by low voter turnout; approximately 25% of the voting-age population and 32% of registered voters voted for the "winner" of the 2000 presidential election. Such institutions as the Federal Reserve, the Federal Communications Commission (FCC), and the Securities and Exchange Commission (SEC) wield significant authority (steering the entire economy, in the case of the Federal Reserve) with neither an electoral majority nor public accountability behind them. And a second-term president is no more accountable to the electorate than a federal judge—neither one will ever face a reelection campaign. This is not merely a fanciful concern: Consider the ability of President Bush to continue a very expensive, very unpopular war despite its strong rejection by the electorate—surely something far beyond the wildest dream of the most activist judge who ever lived.[4]

That some organs of government are more directly responsive to majority opinion than others should not surprise us in a democracy as complex as ours, and it is a mistake to demand the same level of democratic accountability from every institution. Instead we should ask whether the system as a whole is democratically legitimate, and if it is not, the prospect of unelected judges occasionally invalidating a popularly enacted statute is the least of our worries.

Reliance on the countermajoritarian difficulty to critique judicial review is also undermined by the fact that the democratic pedigree of the judiciary differs only in degree, not in kind, from those of the popularly elected branches. (In other words, premises two and three of the dilemma are exaggerations.) The judiciary is nominated by the (more or less) popularly elected president and confirmed by the (more or less) popularly elected Senate—and, in recent times, the political preferences of both branches have played an increasingly large role in the selection process. The popularly elected branches, meanwhile, are not as majoritarian as they might seem on paper. The Senate, as noted, is stunningly malapportioned, and even the House is not perfectly apportioned. (Not only is each state guaranteed a single representative, even if its population would not otherwise entitle it to one, but there are also rounding problems in the calculations that turn out to make a significant difference in state representation.) And as we know from public choice analysis, legislative deviations from majority preferences are common for a whole host of reasons, many having to do with the need to raise money for reelection. Federal judges, while not required to follow the will of the majority, are at least not distracted from their responsibilities by the selfish desire to retain their jobs. Nor does the frequency of elections, which injects fund-raising as a distorting factor, necessarily have the compensating effect of making the legislators more responsive or accountable to their constituents: In the 2002 elections, for example, 90% of House seats were considered virtually uncontested. Finally, some studies of interactions between the legislature and the judiciary suggest that the functioning of the popular branches actually depends in part on the existence of judicial review, either as an impetus for congressional consideration of constitutional issues that would otherwise fall by the wayside or as a way to resolve difficult conflicts that legislators are loath to decide.[5]

This is not to suggest that the courts are just as democratically accountable as the other branches, but merely that the countermajoritarian difficulty is seriously overblown. Nevertheless, it has continued to obsess many constitutional scholars. This obsession has done much to warp modern constitutional theory.

Misguided efforts to escape the countermajoritarian difficulty

The second half of the twentieth century spawned two primary theoretical approaches to the countermajoritarian nature of judicial review. One is to devise an interpretive mechanism that will constrain judicial discretion, and the other is to reduce, eliminate, or downplay the significance of judicial interpretation of the Constitution. Both rest on a dichotomous view of judicial decision making in constitutional cases: It is either artificially constrained or it is purely political. The first approach looks for artificial constraints to control political judges; the second approach denies the possibility of constraint and thus assumes that all judges are political. Neither approach recognizes the possibility that constitutional interpretation might be both flexible (that is, unconstrained by artificial mechanisms) and principled (that is, not primarily political).

Some contemporary constitutional scholars have constructed elaborate, overarching theories of interpretation to constrain judicial discretion. They believe that faithful application of their favorite theory will automatically produce correct and unassailable answers to any given constitutional question. By this method, scholars (and a few judges) hope to eliminate the uncertainty inherent in the constitutional language and thus reduce judicial discretion.

We will describe some of these theories very briefly here, because our purpose is not to critique their individual flaws but their common inability to constrain judicial decision making. Adherents to these various theories will find our treatment simplistic, and they will obviously not be persuaded to abandon their favorite approach. We believe, however, that they, too, should be able to find value in this book. The more nuanced, complex, and sophisticated one of these theories becomes, the more possible that different judges applying the theory will reach different results. Thus, even originalists, textualists, and adherents to other theories of interpretation should be concerned about how to assess whether judges are properly addressing such issues and whether institutional changes could improve judicial performance. So if you are a hedgehog rather than a fox, do not stop reading this book; just skip a few pages so that our discussion of your theory does not raise your blood pressure.

Several of the theories attempt to anchor constitutional meaning in certain privileged points in time. Originalist interpretation focuses on the original, fixed, historical meaning of the Constitution. Originalists look for historical evidence of the public meaning of the constitutional words: What would the language of the original Constitution (or the Bill of Rights) have meant to an eighteenth-century reader? How would a nineteenth-century reader have interpreted the Reconstruction Amendments? Constitutional dualism and translation theories begin with the original historical meaning of the Constitution, but then look for transformative historical changes over time. These theorists would ask, for example, whether the New Deal should alter our interpretation of the Reconstruction Amendments. In our view, these efforts to provide a reliable historical anchor for constitutional law are inadequate because they expect more certainty than history can provide, and because they fail to accept the inevitably of ongoing constitutional evolution.

We find other theories equally unsatisfactory. Textualism closes its eyes to all but the constitutional text itself and demands absolute fidelity to its words. Ideally a textualist would need only the Constitution itself (and perhaps an antiquarian dictionary) to divine constitutional meaning, even for such broad phrases as "the equal protection of the laws." Further research is required only when dictionaries are incomplete, in order to scope out common patterns of word usage in earlier historical periods. More expansively, textualists sometimes consider overall constitutional structure, such as the tripartite division of federal powers between branches of government. Such structural arguments, unfortunately, can often be made on both sides of an issue, depending on how one characterizes the constitutional structure.

Intratextualism is a variant form of textualism. Rather than looking only at the text of the provision to be interpreted, it asks interpreters to compare different parts of the constitutional text in the search for meaning. The comparison is intended to produce a fuller explication than looking at any single part of the constitutional text alone: If one provision includes the word "express" and another does not, for example, its absence tells us something about how to interpret the latter provision. Unfortunately, this approach assumes that the textual language was chosen with great precision and forethought about how it integrates into the entire document, which is not always true.

"Constitutional minimalism" also comes in two varieties, strict and not-so-strict. In the late nineteenth century, Harvard law professor James Bradley Thayer urged judges to hold unconstitutional only legislation that was obviously and egregiously inconsistent with the constitutional text; since legislatures are unlikely to pass patently unconstitutional laws, Thayer's approach leaves the judiciary with virtually no reason to act. More recently, Cass Sunstein—a long-time University of Chicago law professor who has just moved to Harvard—has urged a more restricted form of minimalism. Sunstein would allow judges to interpret the Constitution broadly in certain limited circumstances, such as when "there is a good argument for invalidation on democratic grounds, or [when] the Court has considerable confidence in its judgment." Whatever else can be said about this approach, it obviously calls for considerable judgment on the part of the judges about when to deviate from minimalism. In any event, proceeding cautiously, while often good advice, has more to do with the pace by which judicial doctrine develops than with its ultimate content.[6]

As we have tried to show in earlier work, none of these interpretive methods can succeed in constraining judicial discretion because each contains its own unavoidable ambiguities. The historical analysis that underlies originalism, constitutional dualism, and translation theories often fails to produce clear results and also requires too much historical expertise from judges. Textualism simply reproduces the problems that arise from the uncertainty of multiauthored ancient texts that contain internal contradictions, and intratextualism and translation theories double (or triple) the opportunity for mistaken or conflicting interpretations. Dualism and translation theories compound the weakness of originalism by expanding the historical analysis. Minimalism either—if consistently applied as in the Thayerian form—reduces judicial discretion, but at the cost of increasing the potential for majority tyranny, or—if more flexibly applied as in the Sunsteinian version—allows judges to evade its restrictions through an exercise of discretion. Essentially the problem with each theory is that applying it requires judges to use judgment—which is fine in our view, but also means that the theory fails in its purpose of taming judicial discretion.

Thus these theories fail in their aim to rescue constitutional law by purging the exercise of judgment. It is true that each of them provides some tools that may sometimes be useful in resolving constitutional issues. But none of them can "solve" the problem of judicial discretion. Advocates of these theories may feel that the theories do more than we contend to narrow the degree of discretion. They cannot very well argue, however, that discretion is eliminated, and that being the case, they should be willing to consider our suggestions about how that discretion should be understood and guided.

Perhaps recognizing the futility of such theories, some constitutional scholars—on both the left and the right—have recently tried a different approach to resolving the countermajoritarian dilemma. Abandoning the heavens of interpretive theory, these scholars sometimes see only the abyss of everyday politics. Judges, they declare, reach constitutional decisions (at least in the big important cases) based entirely on their own political beliefs, and thus federal judges are merely unelected legislators in black robes. A few of these scholars ask what all the fuss is about: We need not be concerned about judicial review because the courts "follow the election returns" and generally reflect majority opinions; thus court decisions are ineffectual in either preventing or encouraging societal changes. Most of those who conflate constitutional adjudication with politics, however, urge some form of popular sovereignty or popular constitutionalism, suggesting that modern "activist" judicial review is a usurpation of the people's democratic right to govern themselves. They contend that the Constitution should be interpreted by the people and their representatives rather than by the courts. A few even go so far as to suggest that the illegitimacy of judicial review entitles Congress, the president, or the states to ignore Supreme Court decisions.

But it is a rare (or perhaps nonexistent) advocate of popular sovereignty who extends this critique to *all* exercises of judicial review. Like other constitutional theorists, those in favor of popular sovereignty generally condemn the judiciary only for invalidating "good" legislation—and, indeed, often lambaste the courts for failing to invalidate "bad" legislation. Thus those on the left criticize the Supreme Court for trimming congressional power over various types of discrimination, but may then laud it for striking down antiabortion laws or bans on homosexual sodomy. The conservative wing of the popular sovereignty crowd, on the other hand, thinks the abortion and sodomy cases are unconscionable and countermajoritarian, but then turns around and denounces the Court for failing to strike down affirmative action or the taking of private property. That *both* groups are unhappy with the current state of judicial review might suggest the unsoundness of any view that faults constitutional decision making for being purely an exercise in politics.

Constitutional populism also ignores hard-won lessons about the value of judicial review. Judicial review is no panacea, but the Supreme Court has time and again stood up for fundamental rights that any democracy should respect: the right to equal citizenship regardless of race, the right to criticize the government and denounce the established order, the right to have everyone's vote weighted equally, and (most recently) the right to a hearing before a person is sentenced to indefinite imprisonment. These rulings have helped maintain a free society, not to subject it to judicial tyranny.

Popular constitutionalism also seems vague about how to operationalize the concept. To the extent it contemplates something like the current national political process, popular constitutionalism really means empowering elected officials, since the populace expresses its will in national politics purely through electoral politics. At that point, popular constitutionalism begins to look very much as a practical matter like giving the president or Congress the operational power to decide constitutional issues, and is thus hard to distinguish from legislative or executive supremacy, or at least some form of departmentalism—none of which seem to find much favor with the American people. Unaccountably for popular constitutionalists, most people seem to approve of the Supreme Court as an institution and approve of its constitutional role. Alternatively, popular constitutionalism could refer to the popular will as expressed on the streets, but popular constitutionalists generally eschew this form of lawlessness. All that seems to remain is constitutional populism as constitutional law by referendum. This system has been tried in some American states, such as California, but with results that are decidedly mixed. It would be somewhat foolhardy to give up our current form of constitutionalism for some kind of government by plebiscite merely because of a fear of judicial errors.

In trying to describe these theories and critique them very quickly, we have ignored nuances. Advocates of these theories may feel that we have caricatured their views. In our previous book, *Desperately Seeking Certainty*, we delve into the theories in considerably more depth, and we recommend that book for those who would like a fuller discussion. Here, we are merely trying to reprise the material for readers who are not intimately familiar with these debates.

In part, the countermajoritarian difficulty is as much an attack on constitution-alism as on the specific institution of judicial review. Whether enforced by judges or otherwise, constitutionalism requires that sometimes a current majority cannot adopt the policy that it would otherwise think best, all things considered, because the Constitution has created procedural barriers or privileged certain values over others. It happens that judges are often charged with enforcing these barriers, but the real complaint is that the barriers exist at all. If government by plebiscite is appealing to popular constitutionalists, it is not because it eliminates judicial interpretation (it does not), but because it waters down constitutional protections for minorities. As Justice Robert Jackson noted: "Unrestricted majority rule leaves the individual in the minority unprotected. This is the dilemma and you have to take your choice. The Constitution-makers made their choice in favor of a limited majority rule."[7]

To the extent that the democracy worry focuses specifically on judges, it amounts to a fear that judges are not enforcing existing legal rules but are making up the answers as they go along, engaging in a political rather than legal exercise. It is for this reason that the democracy worry and the "judges are political" worry tend to go hand in hand.

That virtually no constitutional scholar condemns judicial review wholesale—but instead either urges that it be constrained, or critiques individual cases—should also tell us something else. The real majoritarian issue raised by judicial review is not whether it should exist, but to what extent judges should defer to legislative interpreta-tions rather than exercising their own discretion. The answer to that question depends on what it is we think judges are doing when they interpret the Constitution.

In our view, modern laments about a countermajoritarian court diminishing popular sovereignty rest on a fundamentally mistaken view of the nature of con-stitutional interpretation. The crux of our argument in the rest of this book is that constitutional interpretation is an exercise of law, not raw politics, and thus that judges are engaging in essentially the same task when they interpret the Constitu-tion as when they decide any other legal question, such as the interpretation of a statute. Constitutional decision making depends neither on theoretical constraints nor on politics, but on judgment. How judgment functions in the context of constitutional adjudication will take us the next several chapters to explain.

PART II

Discretion and Judgment

4

How to Think About Discretion

WHAT HAVE WE learned so far? First, judicial review is not an anomaly. Rather, it is a key part of our system of government. Complaints about judicial review are really complaints about constitutionalism (the idea of enforceable constitutional limits on government) and the separation of powers (limitations on the power of the legislature). And second, efforts to eliminate judicial discretion by providing recipes for deciding cases, like originalism or textualism, are ultimately frustrated by the inherent limits on the clarity of the constitutional text and constitutional history. Such theories cannot overcome the inevitable patches of vagueness and ambiguity in the Constitution. Consequently, hard cases inevitably involve judicial leeway; this is simply part of the system. Hard cases, almost by definition, require creative, critical thinking, which is not going to be reducible to a formula.

All well and good, you may say. So judges are supposed to have leeway. But how are they supposed to decide cases without the constraint of general theories? And is the resulting degree of judicial flexibility something we can really live with in a democracy? What separates judicial decisions from legislative fiats?

These are hard questions; indeed, it is hard even to work out the best way to frame them. If foundationalist theories (like originalism or textualism, for example) are incapable of producing determinate results, nonfoundationalist theories fare no better. Nonfoundationalist efforts to instruct judges, we find, seem invariably to sound like a bad cookbook: either vague ("season to taste") or banal ("don't over-salt!"). We have spent many a long hour banging our heads against this wall. In the end, we have decided that this is the wrong way of thinking about the problem. You cannot tame judicial flexibility by giving judges a recipe for solving constitutional issues.

Thus, rather than trying to prescribe how judges should search for solutions, we ask how they (and the rest of us) should assess the acceptability of those solutions. We take the existence of judicial flexibility as a given. Our first question, therefore, is: When does a judicial decision fall outside the permissible range of flexibility? Our second question, assuming that a decision is within the permissible range, is: Within that range, are there ways of evaluating the validity of a decision? And finally we ask: Are there characteristics of the judicial process that may encourage responsible judgment within this range? Those three questions are the subject of this section of the book. Later sections consider the forces that tend to keep judges within this range, as well as asking how judges can most responsibly exercise their legitimate flexibility. The first order of business, however, is to explain and justify our approach.

Decision making without recipes

The critics of judicial review whom we discussed in the previous chapter are responding to the fear that without a prescribed formula for judicial decision making, we will be completely at the mercy of individual judges. The law will change from day to day on the basis of political shifts or judicial caprices. What seems to loom looks more like the "rule of men" than the "rule of law." But this fear, while not groundless, overestimates the need for legal certainty and underestimates the degree to which reasonable judges will honor the rule of law.

One function of law is social stability, and one appeal of a formulaic approach is its promise of stability. Fortunately, we can have the stability without having the formula, because stability requires only that most cases be reasonably predictable. Because there are easy cases, most of which never reach the Supreme Court, constitutional law can provide a stable framework for government. (It is important to note that many cases that would have been quite hard when a constitutional provision was adopted can later become easy because they are controlled by precedent.) So we need not fear that the law will be reduced to chaos if we abandon the quest for the perfect decision-making formula. Many cases will be straightforward, and reasonable judges will readily agree on the outcomes. Moreover, the hard cases, while controversial, rarely involve Americans' most pressing concerns: Since at least the 1950s, there has been little overlap between the issues on the Supreme Court's docket and the issues that Americans tell pollsters are most important to them. So most of the law is quite stable, with judicial creativity being exercised only around the edges; only on a few issues is the law genuinely in flux.[1]

This is about the best that any system of decision making can guarantee. Complete predictability is not a possibility, nor is it possible to make outcomes entirely independent of the identity of the decision maker. There is simply no way to train judges into machinelike uniformity and predictability, or to constrain them so that they can reach only a single result.

A judge in a hard case is trying to solve a difficult problem. In general, there is no simple recipe for problem solving, whether the problem arises in law, business, engineering, or medicine. We can help prepare people to solve such problems in various ways—giving them basic tools they need to analyze the problem, talking in general terms about good ways to approach problems, and exposing them to case studies of similar problems. That is, for example, how business schools train corporate managers, and how law schools try to train future lawyers and judges. But there is an element of creativity in finding solutions that simply cannot be reduced to a formula, and efforts at guidance simply fade into platitudes.

No doubt, it would be wonderful to have some recipe for making hard decisions. But we rather suspect that the absence of such a program is simply part of the human condition. Life presents hard choices. In making these hard decisions, people expand their knowledge, revise their understanding of who they are, and better grasp their fundamental values. Of course, a great many decisions in life are easy, and that is an important fact about constitutional law as well. Yet, what is true in personal life is also true in constitutional law: The big decisions cannot be reduced to a formula.

Knowing that there are many easy cases is only a limited consolation, because the remaining cases are often the most important. Those hard cases raise the greatest controversy and evoke the most acute fears of an imperialist judiciary—the fears that motivate much of constitutional theory (except for the theories of scholars who *hope* the imperial judges will share their own views). If we want to claim that courts engage in something more than raw policymaking when they decide hard cases, we need some standard other than our own preferences for assessing those decisions.

In short, if we cannot provide an *ex ante* recipe, at least we need an *ex post* standard of performance.

If we are stuck with the exercise of judgment by courts, and if we cannot give them a recipe that will guarantee correct outcomes, how *do* we evaluate the exercise of judgment? What is the difference between an indefensible opinion and one that is reasonable, even if arguably wrong? In short, what makes law an exercise in reasonable judgment rather than an application of arbitrary force?

Discretion, legislative and otherwise

One appealing but overly simplistic approach is to draw analogies to legislative discretion. A simple model of decision making would say that easy cases are covered by existing legal rules, while hard cases involve gaps in the law where judges exercise discretion, creating new law in much the same way that legislators do.

In its most extreme form, this model of the judiciary is all gaps and no rules. At one point, this was a popular view among left-wing legal theorists in the Critical Legal Studies movement. Their view is oddly echoed in recent writing by the conservative Judge Richard Posner. His view is that, "[f]rom a practical standpoint, constitutional adjudication by the Supreme Court is also the exercise of discretion—and that is about all it is." He also says "there isn't a single" landmark Supreme Court case "that would not have been decided differently but equally plausibly had the Court been differently but no less ably manned." For this reason, he considers constitutional decision making to be "inherently...lawless," situated in an "ocean of discretion." We suspect that he is not alone in thinking this—it is a viewpoint that not infrequently surfaces in discussions by legal academics, although less often found in print.[2]

Posner's description might be right—but only if we *define* a landmark case as one that decides between two previously equally plausible alternatives. (Even then, some options are not plausible in terms of existing law, so that the judge's discretion is limited to choosing between those that remain.) To say that this is true of every landmark case, however, is an unsustainable exaggeration. But unless it is a tautology, this statement is surely false, as virtually any lawyer would agree. If a landmark case is one that becomes the basis for an area of law or one that addresses an important social issue, then it is false that all of these cases involve the lawless exercise of discretion. It simply is not true that both holdings in *Marbury v. Madison* (the case establishing judicial review) were equally plausible, nor was this true of many other leading cases. It is even less true of the run-of-the-mill Fourth

Amendment or First Amendment case decided by the Supreme Court, though these cases can be important.

Judge Posner's comment may be yet another manifestation of the "if not the heavens, then the abyss" syndrome that we discussed earlier. It refuses to see the middle ground between complete constraint and boundless leeway. This perspective, whether coming from the Left or the Right, is too quick to assume that all important cases take place in the domain of unlimited discretion because it finds constitutional law hopelessly indeterminate, at least at the Supreme Court level.

Even in its less radical form—one that recognizes the existence of rules as well as gaps—this model is too simple. First, cases do not fall neatly into two groups, one in which no legal doubt exists and the other in which the law offers no guidance. Almost all appellate cases involve at least a little legal uncertainty (or the lawyers on one side would be fined for wasting the court's time). So we are dealing with matters of degree rather than a dichotomy.

Second, this model is not true to the way judges themselves perceive their work. Judges in hard cases may feel that they are exercising discretion, but they may equally well feel that they are trying to solve a puzzle that really does have a right answer. And in resolving the case, they may feel that they are not reaching "outside the law" for a policy solution, but "inside the law" for concepts and values. Thus the analogy between judicial and legislative discretion is only approximate.

Another problem with the simple model of discretionary "gap filling" is significant. This model does not provide enough of a basis for evaluating judicial decisions. According to the model, in easy cases only one answer is legitimate, while in hard cases any answer is equally legitimate and the only question is whether the judges have made the best policy choice. (In some sense, foundationalists share this model: Their goal is to make as many cases as possible into easy ones because they are afraid of the unbridled discretion invited by hard cases.) Yet, it is not likely that either judges or their would-be evaluators have the kind of information that would allow a confident judgment about policy, leaving the evaluative process adrift. Moreover, the analogy to legislators ignores the completely different institutional and political context in which judges operate.

But there is a better analogy, one that courts themselves recognize. Courts face the problem of evaluating the exercise of discretion whenever they review the work of administrative agencies. Agencies like the Environmental Protection Agency (EPA), the Securities and Exchange Commission (SEC), or the Occupational Safety and Health Administration (OSHA) make decisions of huge social and economic consequence. They also exercise tremendous power over individuals and companies. And yet, one of the main reasons the agencies exist is that Congress is incapable of providing—or unwilling to provide—clear-cut answers to specific problems, leading to a delegation of power to such an agency. This means that the governing law will often provide some guidance to the agency, but will also leave great leeway. For example, a statute might tell an agency to set "reasonable" rates or to prevent "unreasonable" health risks. Courts have grappled with the problem of controlling this discretion without trying to take over the agency's job. The concepts they have developed since the New Deal to control the modern administrative state are also quite revealing when they are applied to courts rather than agencies. In essence, the courts have discovered that even in the absence of definitive legal rules, it is possible to assess whether agencies have behaved responsibly.

What administrative law doctrines provide, in short, is a form of analysis that recognizes the existence of flexibility but tries to get a handle on how to assess its exercise. While agencies are different from courts in a number of quite significant ways—including their relationships with Congress and the president—they share with courts both great flexibility and a potential for abuse of discretion and lawless decisions. Thus, although we do not suggest that administrative law doctrines should be transplanted wholesale to constitutional law, they can give us insights into how to approach the question of judicial discretion.

The administrative analogy

In administrative law, courts scrutinize an agency's decisions to determine if they have exceeded or abused their delegated authority. Like courts, agencies must justify their actions in terms of their legal mandates, though at the same time they have some leeway in applying those mandates. Just as the Court has whatever textual guidance is provided by terms like "due process" and "equal protection," the agency is directed by statute to ensure "reasonable rates" or to prevent "unfair methods of competition" or to "provide an adequate margin of safety." In both situations, the text points out a general direction but leaves a lot to the imagination. In the case of agencies, we know that their discretion has limits; the task is to discover similar limits for courts.

One advantage of the administrative analogy is that it invites us to consider the idea of reasoned decision making in more mundane contexts than abortion or affirmative action, which should leave our thinking less clouded by emotion. For instance, the leading administrative law case about agency discretion involved a fairly humdrum question, the construction of a highway through a park in Memphis. A federal statute barred funding for any highway through a park unless there was "no feasible and prudent" alternative. The agency argued that this phrase (particularly the reference to prudence) was essentially a grant of legislative discretion to the agency. (In technical terms, the argument was that the decision was "committed to agency discretion," or in other words, that "feasible and prudent" means whatever the agency says it means.) The Court rejected that argument, finding that the statutory language had real substance.[3]

Still, what is "feasible and prudent" is generally going to be a judgment call. Thus the agency has real discretion in applying the phrase, although not the unlimited discretion of a legislature to implement its own views of wise policy. How does a court review the exercise of administrative discretion? Here, the Supreme Court called for a two-step process, involving a searching review of the record. The first step is to ensure that the decision was based on a consideration of the relevant factors (and only the relevant factors). This requires a determination that the agency considered all of the evidence in light of the relevant factors. The second step is to determine whether the agency committed a clear error of judgment. Altogether, what the Court required from the agency is a reasonable explanation of how the evidence supported its application of the statutory standard. In the context of the highway decision, this would mean a careful consideration of alternate routes and mustering evidence to show that they were either infeasible for engineering reasons or were unacceptable for cost or other reasons.

In administrative law, the standard applied to review agency actions of this kind is that the agency's decision will be upheld unless it is "arbitrary and capricious." This may sound like a very lax standard indeed. But in reality, the standard has real teeth, and it is not at all uncommon for a regulation by EPA or another regulatory agency to be sent back for further proceedings. The key is the requirement that agencies provide a reasoned justification, based on the relevant factors, for their decisions.

It might be argued that the administrative analogy fails because the Constitution provides the Court with a less intelligible mandate than those that Congress gives administrative agencies. It is true that many modern regulatory statutes are much more detailed and specific than the Constitution. But they still establish some goal and require the agency to make a judgment about how to implement that goal. Similarly, the First Amendment provides a goal (protecting freedom of speech), but leaves it up to the Court to decide how to implement that goal and how to reconcile that goal with other constitutional values.

The administrative analogy could also be criticized on the ground that administrative officials are more democratically accountable than federal judges. (They are less accountable than state judges, who generally have to stand for reelection.)

This is true, but only to a degree. Some administrative officials can be removed at any time by the president (who is not himself electorally accountable in his second term), but others have fixed terms and can only be removed for good cause during that time. In any event, accountability cuts both ways here. It does provide a check on administrative exercise of discretion, to the extent that the administrator's acts are inconsistent with political forces. Yet, at the same time, their accountability to political actors undermines our confidence that administrators are even trying to follow their legal mandates—at least federal judges do not have to worry about losing their jobs if following the law would offend politically powerful groups.

Of course, there are significant differences between administrators and judges. Although it may be helpful to think of judges as "administering" the Constitution, we are proposing an analogy rather than an identity of functions. We find the administrative analogy fruitful because it addresses a fundamental question about the exercise of governmental power. When government officials must carry out rules enacted by others, what determines the appropriateness of their actions? Unlike legislators—but like administrators—judges are charged with implementing legal texts that they did not themselves create.

A broader point is the need to bring our thinking about the judicial role in line with the realities of the modern administrative state. Limiting the abuse of discretion is not an issue unique to judges. The question of how to reconcile the need for decision makers to have leeway with the need to ensure fidelity to legal mandates is pervasive in the modern world. Our legal system has worked out reasonably good ways of attempting this reconciliation for administrative agencies. We can learn from that experience in thinking about the judicial role.

Some will reject the administrative analogy because it seems to allow too much discretion to judges. Even they, however, would surely agree that judicial decisions should rely on legally relevant factors, explain the court's reasoning, and exhibit good judgment in applying those factors. On the other hand, legal realists who think that judges are essentially policymakers should also be willing to apply the same standards to judicial policymakers as to administrative ones. We find the analogy to agencies helpful because it captures a key element of the judicial role: the need to exercise a large element of judgment in implementing legal mandates.

In the next chapter, we turn to how that administrative law model applies to judicial decision making. As with agencies, the admitted discretion of courts does not translate into unlimited leeway or an abandonment of reasoned decision making.

5

Reason and Relevance

R EASONED JUSTIFICATIONS, BASED on relevant factors, are the bread and butter of judicial decision making. Or, as Sir Edward Coke put it several centuries ago, "Reason is the life of the law." True, the bottom line of any judicial decision is the outcome. Someone wins, someone loses; evidence is admitted or excluded; money is ordered to be paid or an injunction is issued requiring or prohibiting a certain action; the case is affirmed or reversed or sent back to a lower court. Sometimes a statute is held invalid or an executive decision nullified. And for many observers, especially nonlawyers, this bottom line may be all that matters. But in Anglo-American jurisprudence, the outcome is only a small portion of the decision actually issued by the court, and it is often not the most important part. At every level of the judiciary, but most prominently in appellate courts, judges write opinions explaining why they reached the result that they did. Judicial opinions are as varied as the judges who write them, but they all serve the same purpose: to present a reasoned elaboration of how the relevant legal analysis produces the particular outcome.[1]

The importance of reasoned elaboration

This reasoned elaboration is both an institutional constraint and a psychological one, and it also provides a way in which we can evaluate a judge's performance. To the extent that a court's authority rests on reason rather than will, unreasoned or poorly reasoned decisions weaken its legitimacy. While a single bad opinion may not have immediate concrete consequences, the cumulative effect of a run of unreasoned decisions on a court's legitimacy may reduce its actual authority: Elected judges may be removed, and judges on an unelected court may face limits on jurisdiction, constitutional amendments, or changes in the way that litigants, the public, or the popular branches respond to judicial decisions. (For instance, lower courts may feel less compulsion to apply appellate decisions generously when those decisions are obviously weakly reasoned.) It is a more serious charge that a court (or a judge) is acting illegitimately than that it is mistaken; reasoned elaboration makes the latter critique more likely than the former.

The additional psychological constraint of the requirement of reasoned elaboration is illustrated by a casual remark made by a federal district judge to one of the authors. Having made a preliminary ruling from the bench, he said, sometimes he finds when he sits down to draft his opinion that his decision "just won't write." It is not that he cannot put together some arguments that support his initial ruling; every first-year law student soon learns that it is possible to come up with logical-sounding arguments for almost any legal proposition. But superficial logic is not enough: The requirement of reasoned elaboration demands arguments that stand up to close and critical scrutiny in the light of opposing arguments. Judges, knowing in advance that they will have to publicly justify their decisions with careful reasoning, are less likely to make wild or idiosyncratic decisions. The best judges, confronting a decision that "won't write," will change that decision. Indeed, according to Justice Blackmun's papers, Justice Kennedy changed his vote—and ultimately the outcome—in an important case in 1992. Having drafted a majority opinion upholding prayers at school graduations, he concluded that the "draft looked quite wrong," and then wrote what became the majority opinion (for a different majority) striking down such prayers as unconstitutional. Weaker judges may instead write weak opinions, but those are subject to public scrutiny.[2]

But what is it that we are to scrutinize? How do we know whether any particular opinion is a sufficiently reasoned elaboration? There is no formula, but there are some basic—and largely noncontroversial—rules.

For an opinion to provide adequate support for a result, it must be a logical and coherent whole. It cannot contain such moves as arguments from religious revelation ("because God said so"), indifference to major inconsistencies (not uncommon in political speeches), or judicial fiat (the equivalent of the parental "because I said so!"). It must rest on what Herbert Wechsler famously called "neutral principles." Wechsler's idea was that a court deciding a particular case must base its decision on principles that would be applicable to all similar cases, rather than on a desire to reach a particular result in that one case. The principles must be "neutral" in the sense that they did not rest on the individual circumstances of the particular case. (For those who are familiar with Wechsler's article, we should note that we do not agree with the way he applied this concept to desegregation, which mischaracterized the issue as one of freedom of association rather than racial discrimination.) In other words, the judge must be willing to extend the reasoning to other cases; an opinion, even though it decides only a single case, can never be a ticket for this train only.

A persuasive opinion must also fit into the existing American political and judicial ethos without doing too much damage to it—it must be coherent in the philosophical sense that it cannot depend on wiping the slate clean, but must instead work within the framework of existing beliefs. The much-used metaphor of a web is useful here, to rule out of bounds any argument that is radically inconsistent with either the judge's own beliefs or with the overall body of existing precedent, history, text, or the various other sources we identify in this book.

Finally, the persuasive force of a reasoned argument must be measured independently of its source: While a great judge might be more likely than a mediocrity to produce a well-reasoned opinion, and a politically compatible judge more likely to produce a result we like, we should give no additional points for authorship. We must be equal opportunity critics. This does not mean that we need to consider all judges' work as equal. Some judges are known for their care, their thoroughness, or their wisdom, and it behooves us to recognize that and perhaps to look twice at their opinions before condemning them on the basis of apparent errors.

Reasoned elaboration in administrative and judicial contexts is similar in a number of ways, then. In both cases, it allows us to meaningfully review whether discretion has been exceeded or abused. We are not faced with a choice between pretending that administrative decisions are value free and saying that anything goes because "it's all political." Like administrative agency decisions, constitutional decisions can involve a human factor (and therefore have some connection with ideology) without being purely political.

What arguments are relevant?

Reasoned elaboration is not the end of the story. As administrative law teaches us, the proper exercise of discretion involves the reasoned analysis of the *relevant* factors. Our next task is to identify the factors relevant to constitutional interpretation. Indeed, much of the dispute in constitutional theory concerns the question of what factors actually are relevant. Everyone agrees that the text and original understanding are relevant factors. (Originalists differ from nonoriginalists only in terms of the amount of weight they would give these factors.) We will discuss later the role of precedent; for present purposes, it suffices to say that almost everyone agrees that this, too, is a relevant factor. The one area where there is a fundamental dispute relates to contemporary social values. Can judges rightfully invoke contemporary values in deciding constitutional issues, or is that too "political" and therefore illegitimate?

For some critics, an intimate connection between values and judicial decisions is seemingly as shocking and distasteful as the adolescent's realization that one's parents must once-upon-a-time have engaged in sex. But discovering law and values in bed with each other should hardly be a shock. Law is a form of social governance, and it would be more shocking if its implementation were somehow conducted in a way devoid of human values. Indeed, the Constitution itself recognizes as much: Its goals include establishing justice, promoting the general welfare, and securing liberty. It would be wrong for constitutional lawyers and judges to ignore these goals, and contemporary values will necessarily color our understanding of justice, the general welfare, and liberty.

Moreover, the need to interpret the Constitution inevitably requires judges to make some sensitive judgments about societal values. To decide a First Amendment case, a judge must decide what counts as speech or religion; to decide a case under the Equal Protection Clause, the judge must decide what forms of discrimination are objectionable. This determination involves value judgments that inevitably evolve—even the most conservative jurists today concede that laws discriminating against women are subject to special judicial scrutiny; the framers of the Equal Protection Clause had different values and probably would not have agreed. Interpreting the Constitution also requires judges to resolve conflicts between constitutional values, such as collisions between freedom of the press and a defendant's right to a fair trial. Thus constitutional decision making inherently involves value judgments by judges.

In saying that judges need to articulate and reconcile constitutional values, we do not mean that they should necessarily do this on an ad hoc basis in every case. Often, it is better to do so by establishing a clear rule. For example, in a land-mark 1964 decision, the Court decided that limitations on libel law were necessary in order to prevent the threat of liability from chilling robust public debate on controversial issues. The Court did not, however, call upon judges to decide on a case-by-case basis whether the interest in robust debate outweighed the harm to the reputation of the person who was attacked. Rather, the Court established a categorical rule that defendants can be sued for knowingly false statements about public officials, but not for statements that they believe have some factual basis.[3]

The real question is not whether values should enter into decisions, but how they should do so. We begin by rejecting what is sometimes considered the prag-matist position, which equates judging with social engineering. (We think that this would be a misinterpretation of pragmatist philosophers like William James and John Dewey, but that is a bit beside the point.) On this "pragmatic" view, judges would play the same role as legislators in pursuing the public interest—or at least the same role that we hope legislators take, when they are not courting interest groups and chasing contributors.

While we do not shy away from the inevitable role of values in judicial decision making, we think judges would be ill-advised to embrace social engineering as the definition of their mission. In *Brown v. Board of Education*, for example, we think the Court was much better situated to decide that racial discrimination, in the post–World War II context, violated the deepest values of American society rather than to plot out the best way to redesign the education system so as to advance the long-term interests of racial minorities.

Courts are also often concerned with a different range of social values than are agencies (and often, but not invariably, legislatures). Social welfare is an important value, but should not be the only judicial concern when value judgments must be made, and less utilitarian concerns about fairness and rights also tend to be central to the work of courts. For example, in considering a claim of employment discrimi-nation, a court may properly be less concerned with the effect of discrimination law on the economy than with ensuring that protected groups are treated fairly.

For all these reasons, courts should not have an open commission to determine or implement social values. Judges should—and usually do—feel a sense of their own limitations when they make value judgments. Nevertheless, asking judges to forget about how their rulings may affect the well-being of their society is unrealis-tic. And asking them to make constitutional judgments without identifying consti-tutional values is impossible.

One commentator was moved to ask one of us whether there were any *irrelevant* factors in constitutional analysis. The most clearly irrelevant factor for judges—but a dominant factor for presidents, members of Congress, and other elected officials—is how a ruling will affect the outcome of the next election. Favoritism or hostility toward particular groups of litigants is also ruled out. In the constitutional setting, some impacts on social policy may be relevant, but others will not be. For instance, in deciding whether to uphold the constitutionality of a unilateral exercise of presidential power—or whether to require the president to receive congressional approval—it is not relevant whether the president has chosen the correct course of action in policy terms. These relevancy determinations are partly shaped by general considerations about the judicial role, partly by considerations of judicial competence, and partly by the considerations that prior law has singled out as deserving consideration when interpreting a particular constitutional provision.

How judges should make value judgments

How, then, should judges go about identifying constitutional values? Obviously, the greater the degree of national agreement about a value, the more comfortable a judge can feel. This may seem like an irrelevancy for a constitutional court, since consensus is presumably reflected in legislation and therefore does not need constitutional protection. But the truth is more complicated. First, on important issues, an overall majority agreement about certain values may exist without being reflected in every region or locality. Two examples were the ban on contraception in a handful of states in the 1960s, and the criminalizing of homosexual acts in a few states in the 1990s. Arguably, a more striking example was Jim Crow segregation, which was entrenched in the South but had little credibility at the national level. (Recall that President Truman had already desegregated the armed forces before the Court even considered the issue of segregation.) The question of how much localities should be allowed to deviate from a national majority is not necessarily easy, but this issue should not give rise to grave concerns about the legitimacy of judicial action.

Second, the existence of a dominant majority opinion does not necessarily mean that legislation will actually reflect that consensus, so judicial intervention may be necessary. Contrary to the vision in which important value issues are fully deliberated through the legislative process before law is made, political actors have significant leeway, which they can use even in the face of a contrary popular majority. Important constitutional interests can be invaded without full debate through executive fiat. A key role of the courts is to combat this risk. An important tool is the canon of interpreting legislation to avoid serious constitutional doubts, which means that the executive must return to Congress for clear authorization before stepping into constitutionally dangerous territory. Even within Congress, constitutional issues can be suppressed, as when a rider is attached to critical legislation at the last minute. Constitutional litigation can help defend widespread public values against such sneak attacks.

How judges should implement values is often thought to be a problem that arises primarily when the Court purports to be protecting unenumerated rights like privacy. It is just as much a problem, however, with enumerated rights like free speech. The constitutional text does not tell us whether flag burning counts as the kind of expression that is protected, any more than it tells us whether the right to an abortion is part of constitutional liberty. (If you are tempted to say that speech only covers vocalization, do you really think that banners, armbands, buttons, and video are not protected?) At the very least, judges should look for whether there is broad support for a value, even if not consensus—for example, whether support for the value cuts across party lines. Free speech (even for flag burners) has supporters across the political spectrum. It is also here that "tradition" plays a role.

Traditions do not come neatly packaged in a way that provides clear answers to constitutional questions. But a judge should be able to show that a value has genuine roots in our traditions. The argument is even stronger if the judge can show that failure to apply a more traditional value, such as personal privacy or freedom of expression, really is relevant in a particular context, but that this traditional value has not been given its proper weight for reasons that do not deserve respect, such as stereotyping, racist or sexist prejudices, or fear of political dissenters.

Conflicts between constitutional values pose equally great difficulties. The lessons of history are often crucial. For example, it is not obvious how we should deal with free speech issues in the face of threats to national security. National security and free speech are both values of constitutional dimension. Indeed, they both get explicit mention in the text itself: in the Preamble's purpose to "provide for the common Defense" and in the First Amendment. Unlike the framing generation, which fumbled the issue in passing the Alien and Sedition Acts, we are in a position to learn from two centuries of experience. The lesson we have learned—from the Alien and Sedition Acts themselves, from the Civil War and World War I, and from the "red scares" of the 1920s and 1950s—is that the government tends to overreact against dissenters in crisis periods. Thus the lessons of history are not limited to positive precedents—sometimes we learn at least as much from past mistakes.

Just as courts must define the boundaries of explicit constitutional values and resolve conflicts between them when such conflicts arise, so they must also sometimes decide whether values deserve constitutional protection in the first place. In *Griswold v. Connecticut*, for example, the Court extended such protection to the right of married couples to use birth control. The large majority of Americans seem to feel that this was warranted and that a contrary ruling would have been absurd.[4]

When we consider some specific cases at the end of the book, one of our main questions will be how the Court handled issues of value. Did the Court make a convincing argument for identifying a value as having constitutional stature? This is a key question regarding the abortion and homosexual conduct decisions. Did the Court identify a reasonable accommodation between conflicting constitutional values? That turns out to be the key question in the "war on terror" cases.

The risk of overreaching

The process of identifying constitutional values can misfire, sometimes badly. In the famous *Lochner* case, for example, the Court held that laws limiting bakers to sixty hours of work per week violated the workers' "freedom of contract." *Lochner*, and its glorification of "freedom of contract" as a constitutional value, remains the classic example of judicial overreaching. Ultimately the Supreme Court repudiated *Lochner* and held that economic regulations of this kind are constitutional whenever they serve some rational purpose. What went wrong in *Lochner*?[5]

To begin with, the Court conspicuously failed to connect its view of "freedom of contract" with constitutional traditions. As *Lochner* revisionists point out today, it might have been able to identify such a tradition in the earlier "free labor" strand of antislavery views and elsewhere. But doing so would have immediately raised the question of whether those earlier nineteenth-century traditions spoke realistically to the new world of industrialization at the beginning of the twentieth century. Many, in both political parties, doubted that they did. A philosophy that might have been credible in 1866 when the Fourteenth Amendment was written rang hollow, as anything but a partisan view, forty years later. *Lochner* can also be recharacterized as a case about special interest legislation, but the Court never developed that connection explicitly nor tried to develop it into a coherent theory of legislative validity. And that theory, if accepted, would tend to suggest that the minimum wage should have included more employees (so as to be less special interest), which is hardly what the Court had in mind.

The *Lochner* Court also ignored the extent to which its values were contested, even at the turn of the century, rather than supported by consensus. It presumed universal support for a viewpoint that was in fact partisan and contested. Indeed, the Court denied that it was making a value judgment at all. It claimed that it would defer to legislative policy judgments, and that it merely looked for rational empirical support for the resulting legislation. Sometimes it did defer to legislative policy, but in other cases—like *Lochner*—it ignored respectable empirical support for the legislative judgment while simultaneously denying making any value choice. As we have said, courts must sometimes make contested value judgments, but when they do so, they should at least be candid rather than hiding behind linguistic formulas like freedom of contract. As we will show in a later chapter, transparency is valuable as both a constraint on judicial overreaching and a method for exposing such overreaching.

And finally, after it decided *Lochner*, the Court refused to listen to what the rest of America was saying. By the early 1930s, it was plain that the *Lochner* vision had been repudiated by a broad spectrum of American society, yet a majority of the Court refused to yield. The justices showed a singular inability to learn from changing events and to hear opposing arguments. Instead, the Court seemingly redoubled its efforts (although even then its decisions were fitful and hard to reconcile). This is in contrast to the abortion issue, where the Court has tried to accommodate opposing values when it became clear that its ruling was deeply opposed.

Lochner illustrates the dangers that can arise when courts undertake to pronounce on fundamental values. Why, then, should we take the risk of allowing the Court to implement constitutional values? There is no easy answer to this issue, but it seems clear that in the United States, as in many other parts of the world, we have decided that the risk is worth running. This may stem in part from what the world learned during World War II about the critical need to protect human rights. The risk of the occasional unnecessary intrusion on political institutions has seemed worth running in order to avoid the opposing risk of human rights violations. In the U.S. system, however, the issue is not seriously in doubt. We have come to rely on the Court to perform this role over the past century. A judicial nominee who explicitly disavowed this role—for example, by arguing in favor of the state's right to ban contraception—would not be confirmable. Indeed, Judge Robert Bork made that very argument and the Senate rejected his nomination to the Supreme Court. His written speculation about a drastically truncated First Amendment also met a cold response; his plea that radical surgery was needed so that judges would not have to make judgments about the value of free expression convinced no one at all. As a society, we are committed to having judges recognize key values and enforce them, much as we may disagree with the results in some individual cases.

Thus we must accept the role of values in judicial decisions, but at the same time we need not surrender to uninhibited judgments by the judiciary. As we will see in the final section of the book, even in hard cases involving controversial social issues like abortion and affirmative action, there is a distinction between reasoned judgment and judicial fiat.

Giving judges discretion, then, does not mean that they are free to decide as they wish. There are limits on both the factors that they can consider and the reasoning that they can use. The limits are neither clear nor formulaic, but they exist and can be captured in the idea of giving a reasoned justification based on relevant factors. We as a society apparently are comfortable with these amorphous limits in the context of agency discretion, and there is every reason to believe that judges are at least as capable of following them as are agencies.

But that does not mean that judges' tasks—any more than agencies'—are easy. Our constitutional system expects judges to perform some very difficult duties, such as identifying the boundaries of fundamental social values. Unlike geometry, the answers cannot be found through deductive logic, nor are the answers always provably right or wrong. In other words, courts must exercise judgment. It behooves us, then, to take a closer look at judgment, and at how good judgments can be distinguished from bad.

6

The Anatomy of Judgment

To be nonarbitrary, a decision must do more than cite text, history, precedent, and values: The decision maker must also offer *some* explanation for how he or she arrived at the decision. The decision itself must result from a reasoned (and reasonable) application of the factors considered. Judgment is obviously called for. What can be said about this type of judgment and how to evaluate it?

It has been said that at one point, aeronautical engineers had proved that it was impossible for bumblebees to fly. Critics today seem to think it is impossible for judges to make reasoned decisions without the benefit of strict legal formulas. But the bumblebees kept on flying, and judges have been engaging in the exercise of reasoned judgment for centuries. If the theorists cannot account for these phenomena, so much the worse for their theories.

Judicial reasoning and the common law

This kind of unstructured but still "reasoned" decision making is certainly familiar to American lawyers. Attention to precedent and policy dominates the common law. Many important bodies of American law, including torts, contracts, and property, are controlled by the common law to this day. Others, such as criminal law, are rooted in concepts originally developed by the common law, or, like antitrust rules, represent common law elaborations on open-ended statutes. At least since Karl Llewellyn—if not since Holmes—American legal thinkers have defended the blend of precedent and policy in common law reasoning, as practiced by the great judges in our legal tradition. We do not regard constitutional law as purely a form of common law, because it is also guided by constitutional history in its various guises. Still, the edifice of common law doctrine does show that reasoned decision making is possible without an elaborate theoretical structure.

Certainly we do not mean to endorse purely ad hoc decision making. The Supreme Court's decisions in the 2000 presidential election illustrate the dangers of such decision making. Apparently motivated by a desire to bring closure to the election, the justices staked out novel legal positions, claiming for the first time the ability to supervise the state court's interpretation of state election laws and the ability to use equal protection law to micromanage state election procedures. These innovations did not flow in any obvious way from recent rulings in allied areas, and indeed seemed at odds with the Court's general view of federalism. Nor did the justices seem to give any thought to how these rulings might operate as precedents; rather, they seemed anxious to forestall the precedential effects of the rulings. The remedial aspects of the rulings—the abrupt grant of a stay and the termination of any recount efforts at the eleventh hour—did not even pretend to provide reasoned explanation. All of this is light years away from the work of common law judges like Justice Cardozo or Judge Learned Hand. A similar decision by an administrative agency would have been instantly reversed as arbitrary and capricious.

Nevertheless, unstructured decision making need not, and usually does not, devolve into ad hoc decision making. What keeps it from doing so is the exercise of judgment. We saw in the previous chapter that a basic part of reasoned decision making is taking into account all of the relevant factors, including making rational responses to the major legal and factual counterarguments. This is something that can be assessed fairly objectively. But merely providing a logical response to criticism is not enough, for it may be possible to cook up a logical but far-fetched reply—that is, a reply that is rational but not reasonable. Knowing what is a *reasonable* argument—rather than what the administrative law cases call a clear error of judgment—is partly a matter of common sense and partly a matter of professional training and experience. Lawyers must constantly decide on the plausibility of legal arguments, and their livelihoods depend in good part on their ability to make such judgments.

Many legal scholars seem uncomfortable with relying on this kind of judgment, and that uneasiness is one of the main motives for seeking grand theories. We understand this discomfort, but there is no avoiding the need for judgment calls in law. Even the most formalist theory will require determinations in borderline cases that will depend on acts of judgment. Moreover, we all constantly rely on experts of various kinds to make judgment calls, but we understand that this does not give them unlimited discretion. What constitutes a reasonable argument is partly a function of time and place, and is subject to change (usually incrementally). And when various arguments pull in different directions, a further act of judgment is required to strike a balance. This should not be too surprising or disturbing: Judges, after all, are people who make *judgments*.

This model of judicial decision making provides some bounds on outcomes. There are some outcomes that simply will not wash. Within the range of permissible outcomes, we are entitled to expect a reasoned decision, attending properly to precedent, constitutional history, and public values. (Of course, we realize that the exigencies of judging will not infrequently lead to shortcomings in opinions— compromises may well have to be made to secure a majority for an opinion, and sometimes the justices will feel tentative about detailed legal theories but certain of the conclusion.) At the end of the day, however, more than one reasonable outcome may exist, and it may be possible to write perfectly decent opinions in opposite directions. We should not overestimate the frequency of such outcomes—even on the ideologically divided Supreme Court today, many opinions are unanimous. But some degree of legal indeterminacy seems, as a practical matter, unavoidable. Where Judge Posner and others go wrong is not in recognizing this fact, but in mistaking an unusual event for a routine phenomenon.

How upsetting should the need for judgment calls be? One question is whether in practice the system will provide enough predictability to satisfy the rule of law. Experience suggests that the answer is yes, and we will later discuss some of the forces that tend to make decisions more predictable. Another question is whether having important decisions turn on judgment calls is fair to litigants. What is fair is partly a function of what is possible; no one can fairly demand something that cannot be supplied. The legal system simply cannot guarantee determinate answers to all legal questions. What it can attempt to provide, however, are reasonable judgments, based on open-minded consideration of opposing arguments, by judges who are doing their best to be faithful to precedent, history, and public values. We do not think a litigant can reasonably demand more, nor can any legal system promise anything better.

On a practical level, this inevitably means that ideology will sometimes affect decisions—not just because appraisals of public values have an ideological component, but because different ideologies produce subtly different interpretations of Supreme Court history and constitutional history more generally. This is to some extent healthy, because it makes the Court responsive to fundamental shifts in American political culture. We do not believe, however, that ideology always (or even often) determines judicial outcomes, or that judges necessarily close their minds to counterarguments. Judgment can be independent and objective.

The idea of objective judgment may seem chimerical, certainly to those who believe that judicial decisions are completely the product of ideology. However, there is good reason to think that, under the appropriate circumstances and from the right judges, we can expect more than recycled ideology from judges.

Improving judicial decision making

What circumstances produce the best decisions? Psychologists have discovered several important features of objective decision making—objective not in some grand philosophical sense, but merely in the sense of being properly responsive to opposing evidence and arguments and less likely to succumb to the various cognitive biases that can negatively affect decision making. Each of these features is reflected in either the structure of the judiciary or the education and professional milieu of lawyers. There is, therefore, reason to think that judges are likely to be about as good as possible—and probably better than most people—at making reasoned legal judgments.

First, individuals do better in general when they feel accountable for their decisions before the fact, but do not know the views of the evaluators. This tends to lead to more careful consideration of a broader range of evidence and arguments. Trial judges are often in this position because they cannot predict the makeup of the reviewing panel in the appellate court. Court of appeals judges do know who sits on the Supreme Court, but most cases are not reviewed by the highest court, so they have to be concerned about how their opinions will be perceived by judges in other circuits, who may refuse to follow their decisions. Indeed, if Supreme Court justices want anything more than the most grudging application of their rulings by lower federal courts and state judges, even they need to think about how those opinions will be received by other judges. Moreover, if justices want to get majority support rather than being relegated to plurality opinions that lack full precedential force, they need to be persuasive to at least four other justices.

Second, homogeneous groups tend to reinforce the existing biases of the members, often ending up with a decision that is more extreme than the initial views of the members. Groups with more diverse viewpoints seem less prone to this tendency toward "groupthink." The implications of this insight for judicial appointments are obvious: We should avoid having an ideologically uniform bench. Fortunately, fluctuations in the political system usually ensure a variety of appointees.

Third, studies of expert judgment show that experts differ from novices in their ability to grasp patterns. For example, chess masters do much better than novices when they are quickly shown pictures of board positions. Interestingly, this advantage only holds when the pieces are in some kind of reasonable strategic order, rather than randomly placed on the board. Even more interestingly, when chess masters make mistakes, they often substitute another arrangement of pieces that has essentially the same strategic attributes. In short, what they spot is the strategic pattern on the board, not simply a compilation of the individual pieces. This ability is acquired by spending many years studying thousands of games and board positions.

This ability to perceive the key pattern is very much akin to what the pragmatic legal scholar Karl Llewellyn called "situation sense" among appellate judges: the ability to isolate the key, relevant aspects of a case before the court. He viewed "situation sense" as a critical judicial skill. Without it, the judge's application of rules will be lame, and the judge will miss important analogies or arguments for reformulating rules. And like chess masters, good lawyers (whether or not they become judges) develop the ability to identify patterns over the course of their professional lives.

Fourth, all individuals are not equal in their ability to move beyond their own biases and take contrary evidence and opposing arguments into account. Studies show that this ability to engage in critical thinking is distinct from (although somewhat correlated with) raw brain power. It is possible to be brilliant and yet mindlessly outcome-driven, with all the intelligence merely going to provide clever rationalizations for predetermined outcomes. Active, open-minded thinking is crucial to good decision making because it can minimize the effect of what are called "cognitive biases," common psychological mechanisms that cause errors in rational thinking. As we will see in a later chapter, critical thinking is stressed in law schools and is also an important attribute for successful lawyers, and thus is likely to be highly developed in many judges.

An especially interesting series of studies involved experts on international relations. Over an extended time period, the studies investigated the ability of these experts to make accurate predictions about important international events. There were major differences in predictive ability. The best predictor of this ability was the ability to "think small," taking into account many factors rather than relying on a sweeping grand theory. Those who embraced grand theories made bad predictions, rarely acknowledged errors, and seemed to learn nothing from new information. Other studies have shown that dogmatism—tenacious adherence to a particular worldview, akin to a grand theory—also correlates with weak critical thinking and the inability to learn from mistakes.

None of these situations involving expert judgment is precisely similar to judicial rulings. It is easy to tell when a chess player is successful, and it is only a little more difficult to tell when a political forecast is incorrect. Determining the correctness of a controversial judicial decision is more difficult. Nevertheless, even without regard to disputes about how much weight text and original intent should get versus precedent and values, we can always ask how well a judge uses the intellectual tools he or she has chosen. The psychology literature strongly suggests that judges who are open to opposing arguments and willing to consider inconvenient facts will do better—whether the disputes are about history, text, precedent, or values.

In other words, judges should be foxes rather than hedgehogs. (A Russian saying, made famous by the philosopher Isaiah Berlin, observed that "the fox knows many little things, but the hedgehog knows one big thing"; Berlin used this as a metaphor for distinguishing between pragmatists and grand theorists.) If we want successful decision makers, says a leading researcher, "we are better off turning to experts who embody the intellectual traits of Isaiah Berlin's prototypical fox—those who 'know many little things,' draw from an eclectic array of traditions, and accept ambiguity and contradiction as inevitable features of life" rather than to the hedgehogs "who 'know one big thing,' toil devotedly within one tradition, and reach for formulaic solutions to ill-defined problems."[1]

Some authors have disparaged the idea that "craft values" or "professionalism" can significantly affect judicial decision making. But the psychology literature shows that decisions are indeed affected in a measurable way by intangibles of this sort. Of course, there are limits, but the existence of these limits is not inconsistent with the very real power of these intangible factors on judges. Ideally, then, we want a regime of judicial decision making that maximizes the presence of these intangible factors.

But intangible psychological factors are not the only constraints on judges. The next two sections of this book discuss the internal and external restraints on judges, which keep them from lapsing into arbitrariness or purely political decisions. We begin with one of the most powerful influences on judicial decisions—precedent—and then consider other judicial practices that moderate temptations toward political decision making. After looking at these more tangible constraints on judges, we will return in part V to the intangible psychological factors. Our topic, in other words, will be how the rule of law coexists with a good deal of judicial leeway.

PART III

Precedent as a Safeguard

7

Respect for Precedent

IF YOU OPEN a random page of the *U.S. Reports* and read a constitutional decision, you will be struck by how much of the space is devoted to discussing the Court's previous rulings. Indeed, the constitutional text may only be mentioned in a footnote, and discussion of original intent may or may not be present—but discussion of precedent is universal and generally thorough. Respect for precedent is also called *stare decisis*, which means roughly "adhering to what has been decided." Some critics decry reliance on precedent, but whatever one may think about it, it is clearly a key part of long-standing judicial practice in countries that follow the common law.

Many discussions of the role of the Supreme Court focus on how an individual justice should decide a discrete case. But the Court is a continuing institution, with continuity provided not only by overlapping membership, but by adherence to precedent. Indeed, in various ways, the Court situates itself in American constitutional history in its rulings. Comprehending the Court as an institution requires an understanding of this aspect of constitutional law. In this chapter we discuss why judges—especially in constitutional cases—should respect precedent, and in the next chapter we explore how this respect for precedent operates in practice.

Precedent and the rule of law

In considering the importance of precedent, we must first consider its relationship to the rule of law. Some observers consider the Court's reliance on precedent to be fundamental to the rule of law, while others sharply disagree. On the one hand, Justice Lewis Powell said that "elimination of constitutional stare decisis would represent an explicit endorsement of the idea that the Constitution is nothing more than what five Justices say it is. This would undermine the rule of law." He also said that the "inevitability of change touches law as it does every aspect of life. But stability and moderation are uniquely important to the law." Powell added that "restraint in decisionmaking and respect for decisions once made are the keys to preservation of an independent judiciary and public respect for the judiciary's role as a guardian of rights."[1]

On the other hand, stare decisis sometimes has been portrayed as a betrayal of the judge's duty to follow the law and thus of the rule of law itself. As Justice Scalia put it, "I would think it a violation of my oath to adhere to what I consider a plainly unjustified intrusion upon the democratic process in order that the Court might save face." He made an exception for "decisions that have become so embedded in our system of government that return is no longer possible," but with that limited exception, he said he agreed with Justice Douglas (a notable liberal activist) that "above all else . . . it is the Constitution which he swore to support and defend, not the gloss which his predecessors may have put on it." In Scalia's view, when the Court is faced with an unsupportable prior decision, "[w]e provide far greater reassurance of the rule of law by eliminating than by retaining such a decision." It should be noted, however, that Scalia does not take this viewpoint to its logical limit, and he does follow precedent when he thinks that overruling would be too violently disruptive. In ordinary cases, however, he does not show much hesitation in refusing to follow decisions with which he disagrees.[2]

For many originalists, then, stare decisis seems in tension with the paramount status of the written Constitution. As one critic says, "If the Constitution says X and a prior judicial decision says Y, a court has not merely the power, but the obligation, to prefer the Constitution." Or as another critic has said, "no court should ever deliberately adhere to what it is fully persuaded are the erroneous constitutional decisions of the past. To do so is to act in deliberate violation of the Constitution."

It is easy to understand the dissatisfaction of originalists with stare decisis. By allowing the views of five justices to displace the true meaning of the Constitution, stare decisis seems to authorize a covert form of constitutional amendment. At the same time, it elevates the mistaken views of five individuals above the true meaning of the law, thereby in a sense replacing the rule of law with the "rule of men."[3]

Rejection of stare decisis presents a theoretical conundrum for originalism. One of the primary arguments for originalism is that it constrains judicial discretion by providing rules that judges must follow. We have already seen that originalism's constraining power is less than one might suppose. Here we will discuss another problem: To the extent that originalism in practice is linked with a type of formalism that celebrates the value of clear rules, the denial of stare decisis deprives originalism of its ability to implement the rule of law. If a majority of justices agree in one case that the original understanding translates into a particular rule, a majority in the next case might distill a somewhat different rule, so that the actual meaning of the Constitution is blurred by competing formulations.

Justice Scalia, the leading proponent of originalism, provides the best illustration of the claim that originalism depoliticizes constitutional law by providing a more rulelike framework. Even a cursory acquaintance with Justice Scalia's work reveals his passion for order and logic. As one leading constitutional scholar has said, "for Justice Scalia, the rule's the thing; originalism and traditionalism are means, not ends." "Here is the codifier at work: first, state the general rule; second, rationalize the existing messy pattern of cases by grandfathering in a few exceptions and doing the best you can to cabin their reach; and third, anticipate future cases in which the rule might be thought problematic and dispose of them in advance by writing sub-paragraphs and sub-sub-paragraphs qualifying the rule with clauses beginning with 'unless' or 'except.'" This passion for rules is tied with Scalia's desire for consistency, which he views as the first of all legal virtues, the "very foundation of the rule of law."[4]

Because of his desire for clarity, certainty, and consistency, Justice Scalia has mixed feelings about the common law. He is uneasy about the common law process, in which law grows, "not through the pronouncement of general principles, but case-by-case, deliberately, incrementally, one-step-at-a-time." In his view, this process is inherently inconsistent with the ideal judicial role: Only by announcing and following clear rules can judicial decisions be respected, and only so can they provide certainty, limit future judicial discretion, and provide uniformity. Indeed, he maintains, judges who do not provide abstract rules but instead rely on the totality of the circumstances are "not so much pronouncing the law in the normal sense as engaging in the less exalted function of fact-finding."[5]

No wonder another leading advocate of the "law of rules" was moved to ask whether the common law qualifies as law at all. Indeed, Scalia himself seems to view the common law with some suspicion, and he regrets that it receives so much attention in law schools. Because law school begins by studying the common law, he says, the students' "image of the great judge—the Holmes, the Cardozo" is one "who has the intelligence to discern the best rule of law for the case at hand and then the skill to perform the broken-field running through earlier cases that leaves him free to impose that rule." The judge manages this task by "distinguishing one prior case on the left, straight-arming another one on the right, high-stepping away from another precedent about to tackle him from the rear, until (bravo!) he reaches the goal—good law."[6]

In an ideal world, where the Court was not already hemmed in by precedents, the right approach for originalists would be to decide every case by considering afresh the original meaning of the Constitution. It is easy to see, however, that this would result in the loss of such virtues as stability, consistency, and clarity—the very virtues that the law of rules is supposed to promote. There are some original-ists, such as Justice Thomas, who are willing to throw precedent to the wayside, but others such as Scalia realize the dangers of abandoning respect for precedent altogether.

Scalia's refusal to jettison precedent is understandable. In the absence of stare decisis, originalism is unlikely to lead to a stable, definitive set of answers to con-stitutional questions. To begin with, views of history, even by professional histo-rians, are subject to revision over time. These changing academic views would be reflected in shifts in constitutional interpretation. Shifts in interpretation could also be expected for two other reasons. Inevitably, even among like-minded judges, there will be some close, difficult cases, where the original meaning of the constitu-tional provision is debatable in its application. These cases may turn on the basis of a single vote, and will therefore be subject to revision whenever a justice approaches the issue anew. Judges are not clones, and originalist judges with different political inclinations will, despite their best efforts at objectivity, be influenced on occasion by their preconceptions. This would remain true even if all of the judges were "conservatives"—some might be social conservatives, others might be libertarians. Such individuals could have strikingly different interpretations of original mean-ing. Moreover, there is also the possibility of discovering new evidence—a study of personal letters by the framers, for example—that could destabilize an originalist interpretation.

Even assuming the existence of no ideological divisions whatsoever, judges could still be expected to have methodological divisions. For example, some might find the *Federalist Papers* a more persuasive source of evidence than others, or at an even finer level of detail, might view Madison's contributions to the series as more reliable than Hamilton's. When these methodological differences turned out to be outcome determinative, an originalist Court's rulings would lack consistency and reliability.

Jurists might also differ in terms of the level of generality with which they defined the original understanding. Again, the result would be inconsistent outcomes, depending on the identity of the judges and how their methodological positions lined up with substantive outcomes in specific cases. Even in the most pristine of all originalist judiciaries, conflicts would still exist between different schools of originalism. Without stare decisis, these methodological disputes would never be settled definitively.

Legal clarity would also suffer from unalloyed originalism. True, individual opinions might lay down clear rules of law based on interpretations of original meaning. But different judges on the same court could well articulate different "clear rules," and today's clear rules might not be those followed in tomorrow's opinions. In practice, if the law at any one time consists of overlapping versions of different justices' clear rules, or if the rules mutate over time, this "rule-based" approach might be incapable of creating clear law.

The dependency of formalism on stare decisis surfaces most strikingly in Justice Scalia's own writings. Justice Scalia has been, on the whole, no fan of stare decisis. Yet he also believes in the primacy of rules in judicial decisions. When writing a majority opinion, he says, he adopts a general rule that constrains not only lower courts, but also himself: "If the next case should have such different facts that my political or policy preferences regarding the outcome are quite the opposite, I will be unable to indulge those preferences; I have committed myself to the governing principle.... Only by announcing rules do we hedge ourselves in." Note that Justice Scalia is speaking here of the cases in which he writes for the majority—he is not concerned with his personal preferences but with the Court's obligations. Thus the picture is that he is bound by the previous decision not only by personal embarrassment over changing his mind, but because the Court's pronouncements are binding rules of law. Indeed, the whole point of the article in which he wrote those words was that law ought, whenever possible, to consist of binding rules.[7]

Yet, without stare decisis, the Court's pronouncements—even when grounded in a vision of original meaning—could not possibly constitute a rule binding on the justices in the future, but would only be at most a revocable command to the lower courts. Lower courts judges themselves would hardly be motivated to follow these temporary promulgations to the letter, knowing that whether their decisions were affirmed or reversed would depend instead on a de novo investigation by the Supreme Court of each new case as it arose. In other words, to achieve the Scalian vision of the rule of law, originalists also have need of stare decisis to protect the decisions of today's originalists against their successors. Thus, even if we could somehow miraculously rewind the clock and ensure that every justice in history practiced the most currently trendy forms of originalism, we would still find that we need stare decisis—if not about legal issues, then at least about the specific tenets of originalist methodology and their application in critical disputes.

Finally, the originalists' own view of the limited value of stare decisis potentially undermines the rule of law. Virtually everyone, including nearly all originalists, acknowledges that certain precedents cannot be undone. Robert Bork, for instance, concedes that some judicial practices are "so accepted by the society, so fundamental to the private and public expectations of individuals and institutions" as to be immune from judicial revision. As we saw earlier, Justice Scalia takes a similar position. But the significance of this concession should not be underestimated. Stare decisis is not peripheral to constitutional law; it fundamentally changes the nature of the enterprise. Bedrock precedents cannot be quarantined; instead, they inevitably affect the system of constitutional law as a whole. Thus to admit that some precedents should be respected is to require that all should be.[8]

The originalist impulse regarding these bedrock but allegedly "wrong" precedents is to say "this far, but not an inch farther." The key precedents will not be overruled for practical reasons, but we will return to first principles in considering new issues. But this is an untenable stance in a legal system that seeks some form of coherence. What sense does it make to say that we can use paper currency but not electronic transfers as money? What sense would it make to say that Social Security is constitutional but that expanding the program to cover expenses for prescription drugs or transforming it into a program of private accounts would not be? Or to try to limit the equality principle of *Brown v. Board of Education* to the Jim Crow laws of the 1950s? It is possible to have a sensible legal system in which a few small patches of doctrine are retained because of practical imperatives, but rejected in principle. But a legal system in which huge swathes of the law are considered unprincipled, while small corners are governed by principle, makes no sense at all. Bedrock rulings cannot be "limited to their facts" if the legal system is to have any claim to integrity; rather, they must be given generative force as precedents. In practice, Justice Scalia has struggled with these issues in many cases, using a series of judgment calls to decide just how far to follow well-entrenched but (in his view) erroneous rulings. He has in effect recognized that "erroneous" rulings can be too embedded in the law to be treated grudgingly in later cases.

Adherence to precedent does not mean simply refusing to overrule past decisions, but taking them seriously as starting points for analysis in future cases. This is partly a matter of reasoning by analogy from similarities between the facts of cases, but more importantly a matter of giving credence to the reasoning in earlier opinions. The willingness of judges to defer in this way to their predecessors—and their expectation of similar deference from their successors—transforms the Court from an ever-changing collection of individual judges to an institution, one which is capable of building a continuing body of law rather than merely a succession of one-time rulings. This kind of decision making, which is familiar to students of the common law system, is structured enough to provide stability and coherence, but flexible enough to allow improvisation and growth. Creating a false dichotomy between precedents—labeling some as unchangeable "bedrock" and others as contrastingly dispensable at will—disrupts the structure and undermines the rule of law.

Two final variants on the relationship between originalism and stare decisis warrant brief discussion. First, some textualists view elaborate recourses to history as unnecessary because they view the text itself as clear. They seem unfazed by the fact that people have been arguing for decades (and in some cases for centuries) about the meaning of phrases such as "the executive power," "due process of law," and "equal protection." Perhaps each of them simply assumes that judges will inevitably adopt their own personal reading of these phrases. But history is to the contrary. What textualism promises is not consensus but a cacophony of confident proclamations about the plain meaning of the document. Expecting these disputes to be miraculously settled when they have existed for such long periods is simply unrealistic. Thus, without stare decisis, this form of textualism will result in the same lack of stability that we have already described.

Some originalists take a more nuanced view of precedent. On their view, clear constitutional meaning remains controlling and precedent is to that extent irrelevant. But when original constitutional meaning is vague, precedent may govern application to specific cases so long as those precedents are not inconsistent with original meaning; moreover, the meaning of ambiguous provisions can be settled by practice, and erroneous practices may have to be left in place when the failure to do so would cause too much disturbance to social arrangements. However, this more nuanced version of originalism does not avoid the problem of instability. Different judges applying the same basic approach to interpretation will reach different conclusions about when meaning is vague or ambiguous and about the extent of the permissible leeway in interpretation, producing interesting theoretical debates on the bench but little in the way of reliable law.[9]

The value of precedent

Having shown that the originalists' skepticism of stare decisis does not hold water, we turn next to the positive case for precedent. The argument in favor of stare decisis is not rocket science. (On the contrary, it takes much more intellectual ability to mount an attack on something that is so obviously in accord with common sense.) Many of the reasons for giving weight to precedent are easily grasped, particularly in the case of bedrock precedents that provide the clearest examples of the need for stare decisis. Nevertheless, those reasons are worth reviewing, partly because they are not universally accepted and partly because they have implications for the way that precedent should be used.

Although precedent seems to have special force for the judiciary, consideration of past decisions is important in other settings. Some reasons for respecting precedent apply to any decision maker, while others particularly apply to courts, and some of those are especially linked with the nature of constitutional law.

There are obvious reasons why a decision maker should consider the views of her predecessors. These reasons apply as much to a school principal or a military base commander as to a justice or a president. One of these universal justifications is efficiency: It saves time and trouble to rely on decisions by predecessors.

A second reason is humility. It would be arrogant to assume that we alone have access to wisdom. The views of earlier decision makers are entitled to a respectful hearing for that reason alone. As even one of the sharpest critics of stare decisis concedes, *some* degree of respect for precedent is hard to avoid: Even without a formal doctrine of stare decisis, jurists would still have "an obligation of due consideration, careful reflection, and deference to the fact that other intelligent and reflective judges have thought about an issue before and taken care to express their reasoning in writing," and past decisions might even get "the benefit of the doubt in cases of uncertainty." Some of those earlier judges are entitled to particular respect—John Marshall, Oliver Wendell Holmes, Jr., and Louis Brandeis come immediately to mind as great figures in the history of the Supreme Court. It is true that this kind of "respect" is less than the most rigid versions of stare decisis might call for, but respect can easily shade into a habit of deference.[10]

A somewhat more subtle set of reasons for entrenching precedents relates to the process of decision making. It is simply unworkable to leave everything up for grabs all of the time. Imagine if, in every First Amendment case, the lawyers had to reargue basic questions such as whether the First Amendment applies to the states or whether it covers nonpolitical speech (both of which have been debated by scholars). Every brief would have to be a treatise, arguing every point of First Amendment doctrine from scratch. Moreover, different judges could adopt completely different First Amendment theories, so a lawyer in a case before the Supreme Court would really have to write nine different briefs based on inconsistent theories of the Constitution. Similarly, the justices would often find themselves unable to discuss the merits of particular cases with each other because they are operating within different conceptual frameworks. Unless most issues can be regarded as settled most of the time, coherent discussion is simply impossible. Surely "it would overtax the Court and the country alike to insist…that everything always must be up for grabs at once."[11]

Another set of reasons applies to some extent to all officials, but much more so to judges. One is the moral desirability of equal treatment. It seems arbitrary for a case to be decided one way this year, perhaps leading to a prisoner's execution or other serious consequences, and for an identical case to be decided the opposite way next year. This call for uniformity is not an unshakeable imperative, but it does caution against departing from precedent too quickly. Given the critical issues that often come before the courts, consistency seems especially important.

A related reason is that only by following the reasoning of previous decisions can the courts provide guidance for the future rather than a series of unconnected outcomes in particular cases. If all we know is that a court affirmed some convictions and reversed others, we can really have no idea what rule applies in the future. By articulating standards that are binding for the future, courts can offer some semblance of what has been called the "law of rules," which is one aspect of the rule of law.

Also relating specifically to the judiciary is the discipline imposed on decision making by the knowledge that a decision will function as a precedent. In deciding a particular case, a judge must provide reasons that will have precedential effect on later cases (both in the same court and in lower courts). Thus the judge is pushed to a form of neutrality—not the neutrality of being value-free, but the neutrality of articulating standards that one is willing to live with in the future: "If the future must treat what we do now as presumptively binding, then our current decision must judge not only what is best for now, but also how the current decision will affect the decision of other…cases." (Recall that Justice Scalia referred to this idea when he called for judicial decisions to lay out clear rules; it is only stare decisis that gives these rules any binding force.) It is in this sense that "neutral principles" are important to judicial opinions. Thus respect for precedent pushes judges to seek generality and coherence in their decisions.[12]

Precedent and the modern constitutional order

At least in certain kinds of cases, precedent gains added importance in the constitutional area. One purpose of having a written constitution is to create a stable framework for government. As even most originalists have recognized, this goal would be undermined if the Court failed to give special credence to bedrock precedents—precedents that have become the foundation for large areas of important doctrine. Some obvious examples involve the rulings of the New Deal era upholding the validity of the Social Security system and other federal taxing and spending programs, and those recognizing federal jurisdiction over the economy. These omelets cannot be unscrambled today, as even the most devoted believers in originalism often acknowledge. Likewise, it is far too late in the day to invalidate independent agencies, as some originalists would like, or to undo the twentieth-century rulings that "incorporated" the Bill of Rights and made it applicable to the states, or to reconsider the constitutionality of segregation.

It is not simply that it would be imprudent to overrule these doctrines, though obviously it would be. But in an important sense, it would run against the purposes of constitutionalism. Overruling these doctrines would create just the kind of uncertainty and instability that constitutions (even more than other laws) are designed to avoid. As one distinguished conservative constitutional scholar explains, "[s]tability and continuity of political institutions (and of shared values) are important goals of the process of constitutional adjudication, particularly 'in a constitution intended to endure for ages to come, and consequently, to be adapted to the various *crises* of human affairs.'" "Moreover," he elaborates, "these values are in part at least among the values that the new constitutional order was specifically designed to secure," and the *Federalist Papers* "even decried appeals to the people in order to 'maintain[] the constitutional equilibrium of government.'"[13]

Originalism can be made more acceptable by acknowledging these bedrock precedents as untouchable, something that Justice Scalia clearly realizes, though it has escaped his colleague Justice Thomas. But even so, there is still something seriously amiss. When originalists agree to accept precedents that diverge from what they consider to be the original understanding, there is really a mixed message. Presumably it would have been better if all these cases had been decided "correctly" in the first place, but now we are stuck with the errors. Thus originalists are asking us to regret that the federal government was given the tools to take the country through the Great Depression, regret that Congress was allowed to pass civil rights statutes, regret that the Court erroneously ruled that states lack the power to set up established churches, and so forth. In our view, however, those decisions are something that should be a cause for pride in American society, not a grudging acceptance of past "errors" that can no longer be undone.

In any event, legitimate or not to some, these modern constitutional doctrines are here to stay as a realistic matter. Plenary federal power over fiscal and economic matters, independent agencies, and application of the Bill of Rights to the states are now integral parts of our system of government; in some ways they are more "constitutional" than some of the more obscure parts of the written Constitution.

Consider the following question: Which would be more shocking, a Supreme Court decision invalidating the Social Security system, or one upholding a requirement that certain homeowners with extra space rent out rooms to military personnel in peacetime? The Third Amendment speaks plainly to the latter situation, in a way that cannot be said of Social Security. Along these lines, one of the most vehement critics of stare decisis in the Reagan era allowed for an exception when overruling a precedent would cause a national crisis. "Surely," he said, "a judge need not vote to overrule an erroneous precedent if to do so would pitch the country into the abyss—if to do so would be on the order of killing the body to save a limb." He pointed to the *Legal Tender Cases*, which upheld the constitutionality of paper money, as an apt example. And admittedly, whatever the framers might have thought about the matter, it is hard to see how a modern economy could survive if only gold and silver coins could be used as a medium of exchange.[14]

The example of paper money also points up another reason for respecting bedrock precedent. Imagine that the Supreme Court did overrule itself and hold that only coinage can be constitutionally used as a medium of exchange. One possibility would be an immediate economic crisis. But perhaps such a crisis would not occur if the political system responded quickly enough. Maybe Congress and the states could drop all other business to pass an immediate constitutional amendment, or perhaps some ingenious solution could be adopted that supported a modern economy while restricting "money" to metal coinage, such as a computerized barter system. Still, even assuming a happy ending, the issue would necessarily take over the public agenda until the solution was implemented. Thus the Court would have preempted legislative attention. Should curing a possible error in an 1870 case really push the legislative agenda off such current issues as the Iraq war, rebuilding cities after Hurricanes Katrina and Rita, or the threat of terrorism? Preempting the normal processes of government for such a purpose seems fantastically misguided.

Bedrock precedents—sometimes called superprecedents—are decisions or lines of decision that are simply too well entrenched to be subject to any serious possibility of challenge. Some examples are the Court's ruling in *Marbury v. Madison* that it had the power of judicial review, its holding in *Brown v. Board of*

Education that segregation is unconstitutional, and the series of post-1937 cases upholding the constitutionality of the modern regulatory state. Once these decisions are accepted as constitutional fixed points, however, they become the bases for wider areas of doctrine, and they also shift the conceptual landscape of constitutional law. There is a certain paradox in the notion that, by entrenching certain doctrines against change, respect for precedent becomes the basis for constitutional growth, much as the skeletons left behind by coral organisms form a reef on which new generations of the organisms take root. By bringing stability to the law, stare decisis—particularly as applied to bedrock precedents—also provides the basis for what has been called the living Constitution.

There are good reasons, then, for respecting precedent in constitutional cases. And the case for stare decisis is only strengthened if we consider the breadth of doctrines that would be ripe for overruling if we were to jettison established precedent in favor of our best guess at the original understanding. The tension between modern judicial doctrine and the original understanding is profound. A partial list of constitutional doctrines that are at least problematic—and possibly untenable—in terms of the original understanding includes the following: the aggressive protection of free speech under modern First Amendment doctrine; the desegregation cases; cases limiting affirmative action, especially at the federal level; cases upholding the power of Congress to regulate the economy, protect the environment, and ban employment discrimination; and cases prohibiting discrimination against women.

Respect for precedent, then, is the best way to ensure stability, implement the rule of law, and protect some of what have become our most cherished rights and traditions. But abstractions will only take us so far. In the next chapter we turn to three questions that arise when we try to apply the principle of stare decisis. First, what counts as a precedent? Second, how should we read precedents: as sources of rules or sources of general principles and analogies? And, third, if we are relying on respect for precedent as a constraint on judicial discretion, what reasons do we have for thinking that it actually works?

8

Explaining Precedent

I**N THIS CHAPTER**, we try to clarify how precedent functions in constitutional law. We begin by suggesting that respect for precedent actually extends beyond previous judicial decisions to include actions and statements by nonjudicial actors. We then explore the question of whether precedents (judicial or otherwise) should be read as establishing specific rules or as providing a source of evolving standards. Finally, we try to rebut the all-too-common belief that judges merely use precedents as after-the-fact rationales for outcomes, exemplified by Justice Scalia's reference to common law judges as running backs who must dodge around precedents in order to reach the goal line.

What kinds of precedents?

Our first task is to determine what counts as a "precedent." It is easy to recognize a judicial decision as precedent (although, as we will see, not as easy to figure out what to do with it). But nonjudicial precedents can also play a significant role in constitutional law. Thus respect for precedent is not merely a way of empowering the judiciary; it also provides a point of entry for other sources of constitutional understanding.

One important source for constitutional law is the *Federalist Papers*, written by Alexander Hamilton and James Madison (with a small assist from John Jay) during the ratification debates over the Constitution. The Supreme Court relies heavily on these essays, supposedly in the service of determining original intent. The essays are not particularly good sources of evidence of intent—they were read mostly in New York at the time and by a relatively small initial audience. It makes much more sense—and is more consistent with the Court's use of the documents—to view these essays as the equivalent of judicial precedents. They are early public interpretations of the Constitution by eminent and exceptionally reliable interpreters, who were not merely writing the equivalent of law review articles but instead were actively participating in the critical public decision of whether to adopt the Constitution. Whatever the specific impact of the *Federalist Papers* themselves, there can be no doubt that Madison and Hamilton played important roles in the ratification campaigns in the key states of Virginia and New York; their publicly expressed views were hardly what political scientists and economists call "cheap talk." In practice, the *Federalist Papers* seem to have much the same status today in judicial decisions as the views of another eminent early commentator, Chief Justice John Marshall, in his pathbreaking opinions for the Court.

For similar reasons, the decisions of the First Congress should also be considered important precedents. The Supreme Court has given special deference to the First Congress on the theory that it was likely to reflect original intent, because many of the members of Congress were delegates to the Philadelphia convention or to state ratifying conventions. Although there is something to be said for this argument based on original intent, political circumstances had shifted significantly by the time Congress met, making congressional decisions an imperfect reflection of earlier understandings. But, like early judicial decisions, these early congressional actions reflected the considered judgments of distinguished constitutional thinkers like Madison, they provided a foundation for many decades of later legislation, and they should be considered important precedents for later decisions.

Another good illustration of the importance of nonjudicial precedents involves the scope of executive power. The extent of executive power is hotly disputed, so what is presented here will be a set of conclusions rather than a full-fledged argument on the subject. The upshot is that the Supreme Court has looked—and should look—to the actual practices of Congress and the executive branch as a source of guidance about the proper delineation of authority.

On a fair reading, the historical record fails to settle what the framers themselves meant by the executive power or how it related to specific grants of presidential authority. As Justice Robert Jackson said in a famous opinion on President Truman's use of presidential power, "Just what our forefathers did envision, or would have envisioned had they foreseen modern conditions, must be divined from materials almost as enigmatic as the dreams Joseph was called upon to interpret for Pharaoh." He added that a "century and a half"—now two centuries—"of partisan debate and scholarly speculation yields no net result but only supplies more or less apt quotations from respected sources on each side of any question."[1]

It is an exaggeration to say that the historical records teach us nothing about the original understanding of executive power, but they clearly fail to provide any precise guidance about the boundaries of presidential power. This is not to say that presidential power was a complete constitutional cipher. The specific grants of power to the president, as well as related grants of power to Congress in military and foreign affairs, give some guidance. The framers built on a history of disputes about executive power. We know that they considered the postrevolutionary governors too weak. We also know that they considered the prerevolutionary governors and the English monarch too strong. Like Goldilocks, they wanted something that was "not too strong" and "not too weak" but "just right." They wanted as much executive energy and initiative as possible without upsetting the proper balance of republican government. But these principles are too general to resolve hard cases. Thus, when particular questions about executive power arise, text and original understanding can provide only limited guidance.

As Madison recognized at the time, there is no way of deducing the limits of executive power from general principles. In *Federalist* No. 37, he said that "[e]xperience has instructed us that no skill in the science of government has yet been able to discriminate and define, with sufficient certainty, its three great provinces—the legislative, executive, and judiciary; or even the privileges and powers of the different legislative branches." He sagely added that "[a]ll new laws, though penned with the greatest technical skill and passed on the fullest and most mature deliberation, are considered as more or less obscure and equivocal, until their meaning be...ascertained by a series of particular discussions and adjudications."[2]

The question, then, is how to find the right balance between energy and efficiency on the one hand, and legal restraint on the other. The president must be free to respond to emergencies, but not too free, lest the category of emergency action swallow up too much of public policy and individual liberty. There is no a priori way to set this balance. Somehow we have managed over the course of our history to find an acceptable balance, and the best the Court can do is to try to maintain that historic balance. It is for this reason that Justice Jackson, in the opinion on presidential power that we quoted above, put so much stress on the practical accommodations reached between Congress and the president over the years. Jackson's opinion has become the foundation for modern thinking about presidential power. As this example shows, respect for precedent need not be based on judge worship—a consistent line of interpretation by Congress and the president is also deserving of respect.

Nonjudicial precedents like the *Federalist Papers* or settled practice by the other branches is important for the present discussion because it illustrates the pull of precedent even outside the courts. Consideration of nonjudicial precedents also reinforces the significance of bedrock precedents. Such bedrock precedents as the post–New Deal understanding of federal power has received the support of the president and Congress over a long period of time; so has the racial integration mandate of *Brown*. These practices rebuff any argument that the precedents in question represent a judicial power grab, and thereby help place their legitimacy beyond question.

What does it mean to follow precedent?

This brings us to the question of how to read precedents. It is one thing to say that a precedent should be followed. It is another to say just what it means to follow a precedent. This is not an easy question to answer. As a writer of an earlier generation remarked, "Yet when one asks, how does one determine the legal significance of judicial precedents?—one finds only fragmentary answers in authoritative materials and no entirely satisfactory theory offered by the writers who have dealt with the subject." That seems to remain true today.[3]

In various legal systems, precedent may be used as the basis for an analogy, or seen as exemplifying a general principle, or taken as establishing a binding rule. Anglo-American law has also been unclear: "The precedent has been viewed as limited to the 'decision' on the 'material facts' as seen by the precedent court, or the same as seen by the nonprecedent court; for others, the term means the 'rule,' formulated by the precedent court; for still others, the term includes the reasons given for the rules formulated."[4]

In rough terms, the dispute over the treatment of precedent can be mapped onto the distinction between legal rules and standards. This distinction itself is not razor sharp, but the gist can be seen by comparing "do not exceed 65 mph" (a rule) with "do not drive faster than conditions allow" (a standard). Thus most American roads follow a rule; the German Autobahn follows a standard.

Justice Scalia's view of precedent—outlined in the previous chapter—calls on courts to lay down clear-cut dictates whenever possible; those rules are then binding as rules on later courts until overruled. If we view precedents as more about general principles than about rigid rules, however, they operate more like standards. The reasoning and result of each case adds to our understanding of the standards, but flexibility is always retained around the fuzzy edges surrounding the core. Doctrine therefore evolves over multiple decisions rather than being laid down as explicit rules in individual cases.

The dispute over rules versus standards is also related to calls for judicial minimalism. The rule approach calls on courts to establish broad rules that will then govern an area of law. Minimalists like Cass Sunstein instead call for courts to take incremental steps, allowing legal principles to evolve with the accumulation of precedent. Thus he seems to want to give opinions very small precedential influence until a sufficient body has accumulated to establish a clear standard.

The general outlines of the standards/rules debate are familiar to lawyers and legal scholars. By creating sharp boundaries, rules have the advantage of being easy to apply and highly predictable. Their application also is supposedly more objective, in the sense that the varying perspectives of decision makers are less likely to affect the outcome. Rules are also more readily applied by lower-level decision makers, an important consideration in cases like *Miranda* where the law must be implemented by low-level officials such as police officers.

But rules also have the defects of their virtues. Creating sharp, easily administered lines comes at the cost of unfair treatment of unusual or borderline cases, which might otherwise warrant individualized treatment. Formal rules invite strategic manipulation—tax law provides the classic example of how efforts to provide clarity and predictability open the way for opportunism. The predictability stemming from formal rules comes at the expense of learning from experience, since new insights can only be incorporated in the law through the relatively radical step of changing the entire rule. "Objectivity" in applying rules may mean that disputes about constitutional values are often disguised as semantic arguments about the meaning of a rule. Surely, constitutional interpretation should not turn on dueling dictionaries or fine-grained word splitting.

Moreover, in the setting of a judicial body, treating precedents as creating rules rather than principles or analogies increases the demands on collective action. It is easier to agree on how to decide a particular case than on a specific rule for the future. If precedents are considered to create "rules," the members of a majority must not only be able to agree on the outcome of the case before them or on a general principle, but on the precise contours of a rule of law. The foreseeable result of a rule-oriented approach to precedent is to have more fractured courts, with fewer majority opinions.

Moreover, treating precedents as rules demands more from later judges in the way of self-abnegation. Judges must feel a stronger sense of commitment to precedent in order to agree to follow not only the outcome and principle of an earlier case, but the precise legal test articulated by the court in that case. The temptation to abandon the rule will be especially strong when the follow-on case involves circumstances that were not contemplated when the rule was established or when a new judge does not agree with the original decision. Thus, because a rule is less flexible than a standard, it is less likely to maintain the allegiance of later judges. Consequently, rulelike precedents have a tendency to evolve into standards. One striking example is the abortion decisions. In *Roe v. Wade*, the Court pronounced rules based on the rigid trimester system. Some twenty years later, *Planned Parenthood v. Casey* reworked the rule-oriented *Roe* opinion into a standardlike undue burden test. In these and other cases, rules have had a way of weathering poorly as precedents.

The frailty of precedent as a source of bright-line rules is a lesson that Justice Scalia has learned to his evident discomfort. In some important majority opinions, he has tried to create strong rules only to discover that other justices regarded these precedents merely as standards. For example, in *Lujan v. Defenders of Wildlife*, he attempted to establish sharp rulelike limits on standing, only to see the Court move back to a standardlike approach in *Friends of the Earth, Inc. v. Laidlaw Environmental Services, Inc.*, and even more strikingly in the climate change case, *Massachusetts v. EPA*. Similarly, he attempted to move takings law away from the standard-based approach of *Penn Central Transportation Co. v. City of New York*, only to see that approach triumphant again a few years later. No doubt these setbacks to his efforts to reduce judicial oversight of the executive and protect property rights have been very frustrating. But even the justices who initially joined his opinions probably thought at the time that they were agreeing only to standards rather than iron-clad rules.[5]

The choice between rules and standards is ultimately a pragmatic one. In the setting of constitutional doctrine, however, standards often have a strong advantage over rigid rules simply because it is easier to gain and then maintain over time majority support for them. Thus there is much to be said for treating constitutional precedents as sources of principles or of fruitful analogies rather than as entrenching rigid rules of law, except in unusual cases like *Miranda* where there is a special need for sharp boundaries.

It may seem that treating precedents as standards rather than rules undercuts the very stability that stare decisis was supposed to provide. But there is a difference between stability and rigidity. Maximizing stability may call for flexibility, as the familiar comparison between the storm-resistant qualities of oaks and willows reminds us.

Stare decisis seeks to preserve stability, but the doctrine must also leave room for innovation and recognition of error. Striking the right balance is not easy. In the end, we prefer a version of stare decisis in which rulings are not overturned except for strong reasons (and only for compelling reasons in the case of what we call "bedrock" precedents). But this version of stare decisis is not rigid, because it sees doctrine as evolving over multiple decisions rather than being laid down as explicit rules in individual decisions. That is to say, our version of the doctrine is strongly against overruling, but leaves more room for good faith reinterpretation of individual decisions.

Does precedent really matter?

Precedent can provide only incomplete constraint, but it still has the capacity to provide real guidance. At the same time, it can provide a foundation for an evolving body of doctrine. Consequently it can give us a constitutional regime that is stable enough to support the rule of law while being flexible enough to adapt to social change. But this assumes, of course, that judges actually follow precedent rather than using it as cover for whatever decisions they wanted to reach anyway. This brings us to our last question about precedent: What reasons do we have for thinking that precedent makes any difference?

Few scholars (and even fewer judges) deny the importance of precedent, but some doubt whether it serves as an effective constraint. There are certainly examples of judges reaching results that are seemingly inconsistent with precedent; indeed, we discuss some examples in later chapters. But the failure often stems more from a lack of transparency than from an inattention to precedent. The very fact that the misuse of precedent is so easily demonstrated illustrates that the justices at issue were not being honest in their application of precedent. Thus how a judge treats precedent can serve as a method of evaluating his or her judicial craftsmanship.

Precedent can be distinguished, read narrowly, revised in light of later cases, overruled, or even misinterpreted and manipulated, but it cannot be ignored. Its very status as precedent makes it both an actual and a psychological obstacle to unfettered discretion. Judges who might wish to write on a clean slate cannot do so without confronting existing doctrine. Precedent is like an old and somewhat unreliable lock. Some keys open it without difficulty, others might need to be turned and jiggled just so, and sometimes you cannot get in without breaking down the door. And both the judge and the reader of the judge's opinions will recognize which method is being employed. A judge who too often uses brute force, manipulating or overruling precedent that stands in her way, will lose respect from her judicial peers, the political branches, and the citizenry.

We do not mean to overstate the influence exerted by precedent. Precedent rarely dictates the result in any particular case, especially at the level of the Supreme Court. Instead, precedent creates both outer boundaries and a place to begin. The development of a body of doctrine over time also provides indications of trends and of underlying values, purposes, and policies.

The idea that precedent is meaningless is based on a rather simplistic view of judicial psychology in which judges care solely about outcomes and evaluate them in purely instrumentalist terms. But this may reflect the psychology of those who advocate that position more than it reflects the psychology of actual judges. We know from many psychology studies that people tend to have a bias in favor of the status quo and that they frame issues in terms of their relationship with that status quo. For similar reasons (not to mention their professional training), it is plausible to expect precedents to shape judges' behavior fairly strongly. The Court also has an institutional interest in adhering to precedent in order to strengthen the influence of its decisions.

A good example of the constraining role of precedent may be found in a relatively recent confrontation between Congress and the Supreme Court, one that had its origins almost half a century ago. Beginning in the 1960s, the Court interpreted the Constitution to provide basic protections for criminal defendants. Prompted largely by the conspicuous failings of a justice system tainted by race discrimination, the Court, in a series of landmark cases, laid out procedural protections to ensure fair trials and prevent police misconduct. These included protections against coercive police interrogations and sweeping searches, access to a lawyer (provided at the state's expense if necessary) at various stages of a criminal proceeding, and the broad availability of federal oversight of state convictions. Then came several decades of fine-tuning: deciding exactly how to accommodate the basic principles of fair treatment and the needs of law enforcement. We do not agree with every choice the Court made, nor would we expect readers to do so. But the end result is a body of doctrine that lays out general (if somewhat underspecified) limits on government actions and provides underlying principles of fairness to guide future decisions.

One of the important cases in this line was *Miranda v. Arizona*, decided in 1966, which held that police must give certain warnings to suspects or else the state will forfeit the ability to use the suspect's subsequent statement in court proceedings. Chief Justice Rehnquist had previously made clear his view that the *Miranda* rules were not required by the Constitution. Congress, too, opposed *Miranda*; in 1968 it enacted a statute that purported to overrule *Miranda*. The statute dictated that the admissibility of a defendant's statement should be governed only by whether it was freely given, regardless of whether the police had given the required warnings. The conflict between the judicial doctrine and the statute finally came to the Supreme Court in 2000. In *Dickerson v. United States*, the Supreme Court invalidated the statute, adhering to its *Miranda* doctrine, in a 7–2 decision that was authored by none other than Chief Justice Rehnquist. Even as the Court refused to hold that the particular warnings themselves were constitutionally required, it credited the basic insight of *Miranda* that *some* protection against coercive police interrogations is necessary; because the federal statute did not provide any alternative to the *Miranda* warnings, that statute could not supplant them. Despite his early misgivings about *Miranda*, then, even Chief Justice Rehnquist ultimately adhered to its core principles.[6]

Another recent example of the importance of precedent is provided by *Randall v. Sorrell*, in which the Supreme Court struck down a Vermont campaign finance law. The Court's basic precedent in this area, *Buckley v. Valeo*, allows the government to regulate contributions to political campaigns but not independent expenditures—in other words, the government has more power to regulate the amount of money that a person can give to a candidate than the money he or she spends to finance advertising that is not controlled by the candidate. Conservatives have long decried virtually all regulation of campaign contributions. Justices Thomas and Scalia have long argued for overruling the part of *Buckley* that allows regulation of contributions, and Justice Kennedy has also expressed considerable skepticism about it. Chief Justice Rehnquist was also opposed to *Buckley*, and Justice O'Connor was the swing vote to uphold campaign finance regulation. With her departure from the Court, it seemed likely that *Buckley* was doomed.[7]

But *Buckley*'s demise has not yet come to pass, despite the opportunity provided in *Randall*. Chief Justice Roberts joined a portion of the plurality that refused to overrule *Buckley*'s limits on expenditures, but that also spoke more broadly about adherence to *Buckley*. He said he could "find here no such special justification that would require us to overrule *Buckley*"—no later cases that had "made *Buckley* a legal anomaly or otherwise undermined its basic legal principles"; no "demonstration that circumstances have changed so radically as to undermine *Buckley*'s critical factual assumptions"; and on the contrary, that "*Buckley* has promoted considerable reliance" by Congress and state legislatures. Roberts emphasized that "[o]verruling

Buckley now would dramatically undermine this reliance on our settled precedent." Justice Thomas's dissent observes that "[a]lthough the plurality's *stare decisis* analysis is limited to *Buckley*'s treatment of expenditure limitations, its reasoning cannot be so confined, and would apply equally to *Buckley*'s standard for evaluating contribution limits."[8]

Thus it seems very likely that Roberts is committed to following *Buckley* and has rejected the Thomas and Scalia argument for overruling it. Justice Alito joined other portions of Justice Breyer's opinion, but wrote separately to say that he did not find it necessary to reach the issue of overruling *Buckley*. At present, however, despite Justice O'Connor's departure from the Court, there seem to be at least five votes to uphold *Buckley*, based in large part on stare decisis rather than agreement with *Buckley*'s reasoning.

We leave for a later chapter the single most striking example of the force of precedent: the Rehnquist Court's refusal to overrule *Roe v. Wade*. After several appointments by Presidents Reagan and Bush, such an overruling seemed all but inevitable. But when push came to shove, Justices O'Connor, Souter, and Kennedy were unwilling to overturn such a critical precedent.

These cases are not merely quirks. A rigorous study of judicial decisions determined that political perspective (measured by the political party of the appointing president) is indeed important. But precedent also counts for a great deal. This study covered all Supreme Court cases decided from the end of World War II to the turn of this century. Citations in later opinions are listed and classified in standard legal reference works, and the study statistically analyzed all of those citations. Based on this massive data set, the authors concluded that "law and policy are…both important considerations that are inextricably linked to one another as the justices interpret and shape the law." Precedent "can be a constraint in that, under certain circumstances, the justices will respond to the need to legitimize their policy choices, and this incentive affects how they use precedent." Precedent can also "represent an opportunity in that it is through the setting and interpreting of precedent that the justices can foster outcomes in society that they prefer." The central conclusion of the research was quite telling: "The main point is that the justices do not change law simply based on their policy preferences or on the existing state of precedent; they do so based on an interactive relationship between these two factors."[9]

Thus precedent has an important role to play in shaping judicial decisions. But it does not stand alone as a bulwark against purely political judgment. In the next section, we will show how other aspects of the judicial system also tend to reinforce the pull of law as opposed to politics.

PART IV

Process Safeguards

9

Deliberation and Multiple Decision Makers

Precedent is not the only constraint on judicial discretion. Other aspects of the structure of the judiciary also play a role. Scholars worried about the countermajoritarian difficulty often focus primarily on two aspects of the judiciary: the way in which judges are appointed and the provisions for controlling or removing them. In the case of federal judges, the fact that judges are not elected, but instead are nominated by the president and confirmed by the Senate, gives rise to the countermajoritarian difficulty. The discussion thus often centers on the extent to which the appointment process incorporates popular will; the relative responsiveness of the judiciary and the popular branches to public opinion; congressional control over the jurisdiction of the federal courts; and the effectiveness of impeachment as a method of popular control of judges. State court judges, on the other hand, are usually elected and are often subject to popular recall or removal procedures. This both reduces concern and provides a standard against which the federal judiciary can be measured.

As we argued in chapter 3, these concerns about the countermajoritarian nature of the federal judiciary are overblown. But a more serious problem with the focus on appointment and removal is that it overlooks other structural constraints. These structural constraints, which operate indirectly to foster adherence to the rule of law, are common to both state and federal judicial systems. One of the simplest, yet most significant, is the multimembered nature of the judiciary.

Tiered, multimember courts

State and federal judiciaries are similarly structured. Trial judges almost always preside singly, but their decisions are reviewed by at least one—and often two or more—multimember panels of appellate judges. In the federal system, the decisions of the district court (trial) judges are reviewed by the courts of appeals. Each geographically defined district court is subject to review by a particular court of appeals, so that, for example, federal judges in Minnesota are always subject to review by the Court of Appeals for the Eighth Circuit, while federal judges in Tennessee are subject to review by the Court of Appeals for the Sixth Circuit. (There are currently thirteen different courts of appeals, and Congress is considering creating one or two more by splitting the current Ninth Circuit into two or three circuits.) Court of appeals judges sit in rotating panels of three, and their decisions can be reviewed by a bench of as many as seventeen judges from the same court. Court of appeals decisions in turn are subject to review by the U.S. Supreme Court, which consists of nine justices. Each level of court—district court, court of appeals panel, and full court of appeals—is bound by the decisions of all the courts higher up the chain. And although they are not bound by the decisions of other courts at the same level—one court of appeals need not follow the decisions of a different court of appeals—rulings by parallel courts often have great influence. State court systems work similarly, containing trial courts and one or two levels of appellate review, and some state court decisions involving federal questions are also subject to review by the U.S. Supreme Court.

Although not every decision is appealed (and very few indeed reach the U.S. Supreme Court), the most controversial, groundbreaking, or significant cases are most likely to be reviewed by multiple courts. Virtually every controversial constitutional issue decided by a trial court will ultimately be decided by an appellate court unless the case is settled. The cases that avoid the appellate gauntlet are usually those that are settled by the parties, involve issues of fact rather than law, or are merely noncontroversial applications of established law. Despite what law students believe, there *are* some easy cases; indeed, more than 90% of court of appeals opinions and more than a third of Supreme Court cases are unanimous. Judicial discretion is only a concern in the less common cases that lack an easy answer.[1]

The combination of hierarchical organization and multimember courts helps restrain discretion in several ways. At any given time, the judges on the federal bench have been appointed by different presidents (and confirmed by different Senates) and have different personalities, backgrounds, experiences, ideologies, and moral intuitions. The only commonality is their mutual faith in the rule of law and their sworn oath to uphold it. Thus, to the extent that a judge needs the agreement of other judges in order to make a decision stick, she will have to appeal to this shared vision rather than to her individual beliefs. And the structure of the federal judiciary means that every judge *does* need to persuade at least some other judges. Except for Supreme Court justices, every federal judge is subject to review by other judges. Not only does this ensure that idiosyncratic decisions are ultimately reversed, it also influences judges to rein in their personal impulses and instead stay as close to previously decided cases as possible: No judge wants a reputation as the most reversed judge in her circuit! At the district court level, a judge does not know which judges will serve on the appellate panel, and thus must make rulings in a manner likely to stand up to scrutiny by the largest possible number of judges. Appellate judges will seek to persuade at least five Supreme Court justices in order to avoid reversal. The farther a judge strays from precedent—in other words, the more radical and less incremental the decision is, or the less faithful to the rule of law—the more likely it is that a reviewing court will overturn it. Thus the sheer fact that lower court decisions are not final ensures a good-faith attempt to adhere to the rule of law and to use discretion judiciously.

But what of the Supreme Court? Although Supreme Court justices do not have to answer to a higher court, they—like all judges on multimember courts—must persuade a majority of their colleagues in order to prevail. As long as the Court mirrors the rest of the judiciary in including judges who vary along multiple personal and political axes, each justice will have the same kind of incentive as lower court judges to rely on shared legal principles rather than on particular moral or ideological views. For example, Justice Kennedy (like Justice O'Connor on the Rehnquist Court) is frequently referred to as a "swing" justice, whose vote can often determine the outcome of a closely divided case. The justices (and lawyers) who seek to persuade a majority of such swing justices are most likely to succeed if they appeal to the sorts of shared values reflected in the principles outlined in chapter 5.

Moreover, unpersuasive opinions may face more resistance from lower court judges, who have considerable leeway because the Supreme Court reviews so few of their decisions. As a practical matter, without the active cooperation of lower court judges across the nation, Supreme Court rulings have only limited effect. And unpersuasive decisions are probably more likely to be distinguished away or even overruled in later Supreme Court cases, limiting their impacts.

We are not contending that these structural constraints are as effective for the Supreme Court as they are for lower courts. The hierarchical nature of the judiciary is irrelevant when it comes to influencing the Supreme Court's behavior, and even the fact that it is a multimember court does not always require the justices to appeal to reason in persuading their colleagues. Nevertheless, the need to convince colleagues exerts some influence. At the end of this chapter, we suggest some institutional changes that might increase the Supreme Court's similarity to lower courts in this respect. First, however, we turn to other structural constraints that apply equally to all courts.

Judicial deliberation

The fact that all appellate courts have multiple judges has another effect besides requiring judges to tether their decisions to shared principles. In order to decide cases, judges on multimember courts must deliberate together, either face to face, by telephone, or by exchanging views in writing (including, now, electronic communication). Deliberation has a number of beneficial effects in cases in which the right answer is not obvious—the kinds of cases in which judicial discretion plays the largest role. The range of views among judges helps to ensure that different viewpoints are aired and that poor or idiosyncratic arguments are identified. Departures from precedent and weak reasoning are similarly subject to expert scrutiny from other judges. If a colleague points out a flaw in one's reasoning, it is (or should be!) more difficult to remain wedded to that reasoning.

Deliberation (like written opinions, which we discuss later in this chapter) thus forces judges to scrutinize their own conclusions and arguments. And, as one judge has pointed out, this self-scrutiny implicates another constraint—"the judge's own self-respect." After all, judges "have to look in the mirror at least once a day, just like everyone else; they have to like what they see. Heaven knows, we don't do it for the money; if you can't have your self-respect, you might as well make megabucks doing leveraged buyouts."[2]

Deliberation also means that judges have an opportunity to persuade each other before their views are made public, and both the act of attempting to persuade and the receipt of a colleague's views serve to clarify disagreements, narrow disputes, and sharpen and strengthen the legal basis for the decision. Thus a judge, in deliberation with colleagues, may find that her initial instincts are inconsistent with the rule of law and change her mind. Historians and others who have examined the papers of former Supreme Court justices—the only source of information regarding that Court's deliberations—have often found examples of justices changing their minds on the basis of discussion or the circulation of draft opinions.

One of our favorite stories along these lines involves Justice Robert Jackson, who served as attorney general before he was elevated to the Supreme Court in 1941. As attorney general, he interpreted the Selective Service Act as allowing the United States to draft visiting foreigners who, for reasons beyond their control, were temporarily unable to return home. That interpretation was challenged in the courts, and in 1950 it came before the Supreme Court—including the former attorney general. Justice Jackson joined the majority in holding that the act did *not* apply to foreign nationals. Having been persuaded by his colleagues to change his mind, he recalled how other judges had dealt with similar situations. An English judge had said, "The matter does not appear to me now as it appears to have appeared to me then," while an early Supreme Court justice had explained that his own former error "can furnish no ground for its being adopted by this Court." After recounting these incidents, Justice Jackson added, "If there are other ways of gracefully and good-naturedly surrendering former views to a better considered position, I invoke them all." As Justice Jackson's experience indicates, the collegial deliberation on multimember courts thus has a strong tendency to moderate individual viewpoints and to produce results that are broadly thought to be consistent with precedent, principle, and the rule of law.[3]

Finally, the process of deliberating can, over time, shape the character of judges. For a ruling to be an act of judgment rather than of will, a judge must be open to new ideas and willing to subject her own views to careful scrutiny. She must be confident enough to risk being wrong but humble enough to recognize and admit it when she is. Long-term participation in a collegial, deliberative enterprise can foster exactly that sort of judicial character. The process of deliberating with others can itself be mind-opening. Listening to other people explicate their ideas and then defend or modify them in the face of counterarguments encourages intellectual flexibility and honesty, as well as an appreciation for moderation and centrism. Discussions grow more sophisticated, nuanced, and inclusive as the participants continue to interact. Even those disinclined to collegial deliberation can be converted: We suspect that all teachers have experienced the situation in which a previously quiet student is somehow drawn into the classroom discussion and then, having had a taste of it, begins to participate more fully.

The role of lawyers in this process should not be overlooked. The adversary system ensures that contesting viewpoints are presented to the court. Even judges who are inattentive to briefs are forced to listen to both sides in oral arguments, and lawyers' responses to questioning may "jump-start" the deliberative process between the judges.

These advantages of the deliberative process are enhanced in two ways by the structure of federal courts. Since federal judges have life tenure, the same group of judges will engage in deliberation with each other over a period of many years. This long-term interaction can draw them closer together and make each judge more willing to compromise—partly out of a spirit of generosity and partly because the next time that judge might be the one who needs cooperation from her colleagues. Of course, long-term interaction can also exacerbate conflicts, and that is where the second structural advantage is manifest: The death or retirement of judges on a multimember court ensures that new members are always being added, changing the dynamics and reducing the potential for long-term conflict. So both the continuity and the change in membership on multimember courts work together to produce better deliberation among judges.

But do the justices really listen to each others' arguments, or do they merely bargain for their preferred outcomes? No doubt both factors operate, and deliberation may be particularly weak on issues where feelings run strong. As a descriptive matter, however, we believe that there are occasions in which judges switch their votes because they find an opinion persuasive. And as an aspirational matter, we think this is the way it should be. If there is not enough deliberation within the Court, institutional changes may be in order to help foster more discussion. For example, a rule might require that other justices withhold formal support until a draft opinion has circulated, and that the Court then have another conference discussion of the case at that time.

There is some evidence that deliberation among judges, especially on the Supreme Court, is decreasing. This is worrisome if true. We think that scholars (and journalists) might be exaggerating the trend: Even if the justices do not seem to talk much, deliberation might still be occurring, primarily through the circulation of opinions and comments on those opinions. Technology has changed the way people collaborate—when we wrote our first three books together, we were in and out of each others' offices on a daily basis, but this one has been written with few face-to-face (or even telephonic) discussions. Ideas may also be communicated through discussions between law clerks. It is therefore hard to tell whether judges are becoming less deliberative.

Other structural supports

Another uniquely Anglo-American aspect of our judiciary also encourages both restraint and deliberation. Unlike judges in many civil law jurisdictions, American judges are not professionalized bureaucrats. There is no "judicial track" in American law, so American lawyers—unlike lawyers in some other countries—cannot choose to go into judging the way they can choose to go into corporate law or medical malpractice or employment law. Instead, judges are drawn from the ranks of generalist lawyers, each bringing different strengths and different visions of the law. The lack of bureaucratization also fosters candor: In chapter 10, we describe the French judicial system as an illustration of one potential consequence of professionalization of judging; judges there have what amounts to a secret handshake—the knowledge that they are making law, not simply applying legislation, contrary to what they tell the public. To the extent that American judges recognize that judging is not a specialist's craft, they are less likely to become possessive and secretive about their task.

Other participants in the decision-making process provide additional, non-bureaucratic perspectives, furthering the inclination toward both openness and principle. The adversary system—for all its faults—brings parties and their lawyers into the adjudicative process. The judge in an inquisitorial system is simultaneously judge and jury, investigator and decision maker, driving the process as well as the result. She alone decides what facts need investigation, which witnesses should appear, and when each issue has been sufficiently aired for her to reach a decision.

Under the American adversary system, by contrast, the litigation process is driven largely by the parties (or their lawyers), and the judge is consciously reduced to the role of neutral arbiter. It is the parties and their lawyers who structure the case, investigate the facts, call the witnesses, and decide which arguments to make and when and how to make them. Judges, moreover, are confined to ruling on questions of *law*; fact-finding is the province of the jury. Finally, the Due Process Clause of the Constitution (and cases interpreting it) specifies minimum requirements of fairness that the proceedings must follow. All of these institutional structures serve to remind judges of their limited role, encouraging them to act according to principle rather than personal beliefs.

Even law clerks can play a part in increasing the likelihood that judges will adhere to the core principles of sound adjudication. Every federal judge (and many state judges, especially at the appellate court level) hires one or more recent law graduates to work as law clerks for a year or two at a time. These clerks work closely with the judge, reading and digesting the lawyers' briefs and doing additional research, conferring with the judge on pending cases, and sometimes writing first drafts of opinions in accordance with the judge's instructions. These are bright young lawyers, already steeped in the culture of the law, but bringing new perspectives to it. There is thus interplay between an established and powerful judge and law clerks with both new ideas and an odd combination of characteristics: They are young enough to be in awe of the power of the law and intimidated by the judge, but arrogant enough (because of their record of academic successes) to press home their points. When the relationship works well, judges and clerks each goad and restrain one another, keeping in check the more extreme or radical inclinations and reducing the likelihood of weak or unreasoned decisions. It works especially well when judges select their clerks—and clerks agree to work for judges—independent of political affiliation, which happens often but not often enough. In chapter 13 we offer some suggestions for increasing the chances of these cross-political affiliations.

The seriousness of formal adjudication and all its trappings also contributes to fostering adherence to the core principles of the rule of law. The fact that a judge puts on a robe and steps behind a bench—with those in the courtroom rising to their feet as she does so—helps to impress upon her the awesome responsibility that she is about to exercise. The process that accompanies adjudication—formal written submissions, arguments made from a podium, witnesses who take an oath, the ability to appeal to a higher court—further distinguishes judicial decision making from individual decision making, making it public and formal and therefore more cautious.

Public scrutiny of judicial opinions

Finally—and perhaps most important—judicial decisions, and the reasons for those decisions, are subject to public and scholarly scrutiny. Most judicial opinions are widely available, especially since the advent of the Internet. The mainstream media report on the most significant cases, often in detail and at a high level of sophistication. Many of the reporters assigned to the courts—and especially those who cover the Supreme Court—are conscientious in attempting to understand and convey to the public the legal doctrines and contexts of the cases, and take advantage of various opportunities to educate themselves further by attending conferences or consulting experts. Some journalists are themselves experts on the law, holding a law degree and combining journalism with a career as a lawyer or a legal academic. At least one major law school offers a special educational program for journalists. Others have become experts through long tenure covering the courts. And there are now many specialized media sources—usually (but not always) online—that provide even deeper coverage, including quite penetrating criticism. The interested lay public can thus easily obtain both court opinions and assistance in interpreting them.

More focused scrutiny can come from more knowledgeable sources, including not only scholars, but lawyers, politicians, and the best of the media. A constant barrage of commentary in both scholarly and popular publications (including widely read blogs) ensures that no judicial misstep goes unnoticed. Serious deficiencies are likely to generate widespread and trenchant criticism.

What good does this scrutiny do? After all, short of impeachment, there is nothing concrete that the public—much less scholars—can do to federal judges (although they can have an effect on those state judges who must stand for election). But judges are human, and, more important, they are members of a learned profession. One does not have to believe—as some scholars have argued—that judges cater to an "intellectual elite" in order to recognize that the prospect of thoughtful, careful, and knowledgeable criticism from their professional peers is likely to make judges think twice about straying too far from the core of current legal thought or trying to pull a fast one in their reasoning. No one enjoys having her mistakes pointed out to her, especially in public.

Today, at least some of the justices are also becoming attuned to another audience. The American concept of judicial review has been adopted in many other places today, and the judges of the world's various constitutional courts have begun to talk with one another. It is not uncommon for decisions in other countries to refer to the U.S. Supreme Court's rulings, either finding them persuasive as to their own constitutions or declining to follow them in some cases. It would not be surprising if American justices have begun to consider whether their opinions will be regarded as persuasive by their peers around the world.

Of course, this beneficial effect of public and scholarly scrutiny depends on several things, some of which we discuss later in this book as in need of improvement. First, of course, a judge who shakes off all criticism through confidence that she is always right and her critics wrong will not be influenced by even the most sophisticated critiques. As we noted earlier, the structure of the judiciary exposes judges to critical review, and we will suggest later some other methods for increasing judges' intellectual humility. We should point out that this form of humility is compatible with a high degree of personal self-confidence: People who are insecure about themselves and their abilities may be all the more reluctant to admit error, while self-confidence may foster a sufficiently healthy ego to learn from criticism.

The other prerequisite for effective public scrutiny of judicial decisions turns on the quality of the criticism. Whether it comes from politicians, the public, the media, or scholars, it must be careful and civil rather than strident and political. Accusing judges of "activism" or "arrogance" without explaining the legal or analytical deficiencies of those judges' reasoning is unhelpful. Attributing a judge's decisions to political motives is affirmatively harmful, to the extent that it incrementally persuades the public or the judges themselves that law is *about* politics and therefore that we should expect judges to be blatantly political. Finally, critics who selectively beat up on disfavored outcomes rather than on departures from good decision making will only convince their readers that the critiques are no more principled than their subjects. We will return in chapter 13 to the critical role of the legal academy in encouraging good decision making by judges.

In this chapter we have discussed some features of the judiciary that may foster open-mindedness, intellectual humility, and group deliberation. We do not mean to paint an unrealistic picture of the judiciary. There are certainly pressures in the opposite direction: large caseloads that prevent judges from carefully considering individual cases or having extended conversations with colleagues; the temptation toward arrogance that comes with high office and feeds upon the eagerness of lawyers to appeal to judicial vanity; the mental inflexibility that can come with advancing age and a cloistered environment. Judges are not saints, nor are appellate courts academic seminars. Our point, however, is that the structure of the judiciary does have a tendency to improve the quality of judicial decision making.

One way of appreciating this effect is to imagine a different institutional setting. Suppose that the Supreme Court consisted of only a single judge. Rather than hearing cases that filtered up through the lower courts, this judge would scan the newspapers for emerging legal questions and then issue dictates regarding their resolution. The judge would not be exposed to academic or public criticism. Obviously, judicial decisions would be far worse in such a world. This thought experiment illustrates how the American legal system's features function to improve outcomes.

Besides the structure of the American judiciary, two other aspects of the American legal regime contribute to judicial restraint. One is the requirement of transparency: Judges must give reasons for their decisions, and are expected to be candid in doing so. The second is our common-law heritage of incrementalism: Although the law changes over time, it does so gradually, one case at a time, rather than suddenly and radically. The next two chapters explore these ideals and their implications for evaluating judicial performance.

10

Transparency

OF THE CONSTRAINTS we explore, transparency is perhaps the least discussed but the most important. In this chapter, we elaborate on the reasons for requiring transparency and offer concrete illustrations of its role in constraining judicial discretion.

First, a note on what we mean by transparency: A judge's written opinions should fairly reflect her actual reasoning. Transparency is the willingness to put forth one's best arguments, without guile (which does *not* mean without craft), for the world to evaluate. Lack of transparency can take many forms: a formalist opinion that disguises the judge's value choice as a result dictated by some mechanical test; a distortion of precedent to make a hard case look easy or to save a flawed doctrine in the face of a challenging application; or a withholding of information or concealing an argument that influenced the Court on the ground that the reader cannot be trusted with it. Transparency also requires that a judge be honest with herself: It is no defense to claim that one really believes implausible or dissembling arguments if that belief is the product of a failure to examine the arguments as rationally and impartially as possible. Weaseling is not excusable, and post hoc rationalizations have no place in adjudication.

Transparency is both an independent value and a necessary concomitant of the other constraints we discuss in this book. If a judge is not candid about what she is doing and why, then it is impossible to know whether she is being faithful to precedent or to the principles of incrementalism. Transparency, as one scholar has pointed out, "is the sine qua non of all other restraints on abuse of judicial power," because the other limitations "count for little if judges feel free to believe one thing...and to say another." In this context, transparency is important not because it necessarily makes judges less prone to error, but simply because it subjects their work to broader scrutiny.[1]

But transparency also stands on its own as a way to produce better decision making. It serves as both an internal and an external constraint, allowing public evaluation of judicial decisions and consequently making the judge herself more cautious. It reins in judicial discretion by exposing that discretion to the light of day. It complements the requirement of providing written reasons for a decision by ensuring that the stated reasons are the actual reasons. Dissembling by government actors always deprives the citizenry of information necessary for deliberation and decision making. Whether motivated by paternalism (the reader cannot be trusted with the truth) or self-interest (the author will be criticized for telling the truth), a deliberate lack of candor is fundamentally antidemocratic. Such dissembling is particularly pernicious in judges, because the visible rationality of a transparent opinion is a necessary substitute for the missing democratic accountability of unelected judges.

Further, a lack of candor transforms the rule of law into the rule of men by allowing judges to reach their preferred results without confronting doctrinal inconsistencies, inconvenient facts or legal sources, or powerful counterarguments. Especially at the Supreme Court level, it creates uncertainty by freeing lower courts from the constraints that consistent and well-reasoned precedent can impose. The charge of ad hoc decision making (or of countermajoritarian tyranny) rings truer where decisions are not transparent. Thus, because transparent, reasoned argument constrains the judiciary, it is a necessary part of the approach advocated in this book; to the extent that it serves both to ensure fidelity to the rule of law and as a stand-in for democratic accountability, its absence is correspondingly fatal to the legitimacy of judicial decisions under any approach.

For all its benefits, transparency is not universally acclaimed, nor is it universally followed. And, like the rest of the limits on adjudication, transparency is not always a matter of black and white. The best judges will subject their own reasoning to a searching examination, but even good judges may—like the rest of us—sometimes be honestly persuaded by weak reasoning. There is also often room for disagreement about whether a particular precedent can be interpreted to foreclose, allow, or require a particular result in a later case. And the need to assemble a majority may require compromises in opinion writing.

Failures in transparency

Nevertheless, two transparency errors can still be identified: explicit or implicit arguments that transparency is somehow unnecessary or dangerous, and—more commonly—judicial reasoning that is so easily exposed as flawed that the judge who puts it forth must be either deceitful (of herself or her readers) or incompetent. In the remainder of this chapter, we examine two sorts of transparency failures derived from poor reasoning. Both involve judicial opinions that purport to be faithful to the rule of law but in fact depart from it. We look first at two opinions that lend themselves to the charge that formalism is being used as a cover for a desire to achieve particular results, and then at an opinion that blatantly manipulates precedent.

While we have suggested in an earlier work, as well as in chapter 3, that formalist approaches such as originalism are both unworkable and unable to constrain judges, there are judges who remain unpersuaded by these arguments. A judge who honestly tries to ascertain and apply the founding generation's original interpretation of the Constitution may be mistaken, but such an opinion may nevertheless meet the requirements of transparency if the judge's rationale is clearly explained. Some originalist opinions, however, are so superficial or inconsistent that they fail to satisfy the requirement of transparency, suggesting that something other than the purported historical evidence has generated the outcome. *New York v. United States* and *Printz v. United States* are two such cases.[2]

In each case, the question was whether Congress could enact a law requiring state government officials to act in a certain way. *New York* involved a federal law requiring state legislatures to enact programs to deal with radioactive waste within the state, and *Printz* involved portions of the Brady Bill requiring state law enforcement officials to perform background checks on handgun purchasers. The Court struck down both federal statutes on the ground that they impermissibly "commandeered" the organs of state government.

In both cases, the majority disclaimed any reliance on policy arguments or judicial discretion in reaching their conclusion. Instead, they purported to rely on the original intent of the founding generation, implying that the Court had no choice but to invalidate the laws. Indeed, Justice Scalia, who wrote the opinion in *Printz*, has often advocated the use of original intent specifically to constrain judicial discretion. Justice O'Connor's majority opinion in *New York* similarly suggested that originalism cabins judicial discretion: The Court's task, she wrote, "consists not of devising our preferred system of government, but of understanding and applying the framework set forth in the Constitution."[3]

In canvassing the historical record, however, Justices O'Connor and Scalia did no more than demonstrate a negative—that an originalist analysis does not unambiguously support a congressional power to commandeer. They made little effort to show that the original intent *rules out* such a power. Justice O'Connor relied primarily on founding-era statements that the new federal government—unlike the national government under the Articles of Confederation—could pass laws directly affecting individual citizens. But it is an open question whether this new power to exercise authority over individuals was meant to replace or merely to supplement the preexisting federal power to pass legislation governing the states themselves. Justice O'Connor provided no evidence that the founders meant to curtail the latter power; scholars have suggested that in fact the founders meant to supplement it. Justice Scalia's historical analysis was even weaker: Faced with dissenting opinions that marshaled historical evidence in favor of an originalist interpretation that *permits* commandeering, he criticized that evidence but provided no countering evidence of his own.

We are not suggesting that we have the correct answer—if there is one—to the question whether the founders intended to permit Congress to commandeer various parts of state government. But an honest examination of the ambiguous and conflicting historical evidence cannot produce the certainty exhibited by the majority in these two cases. A little humility, and a lot less posturing that the Court's hands are tied, would be appropriate even if the outcome remained the same. And to the extent that originalism is relied on specifically because of its ability to constrain judicial activism, it is untenable to invalidate two congressional statutes on the basis of such inconclusive evidence.

The issue in these cases may seem arcane, but the consequences could be most unfortunate. For example, in the case of a threatened terrorist attack, local law enforcement officials cannot be directed to act by the federal government; if a massive attack actually occurred, local officials could not be required to cooperate with federal officers in the aftermath. The Court's analysis precludes it from even considering exceptions to its rule in such extreme situations; indeed, Justice O'Connor's opinion made it clear that even the most compelling circumstances would not allow the Court to make an exception to this rule purportedly mandated by the founding generation.

These cases illustrate a lack of transparency, then, because the outcome of the case cannot really be explained on the basis invoked by the justices. Transparency demands exactly the sort of analysis of constitutional values the Court eschewed: What sort of constitutional balance between state and federal power is optimum in the context of modern regulatory schemes? The failure to engage in such analysis and the cavalier certainty about an uncertain historical proposition suggest a Court trying to pretend that it has no discretion. Lying about the source of a judicial decision does not constitute fidelity to the rule of law.

Distorting history is not the only way that a court attempts to disguise the reasons for its decision. Courts sometimes apply precedent in such an obviously disingenuous fashion that we can only conclude that something else is driving the result.

This type of distortion of precedent is illustrated by a controversial recent decision on gay rights. In *Lawrence v. Texas*, the Court struck down a state law criminalizing homosexual (but not heterosexual) sodomy. Existing precedent—the 1986 Georgia case of *Bowers v. Hardwick*—had already held that criminalizing all sodomy was constitutionally valid. One question before the Court in *Lawrence* was whether *Bowers* was fairly distinguishable from *Lawrence*.[4]

Only Justice O'Connor argued that *Bowers* and *Lawrence* were distinguishable, and thus that the Texas statute could be invalidated without overruling *Bowers*. She suggested that because the Texas law discriminated between heterosexual and homosexual acts of sodomy, it violated the Equal Protection Clause. Moral disapproval of homosexuals, O'Connor wrote in *Lawrence*, could not provide the state with a justification for outlawing their conduct. But Justice O'Connor had previously joined the majority opinion in *Bowers*, which had explicitly accepted moral disapproval as a sufficient justification for prohibiting sodomy. Those challenging the Georgia law upheld in *Bowers* had argued that "majority sentiments about the morality of homosexuality should be declared inadequate" to justify the antisodomy law. A majority of the Court, including Justice O'Connor, *rejected* that challenge. In addition, the plaintiffs in *Bowers* included a heterosexual married couple who alleged that prohibiting sodomy violated their rights. The Court refused to reach their claim, and characterized the case as raising only the question "whether the Federal Constitution confers a fundamental right upon *homosexuals* to engage in sodomy." Thus *Bowers*, like *Lawrence*, raised the question whether a state was entitled to outlaw homosexual sodomy based on moral disapproval. In *Bowers*, the Court said yes. In *Lawrence*, it said no. Justice O'Connor's attempted reconciliation fails the test of candor.[5]

All eight of the other justices squarely confronted the inconsistency, finding the cases indistinguishable. Justice Scalia, writing for himself, Chief Justice Rehnquist, and Justice Thomas, would have followed *Bowers* and upheld the Texas statute. Justice Kennedy's majority opinion concluded instead that *Bowers* had to go: "*Bowers* was not correct when it was decided, and it is not correct today. It ought not to remain binding precedent. *Bowers v. Hardwick* should be and now is overruled." Whether one agrees with Scalia or with Kennedy, both approaches are preferable to Justice O'Connor's obfuscation. Indeed, after a brief spate of conservative attacks and liberal kudos, *Lawrence* has generated little press. The action has moved to state courts and local political bodies—focusing on gay marriage—and the Court, having issued a transparent and comprehensible ruling on a controversial constitutional issue, went back to its more mundane cases.[6]

The sky did not fall, nor would it have done so had Justice Scalia's views prevailed. Had Justice O'Connor's views prevailed, however, both the Supreme Court and the rule of law would have suffered. Pundits who disagreed with the outcomes—either the invalidation of the Texas statute or the refusal to overrule *Bowers*—could attack the Court for its inane reasoning as well as for the results. Police and prosecutors would have retained discretion, under purportedly universal prohibitions, to single out homosexual conduct, in violation of the spirit of Justice O'Connor's opinion. State legislatures would have been mired in debates about the appropriate response: ban all sodomy or none? The popular brouhaha surrounding gay marriage—which does not focus solely on judicial action and which has not involved the Supreme Court at all—provides a glimpse of the sort of nasty political battle that would inevitably have tarred the federal judiciary.

Arguments against transparency

Despite the obvious appeal of transparency and its almost universal acceptance as a legal norm, there have been some dissenting voices. Some scholars have suggested that the public (or, sometimes, government officials) cannot be trusted with various kinds of knowledge. If they know, for example, that ignorance of the law *is* sometimes an excuse—contrary to the popular maxim—they will be tempted to deliberately avoid finding out whether some contemplated course of conduct is legal. Others have argued that the judiciary must hide its reasoning in order to protect its legitimacy or ensure compliance with controversial rulings. Justice Scalia may have gone even further in urging a lack of transparency. He has sometimes seemed to suggest that although originalism is unworkable, judges must maintain the fiction that they are adhering to the original intent in order to "foster a correct attitude toward" constitutional adjudication in judges who might otherwise be too inclined to use their own judgment. Still, however one might carp at some aspects of Justice Scalia's performance, there is little reason to believe that his judicial opinions are anything but candid expressions of his views, often expressed with a minimum of diplomacy.[7]

Occasional attempts to justify judicial lack of candor in America are nothing compared to the apparently massive fraud revealed by a study of the French legal system. Formally, French judges have no discretion at all. The written legal code answers every legal question, and the courts merely apply that code to the particular question. The opinions are very short—often under a page—and follow a format that has not changed since the French Revolution. Each one is a grammatical syllogism: "The Court, (a) given [the relevant parts of the legal code]; whereas [arguments]; (b) on these grounds, [holding]." The opinion is thus a single, logical sentence that "resists any discourse that might hamper its smooth grammatical flow," and therefore "possesses a univocal quality that denies the possibility of alternative perspectives, approaches, or outcomes." There is no citation of precedent, but simply an application of the legal code to the facts. It is, in short, a formalist's dream.[8]

Behind each opinion, however, is an entirely different set of documents, known in different contexts as *conclusions* and *rapports*, which are essentially correspondence among various judges. Unlike judicial opinions, these documents are not available to the public. *Conclusions* and *rapports* are long, conversational, and policy oriented, and contain alternative arguments as well as support for alternative conclusions. They admit to even more uncertainty than the typical American judicial opinion, and can be overtly political (in the broadest sense of the word). One *conclusions* document, for example, in suggesting a particular course of action that would be a departure from earlier precedent, recommends that the court "not . . . choose a discreet, padded [formulation], as if you had misgivings about proclaiming what you are doing, but . . . adopt a formulation that is clear and categorical [and] act in such a way that your decision [will] be a signal and not a wink."[9]

The formalism of the official French approach, and the knowledge that it is a myth, is confirmed by conversations that then-Judge Ruth Bader Ginsburg had with a French colleague who questioned the American administrative law doctrine requiring courts to defer to plausible agency interpretations: "How can that be, a French colleague asked. How can the law have more than one plausible meaning?" But the French judge knew, of course, that the reality was otherwise. So the judge continued: "Or, more accurately, how can a court judgment openly so acknowledge?

The law is the law. There can be but one officially correct reading." And the last comment that cements the deception: "Shouldn't judges, at least in their official pronouncements, make it appear so to the public?"[10]

This bifurcated system allows the French judiciary to continue the fiction, born of Revolutionary mistrust of judges, that judges do not make law. Only the legislature makes law, and there are neither gaps nor interpretive difficulties in legislation. The judges are in on the scam, and apparently so are French academics. It is not clear, however, the extent to which the French public—or even French lawyers—know that what the judges say they are doing and what they are really doing are two quite different things. Nor are they able to evaluate judicial decisions. Presumably no American scholar would suggest moving to the extreme of the French system, but its existence should provide a note of caution for those who are tempted to underestimate the value of transparency.

11

Incrementalism

NEITHER PRECEDENT NOR principle nor reasoning dictates results. Judges must often make choices among plausible applications or extensions of existing doctrine. Those choices will be influenced by myriad factors, including the judge's own policy preferences and views of the judicial role, the persuasiveness of the lawyers, the judge's perception of public or legislative sentiment, and so on. These factors might sometimes counsel restraint and sometimes not. But one factor that influences judges always serves as a brake rather than as a goad: a preference for incremental rather than radical change.

The judiciary is, by nature and by design, the most conservative part of the government. The judiciary's task is to look back on past traditions and simultaneously preserve them and change them to meet the challenges of the present and future. Radical or revolutionary reform is inconsistent with this role. In common law adjudication, incrementalism and adherence to precedent work hand-in-hand to ensure that the law will usually change slowly, through accretion and subtle revision rather than through sudden or fundamental shifts in policy. Constitutional adjudication is similarly constrained.

In praising judicial incrementalism, we do not mean that the Supreme Court should only take "baby steps." What is important is not the size of the individual step, but the fact that each is only one in a series of steps in which the Court works out its path. Just as the common law evolves in a series of decisions, constitutional law is most successful when the Court is able to develop principles over a sustained series of cases rather than trying to emulate a legislature by pronouncing a binding set of rules all at once. In this chapter we illustrate incrementalism by discussing school desegregation and free speech cases.

Incrementalism and school desegregation

The most famous example of constitutional incrementalism is the story of *Brown v. Board of Education*, the case that held racially segregated schools unconstitutional. *Brown* was incrementalist but not minimalist. The *Brown* decision itself was a major, dramatic decision, but the Court had laid the groundwork in previous decisions. The Court moved in cautious steps—some would say too cautious— before it took the plunge of declaring segregation unconstitutional. Although *Brown* is sometimes considered a bolt from the blue, in fact the Court had been moving steadily, if quietly, in that direction for years. For almost two decades before *Brown*, the Court gradually eroded the prevailing doctrine that permitted "separate but equal" schools. In a series of cases largely orchestrated by National Association for the Advancement of Colored People (NAACP) attorneys (including Thurgood Marshall, later appointed to the Court by President Lyndon Johnson), the Court found various segregated educational facilities to be unequal and therefore unconstitutional. The incremental nature of the change is illustrated by the fact that the Court (helped along by the attorneys' choice of cases) began with the most egregious inequalities and the least sensitive education settings—graduate and professional schools rather than elementary schools.

By 1954, when the Court in *Brown* finally declared that even "equal" segregated schools, at the elementary and high school level, violated the Constitution, much of the nation was ready to accept the decision as the next step. Although the South resisted, slightly more than half of Americans overall supported *Brown*; the percentage was as high as 73% among college graduates. As one scholar put it: "By the early 1950s, powerful political, economic, social, and ideological forces for progressive racial change had made judicial invalidation of segregation conceivable."[1]

The *Brown* Court further diluted the radicalism of its holding by signaling a willingness to tolerate delay in implementing it. The original decision contained no order to take any particular action, instead requiring the parties to reargue the question of appropriate remedies. A year later, the Court ordered that schools be desegregated "with all deliberate speed." Although the Court's caution may have encouraged the segregated states to defy the Court, it is not clear whether a more immediate remedial order would have been any more effective; there was not much progress in school desegregation until Congress and the president, in addition to the Court, supported integration. In the meantime, however, the Court quietly went about ordering the desegregation of other public facilities, slowly changing the nation's views on race and perhaps encouraging the movement of the White House and Congress to their more enlightened views.[2]

Brown is instructive on several levels. First, despite southern opposition to integration, the Court's incremental approach had its advantages. In 1938, when the Court first began to find unequal education facilities unconstitutional, most citizens—even in the North—were unprepared to accept integration. Had the Supreme Court tried to outlaw segregation in 1938, the decision would have been met with massive resistance—and not only in the South. Most northern cities were residentially segregated: A 1939 poll found that only 19% of those polled in New England and the mid-Atlantic states, and 11% of those in the Midwest, agreed that blacks should be "allowed to live wherever they want to live." As late as 1952, 56% of whites polled in Detroit advocated residential segregation. As blacks began to move into previously white, working-class neighborhoods in the 1940s and 1950s, there were racially motivated attacks and even race riots in Detroit, Chicago, Philadelphia, Newark, and Cincinnati. Although northern schools were not segregated by law, these residential patterns ensured that blacks and whites rarely went to the same schools. In both the North and the South, many workplaces and occupations were segregated. Professional sports were segregated until the mid-1940s; the armed forces remained segregated until 1949. Attitudes changed slowly, but they did change: President Truman integrated the armed forces in 1949, and the first federal voting rights act was passed in 1957. While we are not suggesting that the Court should take full credit for the changing attitudes, we do believe that it had some influence and that any attempt at more radical reform would have been a dismal failure if not a spark to widespread violence.[3]

The history of the Court's decades-long struggle with segregated schools also illustrates how the combination of adherence to precedent and a preference for incremental change serves to constrain judges. We can see with hindsight that immediate integration—both before and after *Brown*—was a political impossibility. But that fact alone could not have stopped a determined, independent, unelected Court from attempting such a mandate had it been so inclined. That the Court was *not* so inclined is a testament to the inherently conservative nature of constitutional adjudication. Even judges who might have wished to proceed more quickly did not do so, restrained by judicial temperament and incrementalist colleagues.[4]

As *Brown* illustrates, incrementalism is not necessarily inconsistent with boldness. Although the Court had quietly laid the groundwork before *Brown*, and although it developed its remedial strategy only gradually afterward, there is no doubt that *Brown* was a breakthrough decision. But the Court is not a legislature. It cannot create an entire regulatory scheme out of whole cloth and impose it on the nation. It can only decide one case at a time. When it tries to emulate a legislature by imposing comprehensive rules, it is most likely to find itself in trouble, as illustrated by the failed trimester framework of *Roe v. Wade*, which we discuss in chapter 15.

Incrementalism and the First Amendment

Possibly the most robust area of constitutional law is the protection of freedom of speech under the First Amendment. First Amendment doctrine has become very complex as a result of scores of Supreme Court opinions. But the doctrine has evolved over time. The Court gradually identified some core concerns, such as the chilling effect of regulation on speech and the need to avoid discrimination against unpopular viewpoints. The First Amendment is a paradigm case of the success of incrementalism.

The core question that any free speech doctrine must answer is this: What is the best way to balance an individual's right to think and speak freely against the government's need to prevent harms that arise from that speech? The Court's jurisprudence is a classic example of how judicial reasoning processes work incrementally in constitutional law.

In a 1907 opinion by Justice Oliver Wendell Holmes, the Court held that prohibiting prior restraints on speech was sufficient protection for individual rights; the government could always impose a subsequent punishment on speech that it deemed "contrary to the public welfare." Twelve years later, the Court recognized that subsequent punishment for speech might also violate the Constitution—but it took a very narrow view. Writing for a unanimous court in early 1919, Justice Holmes upheld the criminal convictions of antiwar protesters on the theory that their speech posed a "clear and present danger" to the draft.[5]

By late 1919, while the majority still adhered to the narrow conception of "clear and present danger," Justice Holmes himself had recast the test as more speech protective. Dissenting in another antiwar protester case, Holmes wrote that the government should not be allowed to punish speech unless that speech "so imminently threaten[s] immediate interference with the lawful and pressing purposes of the law that an immediate check is required to save the country."[6]

For the next several decades, the Court moved slowly in the direction of Holmes' broad protection for speech. In 1943, for example, Justice Jackson wrote for the court that "[i]f there is any fixed star in our constitutional constellation, it is that no official, high or petty, can prescribe what shall be orthodox in politics, nationalism, religion, or other matters of opinion or force citizens to confess by word or act their faith therein."[7]

The Court finally held in 1969 that subversive speech cannot be restricted or punished unless it is "directed to inciting or producing imminent lawless action and is likely to incite or produce such action." Two decades later, when the Court invalidated a conviction for burning a flag, Justice Brennan's majority opinion explained that the "enduring lesson" of these earlier cases was that "the government may not prohibit expression simply because it disagrees with its message." Step by step, then, the Court recognized that the purpose of the First Amendment is to protect against just this sort of majority tyranny.[8]

These stories—the successful incrementalism in *Brown* and the First Amendment context, and the less successful decision in *Roe*—illustrate the value of incrementalism, but they also teach us something else. It is hindsight that allows us to fully evaluate each of the decisions and its progeny. Had the public and the political branches reacted differently, *Roe* might have succeeded and *Brown* might have failed. The Court might have had to retreat from its First Amendment stance. In short, trying to evaluate judicial decision making by looking at the outcome contemporaneously is doomed to failure. A judgment about whether the Court reached the "wrong" result cannot be made without the luxury of time. And so we return to the process critiques that form the heart of this book: Did the judge adequately consider precedent and other relevant factors? Does the reasoning hold up or is it somehow flawed? Is the decision an incremental step or a radical one?

Just as our guidelines for deciding constitutional cases leave much room for different application, the values we discuss here are imperfect restraints. Even our paradigmatic examples have their flaws. *Brown v. Board of Education*, while (famously) incremental, is (equally notoriously) not transparent: Scholars and judges are still arguing about the reach of the principles underlying the decision. On the other hand, our praise for the transparency of the majority opinion in *Lawrence v. Texas* cannot disguise that it was neither incremental nor faithful to precedent. In *Lawrence*, however, the flaws seem to lie in the particular opinion rather than in the decision. It is possible to imagine—and, indeed, we have previously written—arguments that resonate better with precedent and tradition, but still protect gays from invidious discrimination.[9]

When process fails

Finally, there is *Bush v. Gore*, which betrayed all of the principles discussed so far. In holding that the Florida recount in the 2000 election could not continue, the Republican-appointed majority ensured the election of a Republican president. In doing so, it ignored precedent, which would have suggested (1) that a candidate had no standing to bring a challenge on behalf of voters who could have brought their own challenge, and (2) that the federal courts should not interfere with state court decisions about the content of state law. It betrayed the rule of law by explicitly limiting the reach of its analysis to the single case. And it took the unprecedented step of interfering with the ongoing democratic electoral process, despite constitutional provisions that put the ultimate resolution of any disputes squarely in the hands of Congress. Even the few academic defenders of the Court's decision managed only lukewarm praise for its opinions.[10]

The very rarity of cases as egregiously offensive to the rule of law as *Bush v. Gore* suggests that the constraints, while imperfect, are generally effective. And, as we show in the next two chapters, many aspects of our legal system work to inculcate the values of fidelity to the rule of law, incrementalism, and transparency. In the end, however, there is no substitute for public and scholarly scrutiny.

PART V

Internalized Safeguards

12

Professionalism and the Selection Process

T HE INSTITUTIONAL STRUCTURES we have identified are not the only source of indirect judicial constraints. Oliver Wendell Holmes had it almost right: The life of the law is logic *and* experience. If the institutional structures sharpen the logic, a life lived in the law provides the necessary experience. In that life, the legal culture and professional norms discourage radical, politicized, or idiosyncratic decision making. The judicial selection process ideally should reinforce these professional norms, but today it sadly fails to do so.

Professional norms

Inculcation of these norms begins in law school. Law professors expose law students first to the common law, with its slow and incremental development. We also teach them about process: that how a decision is reached—under what procedures and with what inputs—often matters as much as the substantive result.

(For many litigants, getting one's "day in court" can go a long way toward compensation, even if the end result is not ideal.) Both process norms and the path of the common law tend to discourage intemperate or radical decisions. We also make students confront precedent by presenting new fact patterns and new legal questions against the background of existing cases, rarely letting them begin with a blank slate. They learn to tether their arguments to the past and the present.

The Socratic method, by which professors call on students in class and subject them to sequential questions that force them to think more deeply, further inclines students away from unconstrained discretion. We make them sift and weigh arguments, teaching them what counts as a valid legal argument so that they can separate personal beliefs from principled legal arguments. They are required—at a moment's notice—to develop and consider the strongest arguments on both sides of an issue, preparing them to remain open to persuasion regardless of their initial position. Studies have shown that making people consider opposing arguments is one of the best ways to encourage the active, open-minded thinking that is so crucial to good decision making (and to the avoidance of the cognitive biases that produce bad decision making). The Socratic method also forces students to articulate reasons for their conclusions, something they will have to do as lawyers and that will encourage transparency should they become judges. Inevitably, students listen to and argue with each other both in and out of class. Overall, law schools try to instill habits of careful reading and thought, collaboration, open-mindedness, and a respect for the rule of law. Again, there is room for improvement, and so we will return to legal education when we make suggestions in the next chapter.

The professional norms that are first developed in law school are further reinforced when law students become lawyers, especially if they go into private practice. (We will say more about legal academics and government lawyers later.) Incrementalism is a professional necessity: A lawyer whose primary argument is that the precedent is wrong and should be overruled faces an uphill battle. She is much more likely to be successful if she keeps her arguments for new law within stretching distance of existing precedent. Good lawyers also listen, collaborate, and cooperate with others. Most legal work, whether it involves complex contractual arrangements, negotiation, advising clients, trial strategy, or appellate briefs, is a group project that is honed through discussion and peer review. And lawyers' ultimate positions are dictated by the needs of their clients—and the limits of the law—rather than by their personal beliefs. The best lawyers can see both sides of every issue, enabling them to predict and take into account their opponents' strongest arguments. Transparency, of course, is impossible to avoid. Subjected to questioning by clients, judges, and other lawyers, attorneys must always have reasons and explanations at the ready. Any dissembling is likely to be discovered because there is always someone with an incentive to uncover ulterior motives, half-truths, and other hidden problems.

Judges drawn from the experienced private bar thus have a professional lifetime of acquired tendencies that discourage unchecked discretion. The institutional structures that we have already identified strengthen those tendencies, as do interactions with more experienced judges. Judging is a craft, learned from more experienced colleagues who hand down traditions. Judges also develop a reputation among practicing lawyers, which is enhanced by the careful exercise of well-thought-out judgment and harmed by impulsive, radical, or idiosyncratic decisions. And over time, judges see how their decisions work: how other courts use them or develop them, how they fit with other doctrines, and so forth. This "feedback loop" helps judges gauge—and if needed, fix—the coherence between their decisions and the broader rule of law. This is especially true in the case of the Supreme Court, as the justices see where lower courts take the precedents they hand down.

One example of this feedback loop can be seen in the history of what has come to be called the second Rehnquist Court: the period from about 1994 to 2005, when the Court had no changes in personnel and Chief Justice Rehnquist was clearly at the helm. During the early part of that period, the Court issued some decisions that departed quite radically—in what was usually considered a conservative direction—from earlier cases, especially in the area of federalism. The Court invalidated a record number of federal statutes on states' rights grounds, and rarely reached politically liberal results in nonfederalism cases. Beginning in about 2002 or 2003, however, the Court seemed to soften, not only upholding federal statutes more often, but also reaching liberal results in other contexts, including upholding some affirmative action programs and striking down state bans on sodomy. One way to account for this is to look at it as a natural cycle: In the early years of a new Court, the Court sends a signal that the law is changing, in this case, toward the conservative side of the political spectrum. The lower courts, whose job is not only to apply the letter of the law but also to identify and follow the spirit of recent Supreme Court precedent, take the law ever further in the direction that the Supreme Court seems to be headed.

At some point, however, the Supreme Court looks at where its cases have taken the lower courts, and, if it feels that the change is too radical a departure from the rule of law or the larger body of precedent, makes a correction. The political inclinations of the justices play some role in the initial decision to turn the law's rudder, but ultimately corrective forces come into play. So even at the Supreme Court level, the structure of the federal courts can reinforce the legal culture.

The institutional structures and cultural norms we have described serve to make it less likely that judges will exercise unconstrained discretion. Despite these constraints, however, there are troubling signs that constitutional adjudication may yet become politicized—untethered from precedent and the rule of law—and that future judges may not adhere to the principles that have animated past judges. In the remainder of this chapter, we turn to those signs and suggest ways to prevent judging from becoming just another name for politics as usual.

Judicial selection and politicization

The judicial appointment process is now dominated by the assumption that a nominee's political views matter more than his or her legal acuity or judicial temperament. It was not always this way. Until the late 1980s or so, lawyers were nominated to the federal bench—including the Supreme Court—because they were prominent and respected, as well as usually being stalwart members of the president's party. But party affiliation is not the same as political ideology; in the past, moderate members of the president's party were more likely to be respected by the bench and bar—and therefore more likely to be nominated and confirmed—than were those on the left or right fringes of the party. As one observer notes, the "pre-Reagan generation believed that appointment as a federal judge should come to the deserving in their mid-to-late fifties or early sixties, after a substantial career at the bar."[1]

Justice Blackmun, for example, made a name for himself by quietly practicing law for sixteen years before he was nominated to the Eighth Circuit by President Eisenhower. He was a moderate Republican who had supported Democrat Hubert Humphrey's Senate campaign. In his eleven years on the Court of Appeals, Blackmun earned a reputation as a careful, hardworking, and moderate judge. His Court of Appeals opinions are not particularly ideological, and his nomination to the Supreme Court was probably prompted as much by his long-standing friendship with Chief Justice Warren Burger as by his obvious competence.

Another example of how the nomination process used to work is a current federal district judge, whose open and repeated downward departures from the federal sentencing guidelines in some types of drug cases led to a congressional investigation, Republican lambasting of soft-on-crime judges, and eventually a statute limiting judges' authority to depart downward (which was recently overturned by the Supreme Court in *United States v. Booker*). How did this apparently partisan judge get to the bench? Well, he was a respected local lawyer who managed the election campaign of a successful congressional candidate, which led to his appointment as U.S. Attorney, which in turn led to his nomination to the federal bench. And before you jump to any conclusions: The congressional candidate was a Republican, and the supposedly soft-on-crime judge in question was appointed to both the U.S. Attorney position and the federal judgeship by President Ronald Reagan.[2]

Ideology has now come to have a disproportionate role in the appointments process. Presidents have given more weight to ideology, and positions on some "hot button" issues (especially abortion) have become litmus tests. The result is that within the president's party, members of the ideological wing of the party have an increased likelihood of being nominated as compared with moderates. Even more troubling, some presidents have looked in particular for ideological purity and commitment, trying to weed out any nominees who might be open to opposing arguments. Thus there are now offices within the executive branch charged with the task of identifying true believers, and the slightest hint of ideological impurity will sink a candidate. One scholar has found a correlation between prejudicial service in the executive branch and adherence to ideological commitment on the bench, and suggests that service in the executive branch is being used as a prescreening mechanism for ideological commitment. That recent nominees to the Supreme Court have had significant executive branch experience might therefore provide further evidence of the turn toward ideological nominations.[3]

Everything we have been arguing in this book suggests that a preference for unyielding ideological commitment is likely to lead to poorer judicial performance. Regardless of the particular ideology (left or right), the stronger the ideological commitment, the less open a judge will be to opposing arguments. And the more extreme the ideology, the less a committed judge can contribute to or learn from collegial interactions. In short, committed ideologues, especially at the political extremes, are more likely to be hedgehogs than foxes—and as we suggested in chapter 6, foxes make better judges.

The problem is also deeper than the choice of ideologically committed nominees. The selection process itself may have a deleterious effect on good judging. To the extent that a president chooses nominees for their ideology (especially extremists), ideologically driven senators have responded by blocking nominations from the opposing camp. Press leaks and bitter public disputes are not unusual. This politicization of the selection process influences public opinion, leading more citizens to believe that constitutional law *is* politics by another name.

So now we see such anomalies as an opinion poll (after the death of Chief Justice Rehnquist) asking the public whom they think should be the next Chief Justice of the United States. That is like taking an opinion poll on whether the president needs surgery or the Fed should raise interest rates. Members of the general public simply do not have enough legal expertise to have an informed opinion, any more than they know enough about medicine or economics to respond to our hypothetical polls. Incidentally, the poll results at least partially bear this out: Although Justice O'Connor (who had not yet announced her retirement at the time the survey was taken) was the top pick—a reasonable if not particularly imaginative choice—former New York City Mayor Rudy Giuliani came in second. How in the world does any member of the public know whether Giuliani is a good lawyer or would be a good judge? But the public apparently liked his politics, and if Supreme Court justices are simply legislators in black robes, the average citizen has as much relevant knowledge of potential appointees as anybody else.[4]

Finally, the Supreme Court is not helping matters. As we have argued, we think that most judges, including Supreme Court justices, *do* separate law and politics, at least most of the time. But sometimes they do a poor job of explaining the difference. Some of the cases we criticize in this book mangle principle and precedent so badly that it is unsurprising that both the public and academic observers accuse the Court of playing politics with the Constitution. And judges who devote their spare time to speaking engagements with ideological organizations like the Federalist Society unavoidably create an impression of political partisanship. The most effective method for maintaining or improving the level of judging is to appoint to the bench judges who are likely to exhibit good judgment and an adherence to the constraining principles we have identified. Both the president and the Senate should take seriously the idea that they should be looking for a person of judgment. As former Attorney General Nicholas Katzenbach said, in advising the Senate on the (ultimately unsuccessful) nomination of Judge Robert Bork to the Supreme Court: "Were I in your position... the central question I would be asking is this. Is Judge Bork a man of judgment? Not intellect, not reasoning, not lawyering skills, not ideology, not philosophy—simply, judgment. Is he a wise person?"[5]

How, then, should we identify nominees with good judgment, and distinguish foxes from hedgehogs? Instead of focusing on a nominee's ideology and the depth of his commitment to it, presidents and senators should look for individuals who are open-minded and willing to change their minds in the face of new information, who have an eclectic and open approach to adjudication. They should reject those whose approach to law is rigid and formulaic, who have a tendency to burrow ever deeper in one direction. They should also seek judges who are humble about the correctness of their own views. Judge Learned Hand described the "spirit of liberty" as "the spirit which is not too sure that it is right." A judge who is sure that she is always right can easily become a tyrant. And yet we should also want courageous judges, who are willing to act in the face of the recognition that they might be wrong. The current focus on a nominee's ideology and beliefs about specific cases does nothing to identify such traits; instead, we should look at how a nominee has conducted her professional life.[6]

The press has a role to play as well, although we can offer little more than hortatory suggestions based on our diagnosis of the problems. Perhaps this is spitting into the wind, but might we suggest that the press take seriously its responsibility to educate the public? There are plenty of excellent reporters out there who could serve as role models; we are particularly impressed with the legal acuity and evenhandedness of Linda Greenhouse, who covered the Supreme Court for the *New York Times* for decades, but there are many others as well. Still, there are too many legal reporters—or too many media outlets—who are more interested in getting people riled up than they are in actually informing them. Having reached the limits of our own expertise on this score, we leave the more concrete suggestions on this score to those with expertise in journalism.

Some institutional changes

Whether or not we can fix the selection process, we should at least try to ensure that service on the Court reinforces rather than diminishes professionalism. It is worth noticing that the gradual turn toward politics in constitutional law—which is much slower and less pronounced among judges than among politicians, but still worrisome—has coincided with three changes in Supreme Court procedures.

First, the Court's mandatory jurisdiction has all but disappeared, leaving the Court with almost complete control over its docket. It is therefore completely free to pick and choose its cases. This limits the range of legal issues confronted by the justices and encourages them to think that their job is to change the law rather than to decide cases. Perhaps more importantly, it is probably useful for the justices to have the sense that at least part of their work is not fully within their control, and thus that they are subject to legal rules like the rest of us.

Second, eight out of the nine justices are now in a "cert. pool," so that law clerks—fresh out of a prestigious law school and usually most interested in hot constitutional topics—have greater influence on the choice of cases heard by the Court. Litigants who want their cases to be heard by the Court file a petition for certiorari (or "cert."). In recent decades, the justices have generally had memos from their law clerks summarizing the issues in each case and making a recommendation about whether the petition should be granted. Formerly the justices each received a different memo from the law clerks working in their office, but today, the justices divide up the clerks so that eight of them get the same memo from one of the clerks in each case. The result is that one law clerk's perception of the case acts as a filter for nearly all of the members of the Court. Deciding what cases the Court will hear is among its most important tasks; the screening process should not be delegated to law clerks. In general, law clerks play too large a role; it is hard to see why the justices need so many clerks, particularly when their caseload is sagging.

Third, over the past several decades the Supreme Court has been deciding fewer and fewer cases, down from about 150 a year in the 1970s to fewer than 80 a year in the twenty-first century. One consequence of these three developments is that it makes it more likely that the Court's docket will include a larger percentage of major constitutional controversies. This in turn can encourage justices—unlike lower court judges, who see a full range of legal questions—to view themselves as specialized constitutional arbiters rather than as experts on legal questions. Such an attitude could infect their decision-making process, skewing it toward politics and away from judgment. The smaller caseload also provides the opportunity to devote space in opinions to rhetorical flourishes and theoretical quibbles; a larger caseload might encourage a more businesslike approach.[7]

Two possible responses might help mitigate this tendency toward constitutional specialization by exposing justices to more run-of-the mill—even if difficult—legal questions. Both are a return to previous procedural devices. Congress might reenact earlier jurisdictional rules and enlarge the Court's mandatory jurisdiction, taking away some of its ability to control its own docket. For example, the Court might be required to hear any question of federal law on which there is an identified conflict about an issue in the federal courts of appeals. Perhaps courts of appeals could be given the power to certify to the Court the existence of a serious circuit split on a significant matter of law, requiring the Court to step in. (A certification procedure now exists but is never used; it needs to be replaced by a more robust process.)

Instead, or in addition, Congress might reinstate a practice that was abolished in the late nineteenth century: circuit riding. Justices used to travel around the country sitting with district or appellate court judges, deciding whatever cases came before them. Having a "circuit justice"—who rules on requests for emergency stays and the like—is a remnant of this practice. During the nineteenth century, circuit riding was an arduous job, detested by justices, largely because of the difficulties involved in travel. It would be much easier today, and it might be enlightening for the justices to see more ordinary legal cases on a regular basis. Particularly if their own caseloads remain low, the justices should have plenty of time to ride circuit. They might, for example, sit with circuit judges to hear appeals.

If these suggestions seem implausible or too intrusive on the Court, it may be worth considering three smaller changes in the Court's procedures. First, the current custom is to give each side of the case half an hour for oral argument. This is absurdly short, and leaves little time for discussion of some very important issues. The default rule should be changed to one hour per side, with increases as warranted in more important cases.

Also, the Court has a long-standing custom of finishing all of its work before it adjourns for the summer at the end of the term. This desire to avoid delays and docket congestion is laudable, but it can lead to hastily considered opinions, particularly for cases argued late in the term. Holding a decision over the summer should be allowed if a significant number of justices request the delay—but only one such delay per case, of course, so that opinions are not held up indefinitely.

Finally, we think the justices should be encouraged to keep their distance from high public officials and the temptation to commit themselves to constitutional positions before ideological audiences. Both of these encourage justices to think of themselves as political actors rather than adjudicators. The easiest way to accomplish this would be to revise the statute governing judicial recusals to require federal judges to step aside in any case in which they have a strong social connection with one of the parties (even if the party is sued only in his official capacity) or where they have expressed an opinion on the merits of a dispute before it is heard by the Court.

As legal academics, we are probably less suited than judges themselves to devise appropriate reforms for the judiciary. We are, however, somewhat better positioned to consider how to get our own house in order. In the next chapter, we consider how the legal academy might better contribute to the development of constitutional law.

13

The Role of the Legal Academy

CONTEMPORARY STUDIES SUGGEST that public confidence in the judiciary is considerably higher than confidence in other parts of the government, and that this confidence derives in large part from the perception that judges decide cases on the basis of law rather than politics. The theory of adjudication that we have described in this book comports with the public perception. We have described constitutional adjudication as similar to other types of adjudication: based on the rule of law, and requiring both principled decision making and good judgment. More and more, however, the conventional academic wisdom seems to be that constitutional adjudication is simply politics by another name. The problem is that to the extent that this academic misconception seeps into public and political consciousness, it invidiously begins to influence judges and thus becomes a self-fulfilling prophecy.

Scholarship and popular perception of the courts

Evidence of the contemporary equating of judging and politics comes in many forms. Let us begin with the most sophisticated: the academic literature. Political scientists have argued for years that judicial decisions are determined primarily by the judge's politics (this school of thought is generally called "attitudinalism," because a judge's ideology or "attitude" determines her decisions). Law professors used to take issue with that claim, but many have lately been explicitly or implicitly accepting it.

In this context, consider the "countermajoritarian difficulty," which we described in chapter 3. The term was coined by Alexander Bickel in the 1960s to describe the tension that exists when unelected judges can invalidate the acts of the popularly elected branches. For Bickel, the resolution of the dilemma lay in the recognition that judges and legislatures perform different functions—in other words, that judging is *not* simply politics.

More recently, however, prominent constitutional scholars (on both the left and the right) have appealed to the countermajoritarian nature of judicial review to criticize both judicial review and the Supreme Court. They suggest that in striking down state and federal statutes, the courts are usurping the rights of the people and their elected representatives to interpret the Constitution. Instead of an "activist" or "arrogant" Supreme Court, these scholars urge that we should have "popular constitutionalism." This popular constitutionalism comes in many flavors, from mild exhortations, to proposals for reining in judicial discretion, to arguments that the states and the other branches of the federal government may ignore Supreme Court decisions. All are based on the theory that judicial review, at least as currently practiced by American courts—especially the Supreme Court—is antidemocratic and therefore inconsistent with the American constitutional regime.

Let us leave to one side the fact that the Constitution does not, and was not designed to, create a pure democracy. Also put aside the critics' exaggeration of both the representativeness and accountability of the elected branches and the countermajoritarian nature of the judiciary. (We discussed both of these problems briefly in chapter 3.)

Instead, consider a premise that is implicit in both the countermajoritarian critique of judicial review and the calls for popular constitutionalism: that the Court's constitutional decisions—like legislative enactments—are *political* acts and should therefore reflect the political wishes of the current majority.

This implicit premise becomes clearer if we contrast the criticisms of the judiciary's constitutional decision making with the attitude toward its nonconstitutional decisions. No one complains that judges are acting contrary to the wishes of the people when they rule on whether testimony is admissible, or whether it is an anti-trust violation for a company to conspire with its officers, or when common law doctrines bar a subsequent suit after a judgment is issued in another suit, or how the burdens of production are allocated in an employment discrimination case. Those are *legal* questions, and our society leaves them to legal experts—to judges, in other words. Congress may set the framework by enacting legislation, but we instinctively separate that initial political decision from the myriad legal decisions that must be made in the course of implementing the legislation.

Contemporary critics of judicial review, however, view constitutional questions not as legal questions but as political ones. They think that the courts are doing something different—and suspect—when they interpret the Constitution than when they interpret a statute or a common law precedent or a rule of civil procedure.

This widely held implicit belief that constitutional law is not really law at all, but politics, is also becoming more explicit in the work of some constitutional scholars. Recent scholarship claims that it is not *possible* to separate constitutional law from politics, or that Supreme Court decisions—whether for good or ill—simply mirror popular opinion. If even legal academics now conflate law and politics, it is no surprise that politicians and the public do so as well. The problem will get worse as today's students—steeped in contemporary academic thought—enter the legal profession, and perhaps the judiciary. And it is exacerbated by the fact that for the past 30 years, presidents have had a penchant for appointing legal academics directly to the federal bench. So how did we get into this mess?

The traces of postmodernism

We suggest that two independent but simultaneous developments in legal academia contributed to the change from viewing judges as legal experts to seeing them as just so many political operatives. First, the move toward popular constitutionalism—the argument that the Supreme Court is an antidemocratic usurper of the people's right to interpret their Constitution—can be seen as a domestication of the postmodernism that flourished in legal scholarship in the late 1980s and early 1990s.

Postmodernists, in and out of the legal academy, denied the possibility of objective knowledge, including legal knowledge. They argued that knowledge and reality were socially constructed by those in power. This perspective is not only wrong, but ultimately dangerous, because it encourages the idea that decision making can only be an exercise in power rather than reason. Postmodernist social constructionism in this strong form has faded from legal scholarship, but it has left its traces behind in popular constitutionalism's attack on judicial expertise.

Watering down social constructionism into a democracy-based critique of judicial expertise makes the arguments more palatable. The alternative to a Constitution interpreted by expert judges is no longer just some other socially constructed Constitution, but is now an alternative interpretation by "We the People" themselves with an additional patina of legitimacy because of its democratic origins. Like social constructionism, then, popular constitutionalism is an attack on judicial expertise, but in a much more consumer-friendly package.

There is a historical irony in all of this. The postmodern movement in legal academia can trace its roots back to the legal realism of the early twentieth century. Legal realists rejected the formalist notion that law embodies neutral general principles, which both derive from and determine the results in individual cases. Instead, the realists argued that legal principles are indeterminate, and their application could always vary with the substantive views of the particular judges.

The legal realists counted on expertise to remedy the dangers of legal indeterminacy. Postmodernists, however, took the next step, embracing indeterminacy (legal and otherwise) and concluding that expert knowledge was a myth. Today's democratizers want a return to the legal realists' possibility of certainty but—like the postmodernists—they reject the realists' faith in expertise; instead, they find legal certainty by substituting majority will for expertise. Thus the move toward viewing law as politics is part of a larger movement away from trust in expertise in general and a partial inheritance of the postmodernist movement in legal academia. Popular constitutionalism purports to be a shift in interpretative authority from the courts to the people, but there is little reason to think that the act of interpretation is one best performed through a political mechanism. Popular constitutionalism flirts with replacing the restraints of constitutionalism with a freewheeling reconsideration of all constitutional boundaries at the behest of popular majorities. This approach seems no more likely than the postmodernists' to produce stable and independently defensible constitutional doctrines.

The turn toward novelty

The revised view of constitutional law as politics reflects another important change: the rise of novelty as an academic ideal. Until at least the mid-twentieth century, constitutional scholars generally mirrored the judicial role. They synthesized the existing (sometimes inchoate) intellectual consensus, simultaneously inserting small and subtle innovations that resonated with contemporary beliefs. Their scholarship integrated tradition and change. Scholars such as Alexander Bickel, Harry Kalven, Herbert Wechsler, and, a little later, John Ely, left their mark on constitutional scholarship by breaking new ground—sometimes brilliantly—without completely severing ties to the past. As one modern scholar notes, for example, "Bickel dismisse[d] as philosophical romantics those who promote sweeping institutional reforms for the sake of achieving a closer approximation to some ideal, and vastly simplified, conception of representative democracy." One current law professor describes his 1960s legal education—under the tutelage of these and other thinkers—as emphasizing "that law must be separated from politics and that good arguments are seldom more than one step beyond existing arguments."[1]

How things have changed. The academic milieu now creates incentives to climb out on ever shakier limbs. Novelty has become the ultimate test of an idea's worth. Counterintuitive theoretical ideas divorced from practical reality are too often rewarded. Thus a young faculty member who "brilliantly" turns prior wisdom on its head is more likely to be published and noticed than the humble toiler in an already well-plowed field. As one academic commentator put it, "to build on, refine, or magnify the understandings of the past is likely to be viewed with condescending tolerance," but deconstructing the past "in favor of newly revealed truths that had previously been shrouded from view because of the misconceptions of all of one's predecessors, is surely an impressive achievement."[2]

A nonacademic lawyer hit the nail on the head in reviewing a book by one of the most prominent constitutional scholars (at perhaps the most prestigious law school in the country), suggesting that the scholar and his coauthor were motivated by "not a political agenda, but an academic one," "searching so desperately for a 'new' way to look at the Constitution that they don't mind ignoring two hundred years of accumulated thought on the subject." This academic climate can foster arrogance, self-absorption, and a lack of judgment. These qualities are not conducive to successful judging.[3]

This penchant for brilliance interacts with other factors to ensure that many academics, unlike most lawyers, will not internalize the traits and norms that produce good judicial decision making. Unlike legal work in practice, academic work is a generally solo project, not a group project. In comparison to academics in many other fields, legal scholars show a marked preference for noncollaborative work. Remarks by Justice Scalia, who was a law professor before he was appointed to the federal bench, illustrate the pleasures of academic writing and its difference from much of what judges do. Justice Scalia comments on the joys of being "able to write an opinion solely for oneself, without the need to accommodate, to any degree whatever," the views of colleagues. His concept of "an unparalleled pleasure" is "to address precisely the points of law that one considers important and *no others*; to express precisely the degree of quibble, or foreboding, or disbelief, or indignation that one believes the majority's disposition should engender." We do not doubt that working with a group of other justices to agree on an opinion can be frustrating, like any other committee process. But a failure to "play well with others" is no virtue in a judge, and academic life may simply encourage such "loner" conduct.[4]

Another factor exacerbating the tendency toward novelty is the peculiar publication regime in the legal academy. In most law journals—including the most prestigious—articles are selected for publication by third-year students rather than by legal scholars through peer review. (There are a few exceptions, and we wish there were more.) But this system means that publication often depends on the judgment of unsophisticated neophytes who are likely to be unable to separate the wheat from the chaff and who are therefore likely to be unduly impressed by grand claims and startling arguments.

The legal academy's focus on innovation as opposed to wisdom has broader pernicious effects than simply producing people who make poor judges. As we suggested earlier, law professors can play a crucial role in restraining judges by using their expertise to explain and critique judicial opinions and educating the lay public. Opportunities to do so abound, but legal academics often misuse them. Instead of providing knowledgeable commentary, many scholars use the media exposure to further their own political agendas or personal careers.

Thus we see such phenomena as 430 law professors—most of whom are not constitutional scholars, let alone constitutional historians—signing a letter purporting to instruct Congress on the original meaning of the impeachment clauses of the Constitution, and an environmental and criminal law professor with no constitutional scholarship to his name pontificating as an "expert" on impeachment. Similarly, an e-mail distributed widely among law professors solicited them to sign—purportedly as experts—a letter interpreting an obscure clause of the Constitution, several even more obscure federal statutes, and "the laws of Florida": "[A]ll the expertise" needed, according to the letter, was "a background teaching and writing about the Constitution." With this kind of squandering of intellectual reputation, law professors will soon lose—if they have not done so already—any claim to a role as explicators and critics of the judiciary.[5]

Alexis de Tocqueville noted that "[t]here is hardly a political question in the United States which does not sooner or later turn into a judicial one." Since Tocqueville wrote, we have made progress: Lately, there is hardly a judicial question that does not turn into a media circus. With the explosion of media coverage of legal events—helped by a series of high-profile audience-attracting events such as the Simpson and Jackson trials, the Clinton impeachment, the 2000 election litigation, and the Schiavo litigation—every legal academic can become a pundit. Punditry is too often a game for the clever, not the thoughtful. And those who are successful in today's academic atmosphere often are indeed clever but not always thoughtful. If *academic* reputation depended on the soundness rather than the novelty of a scholar's ideas, scholars might be more thoughtful in their public comments, which might in turn reduce the media demand for entertainment or demagoguery and increase the dissemination of actual information.[6]

Finally, the academic obsession with novelty undermines the very legal culture that helps produce restrained and thoughtful judges, because socialization and professionalization of lawyers begins in law school. To the extent that law professors untether themselves from tradition and favor radical reform, they teach their students that incrementalism is an unnecessary anachronism. Law professors whose classroom, scholarly, and public comments are silly, or simply not thoughtful, can be accused of using politics rather than judgment, demonstrating to their students that ideological attachments are stronger and more important than attachment to the rule of law. And the further from present reality that legal scholarship strays, the less students feel constrained by anything other than their own imaginations.

Suggestions for improvement

So what should we do? It would be helpful if the academy valued incremental, doctrinal, "pedestrian" scholarship a little more, refusing to jump on the latest bandwagon and demanding quality rather than novelty. Law schools might also do well to put less emphasis on hiring scholars in "sexy" fields like constitutional law and give more weight to knowledge of the forbiddingly complex statutory schemes that govern much of the American economy in areas such as pensions, telecommunications, bankruptcy, discrimination law, and taxes. It might also be useful if leading law schools preferred significant practice experience as a qualification for junior faculty, as they once did. Instead, the trend is to require an increasing amount of published scholarship before a person can be hired as a faculty member, which tends to exclude candidates with demanding jobs in legal practice.

As academics, we must take our role as educators—of our students and of the public—seriously. We should push against our students' ideological commitments, even (or especially) if we share them. In advising them on judicial clerkships, we can encourage them to ignore politics in their choice of judges—or even to prefer judges whose politics differ from their own. We should not reinvent the wheel every time we write an article: Let us stand on the shoulders of our giants and acknowledge that we are doing so. Exerting more control over student-run law reviews—or, better still, replacing them with the peer-reviewed journals that exist in every other academic field—would help.

Finally, we should stop teaching the legal realist *cum* critical legal studies notion (now gradually taking over mainstream constitutional law) that the rule of law is really just the political preferences of the judges. Duke law professor Paul Carrington was right some twenty years ago—although much castigated at the time—when he said that ideologically oriented scholars did not belong in legal academia as teachers of future lawyers if they did not believe in even the possibility of a principled and objective rule of law. The point is not that legal academics must uphold the established legal order—far from it—but that they must at least accept the rule of law as an ideal.[7]

In the end, we simply hope that law professors who share our views will hold fast and keep proselytizing (and maybe even assign this book to students!). But a close look at some actual decisions may be more useful than our sermons in rebutting the reductionist view of judging as a form of politics. We have called upon judges to respect precedent and provide candid, well-reasoned explanations of their decisions. At a more fundamental level, we have also called on them to be responsive to social values and to find sensitive accommodations of conflicting values. Examples are worth more than abstractions in understanding this process. For that reason, we close the book with case studies of how the Supreme Court has handled three of our society's most pressing and controversial social issues: terrorism, abortion, and affirmative action.

PART VI

Case Studies

14

Terrorism

BEFORE TURNING TO our case studies, a brief reprise may be helpful. We have argued that except in easy cases, judges find themselves faced with leeway in applying constitutional provisions, but that they have an obligation to give reasoned accounts for how they resolve the cases. We have emphasized the need for transparency and candor in judicial decisions, as well as the obligation to provide a reasoned elaboration. Where relevant, decisions must take account of text, history, and precedent. Where these fail to provide sufficient guidance, there is a need for the judiciary to make value judgments, rooting those value judgments as much as possible in American constitutional traditions and contemporary norms.

The need to articulate and reconcile constitutional values is exemplified by the *Hamdi* case. *Hamdi* was one of the cases growing out of the "war against terror." Because it involved a complex set of intertwined statutes and executive orders, we must begin with some background information.[1]

One week after the terrorist attacks of September 11, 2001, Congress passed a resolution—the Authorization for Use of Military Force (AUMF)—authorizing the president to "use all necessary and appropriate force" against "nations, organizations, or persons" that he determined "planned, authorized, committed, or aided" the attacks. On November 13, 2001, President Bush issued a "military order" regarding the detention of terrorists, which was supplemented three months later by a classified presidential memorandum (not fully declassified until June 2004).[2]

The original order invokes the president's powers as "President and as Commander in Chief of the Armed Forces." After making various findings about the necessity of detention and trial of terrorists, it authorizes the detention of any person whom the president has "reason to believe" is a member of al-Qaeda, has engaged in acts of international terrorism against the United States, or has harbored such individuals. It specifies that these prisoners are to be "treated humanely" and "afforded adequate food, drinking water, shelter, clothing, and medical treatment." The order then provides for trial by military commission, but relaxes the procedural safeguards that accompany both civilian trials and military courts martial. For example, section 4 of the order suspends all rules of evidence except relevance, provides for conviction and sentencing by two-thirds of the members of the commission, and gives wide power to the commission to prevent unauthorized disclosure of information—even depriving the accused and his lawyer of the right to see certain types of evidence used against him. And section 7 prohibits the accused from seeking any judicial relief from detention. Thus the order allows detention on the say-so of the president, and provides minimal procedural protections.[3]

Having eliminated ordinary domestic procedural protections in the November order, the president focused on international protections in the supplemental memorandum. In this January 2002 memorandum, President Bush rejected the application of the Geneva Conventions to supporters of al-Qaeda, whether captured during the Afghanistan conflict or elsewhere. This memorandum was based in part on the advice of Alberto Gonzales, who was then White House counsel. Gonzales stated that "the war against terrorism is a new kind of war." As is well known, the Gonzales memo was sharply contested by the legal adviser to the State Department, William H. Taft IV, who argued that the Geneva Conventions should apply to Taliban detainees captured in Afghanistan. But the president ultimately sided with Gonzales, and thus concluded that those captured in Afghanistan had only the rights the executive branch chose to give them.[4]

The president's supplemental order had the effect of eliminating certain hearing requirements mandated by the various Geneva Conventions. Under Article 84 of Geneva III, prisoners of war (POWs) may be tried only by a "military court" unless the detaining power's laws explicitly permit the use of a civilian court, and any procedure must "offer the essential guarantees of independence and impartiality as generally recognized." Moreover, under Article 106, the prisoner must have the same right of appeal as a member of the detaining power's own armed forces. These provisions might arguably apply at least to some Taliban soldiers. And pursuant to Article 5, "[s]hould any doubt arise as to whether persons, having committed a belligerent act and having fallen into the hands of the enemy," constitute POWs, "such persons shall enjoy the protection of the present Convention until such time as their status has been determined by a competent tribunal." Article 5 might apply to Taliban and perhaps to some of their al-Qaeda supporters in Afghanistan. Common Article 3 imposes other requirements in an "armed conflict not of an international character occurring in the territory of one of the High Contracting Parties." In such conflicts, punishment is not allowed "without previous judgment pronounced by a regularly constituted court affording all the judicial guarantees which are recognized as indispensable by civilized peoples." Thus, where they apply, the Geneva Conventions not only provide substantive protection, but require significant procedural safeguards beyond those promised in the president's detention order.

That is how the law stood when the Court was confronted with the *Hamdi* case. Hamdi, an American citizen, was captured in Afghanistan and after some intermediate stops was detained at a naval brig in Charleston, South Carolina. No charges were filed against him, but the government claimed the right to detain him incommunicado indefinitely as an "unlawful combatant." His father filed a petition for a writ of habeas corpus (the traditional method of challenging confinement) on his behalf. His father asserted that Hamdi went to Afghanistan to do "relief work" less than two months before September 11 and could not have received military training. In response to the petition, the government filed a declaration from Michael Mobbs, a Defense Department official. The Mobbs declaration alleges various details regarding Hamdi's trip to Afghanistan, his affiliation there with a Taliban unit during a time when the Taliban was battling U.S. allies, and his subsequent surrender of an assault rifle. After some back and forth between the federal district court and the court of appeals, the latter concluded that the Mobbs declaration was sufficient to support Hamdi's detention, and no further inquiry was necessary.

A badly divided Supreme Court reversed the court of appeals and remanded for further proceedings. Four justices, led by Justice O'Connor, held that Hamdi was entitled to some form of due process hearing to challenge his detention. Four other justices, in two different opinions, would have held his detention squarely unlawful. Two of those justices joined portions of O'Connor's opinion in order to provide a majority for some disposition of the case. The remaining member of the Court, Justice Thomas, agreed with the government's view that the Mobbs

declaration (which the lower court had characterized as conclusory hearsay) provided a sufficient basis for Hamdi's indefinite detention.

We are no fans of the Bush Administration's handling of terrorism issues or
foreign policy, but the case obviously presented a very serious and difficult constitutional issue. On the one hand, the potential for abuse in allowing arbitrary
detentions is plain. On the other hand, the threat of terrorism (at least of the kind
represented by al-Qaeda) is a new one; we do not know its exact parameters or
the appropriate response, and other democratic nations such as Britain and Israel
have found it necessary to make some sacrifices of civil liberties to combat terrorist
campaigns.

Of the various opinions, Justice O'Connor's made the most serious effort to
reconcile the two interests. She explicitly recognized the need for sensitive treatment of the interests on both sides. She acknowledged that "[s]triking the proper
constitutional balance here is of great importance to the Nation during this period
of ongoing combat." "But it is equally vital," she said, "that our calculus not give
short shrift to the values that this country holds dear or to the privilege that is
American citizenship." She emphasized that it is "during our most challenging and
uncertain moments that our Nation's commitment to due process is most severely
tested; and it is in those times that we must preserve our commitment at home to
the principles for which we fight abroad."[5]

Justice O'Connor found authorization for the detention in the Congressional
resolution, ducking any need to consider inherent presidential authority. But she
was only willing to endorse the detention power in cases like Hamdi's, involving
enemy action in a war zone, leaving other cases to the future, but implying that the
category of enemy combatants was narrow. For reasons that one of us has discussed
elsewhere, we believe that this is a correct reading of the precedents and of our
constitutional history.[6]

Thus Justice O'Connor both acknowledged a power of detention and also
began to stake out limits: For example, detention cannot be solely for the purposes
of interrogation and cannot extend beyond the armed conflict in question. Because
of those limits, she had to face the difficult question of how to determine whether
Hamdi fell within what she called the "narrow category" of unlawful combatants.
Here, too, she tried to accommodate both security and liberty. She attempted to
provide a fair process for determining the facts, allowing the government to begin
the process by filing factual affidavits like the Mobbs declaration but then allowing
Hamdi the chance to provide evidence in rebuttal.

The other justices grappled with the issues but were less successful in reconcil-
ing the competing values of liberty and security. Like Justice O'Connor, Justice

Souter (joined by Justice Breyer) made some effort to accommodate national security needs and civil liberties. He recognized—properly, we think—that the president may have *some* emergency detention powers even apart from statute. But he also observed, again appropriately, that the long-term detention of Hamdi and others could hardly be considered an emergency action. Justice Souter's opinion was not without appeal, and we consider it as being within the range of reasonable assessments of the case. Yet his opinion was less successful than Justice O'Connor's because he failed to separate the analysis of the government's right to detain Hamdi from the question of the conditions of confinement. He reasoned that the detention *itself* was illegal because of the government's failure to abide by Geneva Conventions' rules on the *conditions* of confinement.

The other justices were more rigid. Justice Thomas, as we read his opinion, came close to giving the president a blank check to override civil liberties. Justices Scalia and Stevens may have erred in the opposite direction. They denied the existence of any right to treat American citizens who fight for the other side as prisoners of war. In their view, after it detains citizens who were in combat with enemy forces, the government must either bring criminal charges promptly or release them. Apart from what we think are its dubious historical roots, this view would straightjacket the government without regard to changing conditions. Scalia and Stevens recognized only one source of flexibility, the power of Congress to suspend the writ of habeas corpus. Not only is this a draconian remedy, but if invoked it might be far more destructive of civil liberties than a judicially defined solution.

We do not claim that Justice O'Connor's opinion was ideal, or that it was the only reasonable approach. She might have done more to define the permissible category of unlawful combatants and to make it clear that any inherent power of the president was very narrow. ("Take the keys and lock him up" is fine in nursery rhymes but it is no way to run a democratic society.) Her suggested procedures apparently did not turn out to be as workable and fair as she suggested, and she might have done better to emphasize the role of the courts in reviewing detention decisions. By suggesting that administrative hearings could substitute for a judicial assessment of the validity of a citizen's detention, she may have weakened some of the historic function of the "great writ" of habeas corpus. Thus Justice O'Connor's resolution of the case is not necessarily ideal. Nevertheless, her opinion is admirable for its principled stand against arbitrary arrests and for its effort to find a solution that also respected our constitutional history and the need for some flexibility in protecting national security.

In praising Justice O'Connor's opinion, we do not mean merely that it was an astute compromise between opposing forces on the Court and in society, nor simply that it was good government policy. The case involved a clash between two strong, constitutionally rooted concepts: the core right of every individual to a fair hearing, and the imperative need for governmental authority to respond to severe threats to national security. Failing to give some appropriate weight to each of these factors would not merely be bad policy or poor politics, it would be a failure to understand the constitutional interests at stake.

Hamdi is also notable as evidence that ideology is not everything, even in the hardest constitutional cases. The critical vote for Justice O'Connor's position was Justice Breyer, commonly considered a member of the liberal block. Chief Justice Rehnquist, a strong conservative voice, also allied himself with O'Connor's centrist views. In the meantime, the two most conservative members of the Court (Thomas and Scalia) came to diametrically opposite conclusions, and Scalia was joined by Justice Stevens, the most liberal member of the Court.

Whatever one might say about the various individual opinions, we have no doubt that each of the justices did his or her best to consider all of the arguments and to reason to the best answer possible. The outcome was a decision that respected the important critical values at stake and that gave weight to precedent and constitutional history. As *Hamdi* shows, this process may not be ideal, but it does fulfill the demands of judicial review in a constitutional democracy.

In a later case, *Hamdan v. Rumsfeld*, the Court again rebuffed the administration's efforts to evade legal restrictions. *Hamdan* involved the use of military commissions to try enemy belligerents under the presidential order discussed earlier. In an opinion by Justice Stevens, the Court held that the president lacked the power to establish the military tribunals under congressional enactments and under the Geneva Conventions. Again, the president's effort to operate free from outside legal restrictions was rebuffed.[7]

After *Hamdan*, Congress responded with legislation that deprived the courts of jurisdiction to hear habeas cases of this kind. Just as this book was going to press, the Supreme Court held the jurisdictional limitation unconstitutional in *Boumediene v. Bush*. Justice Kennedy's majority opinion canvassed the history of habeas corpus and echoed Justice O'Connor's careful balancing of government needs against individual rights. "Security," he wrote, "subsists, too, in fidelity to freedom's first principles," of which the most important are "freedom from arbitrary and unlawful restraint and the personal liberty that is secured" by judicial review of executive detentions.[8]

Hamdi, Hamdan, and *Boumediene* provide a perfect illustration of why, despite all its shortcomings, judicial review is better than the alternative. These decisions imposed the only roadblocks to a deliberate assault on the rule of law by the executive branch, which Congress had done nothing whatsoever to block. Those who think we could be better off if the ultimate decisions about the meaning of the Constitution were left exclusively in the hands of the executive branch or Congress would do well to ponder these three cases and to keep a close watch on the Court's future responses to executive overreaching in the war on terror. Given what we know so far about the neglect of civil liberties in the war on terror, we should all hope that the Court continues to stand firm.

15

Abortion

P ERHAPS THE MOST important—or at least the best-known—case that the
Supreme Court has decided in the past forty years is *Roe v. Wade*, in
which it recognized a constitutional right to abortion. Few cases in the Court's
history have given rise to such controversy. For almost twenty years after *Roe*, the
Court expanded and then contracted the right it had recognized in *Roe*, the justices argued among themselves about its validity, and scholars often predicted that
it would soon be overruled. But in 1992, in *Planned Parenthood of Southeastern
Pennsylvania v. Casey*, the Court surprisingly reaffirmed the existence of the constitutional right but altered the structure of its analysis. Both cases can be evaluated
under our standards.[1]

In light of the controversy over *Roe*, it is easy for the actual decision to get lost
in the rhetorical fireworks. It behooves us to begin by taking a close look at the
original ruling itself. The first thing to observe is that what we call "*Roe*" was actually not one case but two: *Roe v. Wade* and *Doe v. Bolton*. The extent to which the
justices regarded the two as interconnected is shown by the haphazard way that the

separate concurring and dissenting opinions are scattered between the two cases.
Yet we generally read the opinion in *Roe v. Wade* without taking into account its
Siamese twin, the *Doe* opinion, which struck down most of Georgia's abortion
statute.[2]

The Georgia abortion statute was newer and more liberal than the Texas
statute invalidated in *Roe*. However, the statute imposed an onerous medical
approval process. The Court rejected the statute's burdensome procedure, but it is
also important to recall the portion of the Georgia statute *upheld* by the Supreme
Court. This aspect of the decision has generally been overlooked. Given that the
district court had struck down the list of permissible justifications that must be
certified by the physician, all that was left was this: "[I]t still remains a crime for a
physician to perform an abortion except when…it is 'based upon his best clinical
judgment that an abortion is necessary.'" This truncated provision was challenged
before the Supreme Court as being unconstitutionally vague.[3]

The Court not only rejected the vagueness attack but went out of its way to
endorse the provision. As the Court interpreted the truncated provision, it required
the physician to make this decision in the "light of *all* the attendant circumstances,"
ranging "farther afield wherever his medical judgment, properly and professionally
exercised, so dictates and directs him." As the Court said, "Whether, in the words
of the Georgia statute, 'an abortion is necessary' is a professional judgment that the
Georgia physician will be called upon to make routinely." That judgment was to be
"exercised in the light of all factors—physical, emotional, psychological, familial,
and the woman's age—relevant to the well-being of the patient." As the Court
pointed out in *Roe*, if "an individual practitioner abuses the privilege of exercising
proper medical judgment, the usual remedies, judicial and intra-professional, are
available."[4]

The familiar trimester system was announced in *Roe*: no state regulation in
the first trimester, health regulation in the second trimester (because the abortion
is then riskier than full-term pregnancy), and limitation to life or health justifications in the third trimester (because the state's interest in protecting potential life
becomes compelling after viability).

Read in the context of *Doe*, the trimester system has a subtle twist. The state
can insist all the way through pregnancy that abortions be based on medical considerations (i.e., life or health of the mother, broadly construed). What the third
trimester marks is *not* a change in the types of allowable abortions, but rather a
change in how the state can implement the restriction. In the first two trimesters,
the state must delegate implementation to physicians, reviewing their decisions
only to the same extent as other medical decisions. In the final trimester, the state

can police more aggressively, using the criminal law to ensure that a medical justification exists.

The dissenters characterized the holding broadly, calling it an endorsement of abortion on demand. The dissent read the opinion as holding that "[d]uring the period prior to the time the fetus becomes viable, the Constitution of the United States values the convenience, whim, or caprice of the putative mother more than the life or potential life of the fetus." Chief Justice Burger's concurrence took a narrower view of the holding: "[T]he dissenting views discount the reality that the vast majority of physicians observe the standards of their profession, and act only on the basis of carefully deliberated medical judgments relating to life and health."[5]

Given that in *Doe* the Court had upheld criminal punishment for physicians who performed abortions without determining them to be medically appropriate, Burger's characterization clearly seems the more accurate. (Indeed, at one point in *Roe* the Court quotes an American Medical Association [AMA] abortion resolution emphasizing "'the best interests of the patient,' 'sound clinical judgment,' and 'informed patient consent,' in contrast to 'mere acquiescence to the patient's demand.'") Certainly, the Court did not seem to regard abortions as elective in the same sense as cosmetic surgery. So far as we know, no state has ever made it a criminal offense to perform a nose job or tummy tuck without first making a written determination of medical necessity. If a state did so, no doubt this would be regarded as a substantial restriction on the availability of these procedures.[6]

The upshot of *Roe* and *Doe*, then, was this: The state may limit abortion to cases of medical necessity in the first two trimesters, but it cannot exclude any factors that a reasonable physician might find relevant and it cannot single out abortion decisions for special oversight beyond that accorded other medical procedures. In the third trimester, the state can be more intrusive by forbidding abortions and using the criminal law to oversee the decision. In assessing what the Court did in *Roe*, we must begin with what the Court said it was doing, not with the dissent's characterization. The Court's decision was simply less radical than it was often portrayed. Perhaps this is understandable, since the somewhat restricted right recognized by the Court was treated as a blank check by abortion advocates, and the press largely accepted the portrayal of the decision by the dissent as endorsing abortion on demand. Still, it is a bit unfair to read these later developments into the Court's opinion.

In order to uphold even a qualified right to abortion, the Court had to do two things. First, it had to find some basis for recognizing abortion as a constitutionally protected decision. Then, it had to take into account the state's interest in protecting the unborn and determine whether or when that interest was sufficient to justify abortion restrictions under the applicable test. How well did the Court perform those tasks?

We suggested earlier in this book that it can be helpful to compare courts with administrative agencies. Thus we might ask whether a similarly reasoned decision by an agency would have been upheld or struck down by the courts under the arbitrary and capricious standard. Was *Roe v. Wade* arbitrary and capricious?

In our view, *Roe* falls short in terms of reasoned evaluation. In *Roe*, the core of the opinion—leaving aside a long and largely irrelevant history of abortion laws—consists of three parts, each of which is unsatisfactory from the perspective of reasoned elaboration. First, Justice Blackmun attempts to use precedent to find a right of privacy in the Constitution. All he does, however, is cite a string of unconnected cases, without explaining what privacy means or how these cases are linked together. The second step is even more conclusory: The opinion states with little elaboration that "[t]his right of privacy . . . is broad enough to encompass a woman's decision whether or not to terminate her pregnancy." Only a fig leaf—a paragraph on the detrimental effects of an unwanted pregnancy—keeps this statement from being naked judicial fiat. Finally, the notorious trimester scheme (which would make fine *legislation*) is insufficiently connected to the first two parts, and looks far too much like ad hoc decision making.[7]

Justice Blackmun conceded that the Constitution does not contain an explicit right of privacy. He relied, however, on a series of rulings finding some aspect of privacy to be protected by the First, Fourth, Fifth, and Ninth Amendments, and by the concept of liberty in the Fourteenth Amendment. He viewed these cases as showing that only fundamental rights or those inherent in ordered liberty are protected, and that privacy extends to aspects of "marriage, procreation, contraception, family relationships, and child rearing and education."[8]

Assuming that there is some kind of right to privacy, is abortion encompassed within that right? Justice Blackmun was correct to identify a cluster of cases protecting various aspects of privacy, and a tighter cluster relating to intimate relations and reproductive choice. This suggests that a plausible rationale for *Roe* could have been identified. Still, the analysis of precedent seems strikingly incomplete. In this respect, Justice Stewart's concurring opinion is more satisfactory. Justice Blackmun's discussion of the consequences of unwanted pregnancy might also contain the germs of a privacy-based argument, if one could argue that those particular types of harms are peculiarly "private" and akin to those involved in earlier family and reproduction cases. Thus while this part of the opinion was not as well presented as it might have been, the underlying argument—if better elaborated—was reasonable and judicious, and, as we will see later in this chapter, much better fleshed out in a subsequent case.

The trimester system was probably the most vulnerable part of the opinion. To some extent, any effort to accommodate conflicting interests will involve drawing somewhat arbitrary lines, as the justices seem to have realized at the time. But the trimester system seems more arbitrary than most, with only a single sentence in the opinion to justify it. There was certainly nothing inevitable about this choice. As we now know, the justices had considered drawing the line after the first trimester, but the majority decided not to, in part because women might not see physicians until near the end of the first trimester. To the end, Justice Douglas preferred the first-trimester dividing line.[9]

It seems inconceivable that an administrative agency, dealing with such questions as air pollution regulation, telecommunication, or even standards for workplace toilets, would get away with such casual resolution of an important issue. It is little wonder that this aspect of the decision was soon eroded and ulti-mately rejected. It simply failed to cross the threshold of reasoned decision mak-ing. A more flexible approach, such as the "undue burden" test later adopted in *Casey*, would have given the Court the opportunity to learn the facts it needed to reach a sound accommodation between women's rights and the countervailing state interest.[10]

What does it take to make a constitutional ruling defensible (even if neverthe-less debatable)? The analogy to administrative law indicates that the ruling must rest on a reasoned application of the relevant factors—in constitutional law, those factors include precedent, history, and public values. It is unrealistic to expect judges to produce perfectly crafted opinions, and some cases do not require a full consider-ation of each of these factors. Still, in hard cases, a responsible Court should provide a coherent, believable claim in these terms. This does not guarantee the correctness of the decision, but does make the decision something other than an exercise of raw judicial power; whether or not we agree with the result, we must agree that the justices have done their job.

Roe v. Wade is only a partial success under this standard. Its argument for recognizing a fundamental right works in the proper direction, but was badly in need of elaboration. More seriously, the Court made almost no effort to justify the trimester system. That failing was all the more serious because it was gratuitous. The trimester system was an ill-advised effort at judicial legislation. All the Court needed to do in *Roe* and *Doe* was to (a) rule the procedural safeguards excessive and overly intrusive in the Georgia case, (b) uphold Georgia's requirement that the physician certify medical necessity, and (c) affirm the lower court's declaratory judgment against Texas's sweeping abortion ban because it prohibited medically necessary abortions. The rest could have been left to the states and the lower courts in the first instance, allowing a much better developed factual record and far more complete analysis of the various options.

Given the stark emotions raised by the abortion issue, it is not clear whether this course would have done the Court much good politically. Still, giving the states more flexibility and making clearer the role of medical necessity as a restriction might have ignited less of a firestorm. But in any event, a decision along those lines would have had a better claim to represent reason rather than fiat. Of course, hindsight is always easy, and we have now had many more years to consider the constitutional dimensions of the abortion issue. The point is not to blame Justice Blackmun and his colleagues for issuing an imperfect opinion thirty-some years ago. Rather, it is to urge the Court to do better in the future.

As it turned out, the Court's effort to freeze abortion doctrine for all time was not successful. Later decisions began to interpret *Roe* in a more flexible way. At the same time, some judges began to question the very foundations of constitutional protection for abortion. In the sixteen years after *Roe*, the Court decided numerous abortion cases. The Court generally struck down state requirements that had the effect of making abortions more expensive or forcing them to be performed in hospitals rather than clinics. On the other hand, it consistently held that the government has no affirmative obligation to pay for abortions, even if it does pay for childbirth. Another recurring issue involved consent requirements. In a 1983 case, *Planned Parenthood Association v. Ashcroft*, the Court upheld a state law requiring a pregnant minor to obtain either the consent of her parent or judicial approval, while in the 1981 case of *H.L. v. Matheson*, the Court upheld a requirement that the minor's parents be notified whenever possible (at least as applied to nonemancipated minors).[11]

During this period, *Roe* came under continuing attack from some of the justices. In *Akron v. Akron Center for Reproductive Health*, Justices O'Connor, White, and Rehnquist indicated their willingness to reconsider *Roe*. Chief Justice Burger and Justice Powell, along with Justices Brennan, Marshall, Blackmun, and Stevens, continued to support *Roe*. But after Burger and Powell were replaced by Justices Scalia and Kennedy, *Roe*'s future seemed clouded. By 1989, when the *Webster* case, discussed below, was pending, it was widely thought *Roe* would be overruled.[12]

In *Webster v. Reproductive Health Services*, a Missouri law required doctors to determine viability before performing an abortion after the twentieth week of pregnancy. The main opinion in the case, written by Chief Justice Rehnquist, declined to revisit *Roe*'s holding that abortion has some constitutional protection, conceding that it involved a "liberty interest protected by the Due Process Clause." Rehnquist then contended that the trimester system should be rejected. Applying an unspecified level of review, he concluded: "The Missouri testing requirement here is reasonably designed to ensure that abortions are not performed where the fetus is viable—an end which all concede is legitimate—and that is sufficient to sustain its constitutionality."[13]

The Court was badly divided in its approach to the case. Interestingly, in light of later developments, Justice Kennedy joined Rehnquist's opinion. Justice O'Connor concurred separately on the basis that Missouri law did not impose an "undue burden" and in any event was consistent with the Court's previous decisions. Her support for *Roe* remained unclear, however. In an angry concurrence, Justice Scalia berated the majority for refusing to overrule *Roe* outright. Justices Blackmun, Brennan, Marshall, and Stevens dissented on the ground that the Court's ruling was inconsistent with *Roe*.

The final abortion case preceding *Casey* was *Hodgson v. Minnesota*. Based upon *Ashcroft* and subsequent cases, thirty-eight states enacted laws requiring notification or consent of one or both parents before a minor could obtain an abortion. Arguably the most restrictive law was that of Minnesota, which required notification of both parents (one of eight states to do so). Virtually the only loophole was an alternate procedure for judicial approval if parental approval was impractical, as required by *Danforth*. Justice Kennedy's opinion for the Court simply applied *Ashcroft* and the other precedents upholding parental notification and consent requirements that gave pregnant girls the opportunity to get permission from a judge instead of their parents. Concurring, Justice O'Connor maintained that the two-parent notification requirement was in fact an undue burden on a minor woman's right to abortion, but she agreed with the Court that the availability of a judicial bypass saved the statute.[14]

When President George H. W. Bush replaced Justices Brennan and Marshall with Justices Souter and Thomas, the future of *Roe* seemed dim. When *Casey* was argued, the U.S. Solicitor General and the State of Pennsylvania both asked the Court to overrule *Roe*. Planned Parenthood, which challenged the state restrictions on abortion, asked the Court to overrule *Roe* if it was not willing to give the right of privacy real bite. This set the stage for the most important abortion decision since *Roe* itself.

It was widely expected that, as a result of Reagan- and Bush-era appointees, *Roe* was doomed. But the Court took a surprisingly different path. *Casey* is by far the most notable and controversial application of stare decisis in recent years. In part, this is because the Court's willingness to stand by precedent came as such a surprise: After all, "[t]he last thing one would have expected the Rehnquist Court to do was to reaffirm *Roe v. Wade*."[15]

But *Casey* is a far cry from *Roe* in terms of judicial craft. Recall that Justice Blackmun's opinion in *Roe* used unadorned case citations to support the conclusion that the Constitution protects a right of privacy. Contrast this barebones approach to the lead opinion in *Casey*. It sets the stage by fleshing out the breadth of the Fourteenth Amendment's protection of liberty: "It is... tempting... to suppose that the Due Process Clause protects only those practices, defined at the most specific level, that were protected against government interference by other rules of law when the Fourteenth Amendment was ratified." The lead opinion rejects this temptation as "inconsistent with our law" and with the "promise of the Constitution that there is a realm of personal liberty which the government may not enter." Quoting Justice Harlan, the Court in *Casey* notes that liberty "is not a series of isolated points pricked out" in the text of the Constitution. Instead, liberty is "a rational continuum which, broadly speaking, includes a freedom from all substantial arbitrary impositions and purposeless restraints" and recognizes that "certain interests require particularly careful scrutiny of the state needs asserted to justify their abridgement." The opinion uses the same cases cited by Justice Blackmun to illustrate this principle, but context makes this use of precedent more coherent and intelligible.[16]

When it comes to placing abortion on this continuum of interests, the *Casey* opinion again ties the question to precedent and to principle. The opinion observes that the Court's precedents "have respected the private realm of family life which the state cannot enter"—a realm "involving the most intimate and personal choices a person may make in a lifetime, choices central to personal dignity and autonomy." Central to the liberty protected by the Constitution, the opinion said, "is the right to define one's own concept of existing, of meaning, of the universe, and of the mystery of human life." Thus, the opinion continued, a pregnant woman's "suffering is too intimate and personal for the State to insist, without more, upon its own vision of the woman's role, however dominant that vision has been in the course of our history and our culture." Rather, her destiny "must be shaped to a large extent on her own conception of her spiritual imperatives and her place in society."[17]

The lead opinion in *Casey* thus takes seriously the obligations imposed by fidelity to the rule of law: to look at precedent, at society, and at the underlying promises of the Constitution in order to create a coherent and principled elaboration of the reasons for the decision. And the opinion explicitly recognizes both that the Court has this obligation and that there is room for disagreement: "The inescapable fact is that adjudication of substantive due process claims may call upon the Court in interpreting the Constitution to exercise that same capacity which by tradition courts have always exercised: reasoned judgment. Its boundaries are not susceptible of expression as a simple rule."[18]

Reasoned elaboration as a constraint on judicial decision making is particularly telling in the context of abortion. Prior to *Casey*, Justice O'Connor had indicated that she believed *Roe* to be wrongly decided and ripe for overruling. So why did she vote to uphold *Roe*, authoring parts of the lead opinion in *Casey*? Perhaps when she sat down to draft an opinion overruling *Roe*, the opinion "wouldn't write." Or perhaps she found the reasoning of the lead opinion persuasive. Or perhaps, when she was finally presented with the question of overruling *Roe*, the pull of precedent was too strong. In any case, her vote in *Casey* shows that the rule-of-law requirement of reasoned elaboration influences judges and may cause them to reach decisions that are contrary to their own personal beliefs.

Casey is also notable because of its very self-conscious application of stare decisis. In particular, the *Casey* opinion by Justices O'Connor, Kennedy, and Souter—in a section joined by a majority of the Court—placed considerable stress on the notion that part of *Roe* was entitled to special precedential force. To understand *Casey*, it is important to keep in mind that this enhanced version of stare decisis was applied only to one part of *Roe*. This was the "central holding" that "viability marks the earliest point at which the State's interest in fetal life is constitutionally adequate to justify a legislative ban on nontherapeutic abortions." According to *Casey*, the only debatable aspect of that holding was the "strength of the state interest in fetal protection," *not* "the recognition afforded by the Constitution to the woman's liberty." Thus the special weight of stare decisis was only relevant to the question of whether the interest in fetal life was sufficiently compelling to overcome in every case a woman's right to abortion assuming she had such a right; stare decisis played no role in upholding the basic right itself.[19]

The *Casey* opinion emphasized that the "Court must take care to speak and act in ways that allow people to accept its decisions on the terms the Court claims for them, as grounded truly in principle, not as compromises with social and political pressures having, as such, no bearing on the principled choices that the Court is obliged to make." Hence, "the Court's legitimacy depends on making legally principled decisions under circumstances in which their principled character is sufficiently plausible to be accepted by the Nation."[20]

The Court then explained why, in its view, overruling *Roe* would impair judicial legitimacy. When "the Court decides a case in such a way as to resolve the sort of intensely divisive controversy reflected in *Roe* and those rare, comparable cases," the ruling "has a dimension that the resolution of the normal case does not carry." This extra dimension is "present whenever the Court's interpretation of the Constitution calls the contending sides of a national controversy to end their national division by accepting a common mandate rooted in the Constitution." In such circumstances, the Court said, "to overrule under fire in the absence of the most compelling reason to reexamine a watershed decision" would appear simply to be "a surrender to political pressure, and an unjustified repudiation of the principle on which the Court staked its authority in the first instance."[21]

Even before the Court's reaffirmation of *Roe* in *Casey*, a leading legal scholar had argued that "*Roe* provides a ready example" of why "departure from precedent may sometimes threaten the stability and continuity of the political order and should therefore be avoided." More generally, he argued, "adherence to precedent can contribute to the important notion that the law is impersonal in character, that the Court believes itself to be following a 'law which binds [it] as well as the litigants.'" For, he said, the Court's "institutional position would be weakened were it generally perceived that the Court itself views its own decisions as little more than 'a restricted railroad ticket, good for this day and train only.'" The question then is whether "judicial self-protection is a legitimate criterion that should be taken into account in deciding whether to adhere to a challenged precedent," a question he tentatively answered in the affirmative.[22]

Under this view, deviation from precedent may cast doubt on the Court's integrity, particularly when the precedent has come under heavy political fire. Indeed, for some justices, this may have been more than just a question of *institutional* standing, it may also have involved individual self-respect. A plausible suggestion is that in authoring the joint opinion in *Casey*, Justices O'Connor, Kennedy, and Souter were "concerned, perhaps above all else, with public perceptions of their personal integrity: They wanted to make it clear that their votes were never precommitted to overruling *Roe*."[23]

Yet, such reference to political factors in applying stare decisis is also troubling. Apart from the empirical question of whether the Court's public legitimacy would indeed be threatened by a reversal of course, there is also a paradox to giving the most controversial decisions additional precedential weight. For the result is that the more questionable a decision was and the more contrary to public opinion, the more the Court would cling to it.

One could argue with at least equal persuasiveness that heightened controversy should lead the Court to reconsider its constitutional position with particular care for two reasons. First, such controversy demonstrates that the issue is one where the political process might well reach conclusions at odds with the Court's, making more crucial the question of whether to block that process. Second, the controversy may be a sign that the societal stakes are high, so that an error is especially undesirable.

The arguments for either adhering to controversial precedents more firmly or reconsidering them more freely cancel each other out. Such precedents should get the same weight as other decisions, no more and no less. Understandably, individual justices may be troubled by the perception that they are acting in response to political pressure or to undisclosed commitments to the presidents who appointed them. The proper response, however, is for those justices to consider the merits of the case with particular care, to guard against any unconscious influences from political pressures one way or the other, and then to explain their reasoning with clarity to the public.

The dissenting opinions expressed a more measured approach to stare decisis. Chief Justice Rehnquist wrote the main dissent. "Our constitutional watch," Rehnquist said, "does not cease merely because we have spoken before on an issue; when it becomes clear that a prior constitutional interpretation is unsound we are obliged to reexamine the question." "[J]ust as the Court should not respond to [public] protest by retreating from the decision simply to allay the concerns of the protesters, it should likewise not respond by determining to adhere to the decision at all costs lest it *seem* to be retreating under fire." Justice Scalia was even more forthright: "I cannot agree with, indeed I am appalled by, the Court's suggestion that the decision whether to stand by an erroneous constitutional decision must be strongly influenced—*against* overruling, no less—by the substantial and continuing public opposition the decision has generated." Besides being appalling, he exclaimed, "the notion that we would decide a case differently from the way we otherwise would have in order to show that we can stand firm against public disapproval is frightening." The dissenters were right on this score, though we think they were quite wrong on the merits of the abortion decision.[24]

On the whole, then, *Casey* seems to have gone too far in describing the special weight that should be given to controversial precedents. But in the end, the opinion's inflated description of stare decisis was important only at the margins. On perhaps the most fundamental question before it, whether liberty encompasses the woman's decision to carry or not carry a pregnancy to term, the Court did not rely on stare decisis. The *Casey* Court's view was that women's reproductive rights are constitutionally protected, not simply because previous precedents had said so, but because that was actually the best interpretation of the Constitution. If, as Justice Scalia and others have argued, this aspect of *Roe* had been based on a completely unfounded conception of constitutional liberty, stare decisis should not have been enough to save it. But the Court did not agree with the dissenters on the merits of that constitutional issue, regardless of precedent.

Rather, the Court applied stare decisis only to the subsidiary holding in *Roe* that the state's interest was insufficiently compelling to justify a complete ban on abortion. Here, stare decisis seems to have a greater role. Determining the weight of a government interest inevitably involves an element of judgment. The fact that many justices over a prolonged period of time have assessed an interest as noncompelling makes that judgment more plausible. Thus the way the *Casey* Court actually employed stare decisis was a good deal better than some of the rhetoric the Court used to describe what it was doing.

The Court went on to uphold many aspects of the Pennsylvania law, with the notable exception of a spousal notification requirement. The Pennsylvania statute required, with certain exceptions, that a married woman sign a statement indicating that she had notified her husband of the abortion decision. Regarding the spousal notice provision, the majority viewed this requirement as an intrusion on the autonomy of women and an invitation to coercion by their husbands. But the Court upheld a requirement that the doctor provide specified information about the fetus, a twenty-four-hour waiting period after providing the information, and a parental consent provision (with a judicial bypass, so a minor could explain to a judge her reasons for not notifying her parents). Upholding the parental consent provision was giving the government the benefit of the doubt—perhaps unduly so, as there was strong evidence that many adolescent girls legitimately fear violence or coercion from their fathers and are too intimidated and humiliated to tell their fears and reasons to a judicial stranger.

We do not suggest that *Casey* was an ideal opinion. In rejecting the argument that the interest in protecting fetal life was strong enough to allow a complete ban on abortion, it properly relied on the doctrine of stare decisis for support, but the Court's discussion of stare decisis was not well considered. Moreover, in applying its "undue burden" test, the Court may well have gone astray, particularly with regard to the parental notification requirement. As with *Hamdi*, however, we think the Court deserves great credit for its effort to articulate constitutional values and translate them into a workable legal standard.

Casey, unlike *Roe*, has weathered well. For one thing, the flurry of state legislative attempts to restrict abortion in the 1980s died down after *Casey*. Like *Lawrence v. Texas*, discussed in chapter 10, *Casey*'s forthright and transparent opinion created a short-lived sensation, but longer-term peace. There are still questions at the margins (and still public controversy about abortion itself), but the *Casey* approach seems well suited to answer them.

As this book goes to press, the most recent Supreme Court abortion decisions bode moderately well for *Casey*'s continued success (albeit a bit less well for continued transparency). The most potentially significant development since *Casey* is the replacement of one of *Casey*'s authors, Justice O'Connor, with Justice Alito. (Chief Justice Roberts has also succeeded Chief Justice Rehnquist, but Rehnquist dissented in *Casey*.) Two cases considering very similar statutes, one decided with Justice O'Connor on the Court and the second after Justice Alito joined, reached different conclusions—but *Casey*, stare decisis, and reasoned elaboration played a role in both.

The two cases involved the extent to which the government could regulate the procedures used to perform abortions. After *Casey*, several states—and ultimately Congress—banned what is called "dilation and extraction" (D&X), "intact dilation and evacuation" (intact D&E), or "partial birth abortion." In 2000, in *Stenberg v. Carhart*, the Court struck down Nebraska's prohibition on the D&X procedure. The majority opinion was written by Justice Breyer, and joined by Justices Stevens, O'Connor, Souter, and Ginsburg. The Court found the statute unconstitutional for two reasons. First, the language of the statute was sufficiently imprecise that it might also make illegal the most common procedure for second trimester abortions, dilation and evacuation (D&E), thus imposing an undue burden on women's access to abortions. In addition, even as applied to third trimester abortions, the Court held the statute invalid because it lacked an exception—required under *Casey*—for abortions "necessary, in appropriate medical judgment, for the preservation of the life or health of the mother." (Notice how this requirement of an exception for medical necessity goes back to the emphasis on medical necessity in *Doe*.) Relying upon the district court's findings that in some circumstances the D&X is the safest procedure, the Court rejected the state's argument that no exception was required because other safe abortion procedures were available. The Court emphasized the judicial need to tolerate reasonable differences in medical opinion.[25]

Justice Kennedy, one of the authors of the lead opinion in *Casey*, wrote a lengthy and emotional dissent, joined by Chief Justice Rehnquist. (Justices Scalia and Thomas also dissented.) The dissent argued that the statute prohibited only the D&X procedure, not the D&E procedure. Justice Kennedy also insisted that the state should be allowed to make the moral decision that killing the fetus outside the womb (D&X) is more gruesome or horrifying—more like infanticide—than killing it in the womb (D&E). Finally, he contended that the D&X was highly controversial even within the medical community, and that restricting pregnant women to the D&E would deprive none of them of a safe abortion. The state, the dissenters concluded, should be able to take sides on a disputed medical question.

The D&X question did not go away. In 2003, Congress passed the Partial-Birth Abortion Ban Act. After several lower courts invalidated it based on *Stenberg*, it came before the Court in 2007. In *Gonzales v. Carhart*, the Court upheld the act, with Justice Alito joining Chief Justice Roberts and the three remaining *Stenberg* dissenters to form a 5 to 4 majority. Knowing only that fact, one might wonder about *Casey's* long-term future.[26]

Justice Kennedy's majority opinion, however, was in large part attentive to stare decisis and the rule of law. It reaffirmed *Casey*, and did not overrule *Stenberg*. Instead, it attempted to distinguish the federal statute from the previously invalidated Nebraska law. Our view is that it was successful in doing so for one of *Stenberg's* two grounds, but not for the other. Justice Kennedy carefully parsed the language of the federal statute to show that it prohibited only the D&X procedure and did not trammel either women's rights or doctors' judgments regarding D&E abortions. If we focus on the constitutional problem of imprecise language imposing a burden on women's rights, the federal statute was an example of how judicial review should work: The Court identified a problem with the Nebraska statute, and Congress learned from the Court's opinion so it could avoid Nebraska's error.

Justice Kennedy's opinion was not as successful in distinguishing *Stenberg* on its second ground. Like the Nebraska statute, the federal statute lacked an exception for D&X procedures necessary to protect the woman's health. But where *Stenberg* held that any dispute among doctors about the necessity of the procedure required the government to defer to the individual physician's judgment, *Carhart* concluded that "medical uncertainty over whether the Act's prohibition creates significant health risks" allowed the government to regulate the procedure. In other words, the Court had changed its collective mind about whether the government could take sides in a disputed medical question. Or perhaps not completely. Justice Kennedy left open the door to "as applied" challenges to the statute in situations of medical necessity. Such challenges presumably would apply to the specific facts of a particular case rather than involving the validity of the statute as a whole, though it is unclear just how these challenges would work in this setting.[27]

This part of the opinion fails our arbitrary and capricious test in two ways. First, it was not candid in its treatment of *Stenberg*. *Stenberg* made quite clear both that an exception for the woman's health was always necessary, and that a lack of medical consensus puts the issue in the hands of doctors rather than the legislature. Justice Kennedy's opinion never confronted these two inconvenient holdings, and thus did not give adequate reasons for allowing the law to stand despite the absence of a health exception. Perhaps even more troubling is that in finding a lack of medical consensus, the Court relied on partisan and uninformed sources of information that have been thoroughly discredited by other evidence. Congress's finding of a lack of medical consensus, for example, was castigated by the lower courts as incorrect. The lower courts pointed out that "none of the six physicians who testified before Congress had ever performed an intact D&E," several did not perform abortions at all, and one was not even an obstetrician or gynecologist. Thus, "Congress arbitrarily relied upon the opinions of doctors who claimed to have no (or very little) recent and relevant experience with surgical abortions, and disregarded the views of doctors who had significant and relevant experience with those procedures."[28]

As Justice Ginsburg pointed out in dissent, Congress also ignored statements—entered into the congressional record—from nine medical associations, including the American College of Obstetricians and Gynecologists and the American Public Health Association, "attesting that intact D&E carries meaningful safety advantages over other methods." The majority nevertheless chose to disregard both the lower courts' finding of fact and the overwhelming medical consensus by holding that Congress was entitled to conclude that D&X was never a safer alternative. An administrative agency would never get by with this sloppy treatment of the evidence.[29]

Despite this serious lapse, however, *Carhart* offers some hopeful signs. Admittedly, continuing to reject thirty years of precedent, Justices Thomas and Scalia, in addition to joining the majority opinion, wrote a separate concurrence to "reiterate [their] view[s] that the Court's abortion jurisprudence, including *Casey* and *Roe*...has no basis in the Constitution." But as noted earlier, the majority did not overrule any cases, and it did carefully distinguish the *Stenberg* precedent. Significantly, neither Justice Alito nor Chief Justice Roberts joined in the Scalia and Thomas disavowal of established precedent. Perhaps Justices Roberts and Alito understand that precedent is more important than politics. Let us hope so.[30]

16

Affirmative Action

A PAIR OF recent and controversial Supreme Court opinions illustrates ways in which transparency—or the lack of it—can manifest itself through the use of precedent. The two cases also provide an example of the potential consequences of a judicial lack of candor.

The constitutionality of affirmative action in higher education is one of the most disputed questions in recent Supreme Court history. After a fractured Court invalidated what it called a "quota"—which had set aside 16 places out of 100 for minority applicants—in the 1978 case of *Regents of the University of California v. Bakke*, the Court remained silent on the issue for twenty-five years. Then, in 2003, it decided a pair of cases challenging admissions policies at the University of Michigan: In *Gratz v. Bollinger*, it invalidated the university's affirmative action program in undergraduate admissions; in *Grutter v. Bollinger*, it upheld the university's somewhat different program for law school admissions.[1]

A quick reprise of the Court's previous affirmative action jurisprudence is in order here. *Bakke*, the Court's only previous encounter with affirmative action in higher education, was a 4–1–4 decision, with Justice Lewis Powell as the decisive swing voter. Justice Powell contended that affirmative action should be subject to strict scrutiny, just like government actions discriminating against racial minorities. Hence an affirmative action plan was constitutional only if it was necessary to achieve a compelling government interest. Justice Powell rejected several possible government interests, such as remedying societal discrimination. He did, however, identify one interest as compelling: the institution's interest in maintaining a diverse student body. In pursuit of diversity, he said, a university could consider race as a "plus factor" in making a holistic determination of the merits of individual applicants. (Justice Powell also agreed that remedying past racial discrimination by the institution in question was a compelling interest, but he found this inapplicable to the case before him.)

Although no other justice joined his opinion, it was generally received as representing the Court's position because the remainder of the Court was split 4–4 on the outcome. Later rulings (not involving higher education) endorsed portions of his analysis, particularly his views that affirmative action is subject to strict scrutiny and that remedying societal discrimination is not a valid basis for affirmative action.

In both *Gratz* and *Grutter*, the Court specifically reaffirmed (and purported to apply) two principles from earlier cases. First, it reiterated that while some consideration of race is acceptable in the admissions process, a school may not apply either a numerical "quota" to achieve a particular racial balance or a numerical formula to assign weight to an applicant's race. Instead, as Justice Powell had indicated, the school must give each applicant individual consideration, using race as one factor among many to determine whether admitting the student will benefit the school's educational mission.

Second, again following in Justice Powell's footsteps, the Court adhered to its precedent that *all* racial classifications—even those allegedly benefiting disadvantaged minorities—should be tested by "strict scrutiny": To be upheld, the classification must be narrowly tailored to achieve a compelling governmental goal. The key terms are "narrowly tailored," meaning that the program must be carefully designed to do no more than necessary to reach its goals, and "compelling," meaning that the goal itself must be of the highest order. In both *Gratz* and *Grutter*, the Court quoted its own precedent to explain that strict scrutiny required a "searching" judicial inquiry into the government's justifications for its use of race to prevent the pernicious use of racial classifications.[2]

These principles led a majority of the Court to invalidate the undergraduate affirmative action program challenged in *Gratz*. That program used a numerical point system to make admissions determinations. An applicant's total number of points determined whether he would be admitted, rejected, or postponed for later decision. Points were awarded for grade point average (GPA), standardized test scores, and other academic factors such as the quality of the applicant's high school and the rigor of the applicant's particular high school curriculum. Additional points were then added based on such things as in-state residency, alumni relationship, personal essay, leadership, and race. All applicants who were members of an "under-represented racial or ethnic minority group"—African Americans, Hispanics, and Native Americans—were automatically awarded 20 points on the 150-point scale. By comparison, a perfect Scholastic Aptitude Test (SAT) score (1600) was awarded only 12 points, Michigan residency 10, "legacy" status 4, and an outstanding personal essay only 3. Although the Court held that maintaining a racially diverse class constituted a compelling governmental interest, thus satisfying half of the strict scrutiny test, it found the undergraduate point system insufficiently individualized and therefore not narrowly tailored.[3]

The law school affirmative action program differed in several respects. Rather than a rigid numerical system, the law school evaluated each individual applicant based on all of the information in his or her file. The officially adopted policy aspired to "achieve that diversity which has the potential to enrich everyone's education and thus make a law school class stronger than the sum of its parts." In implementing that aspiration, the law school sought to enroll a "critical mass" of African Americans, Hispanics, and Native Americans to attain the educational benefits of diversity and to ensure that individual members of those groups would not feel "isolated or like spokespersons for their race." The law school also considered other diversity factors besides race or ethnicity. Based on these statements of policy, a bare majority of justices found that the law school admissions program satisfied strict scrutiny because it was narrowly tailored to achieve the compelling interest in a racially diverse student body.[4]

This superficial examination of the differences between the two policies might suggest that the law school's policy was constitutionally distinguishable from the undergraduate program. Strict scrutiny, however, as dictated by the Court's precedents, requires not superficial but searching examination. And a closer look at the law school admissions policy raises serious questions about the Court's purported adherence to precedent in *Grutter*.

Consider first the law school's representation that it did not attempt to implement a forbidden "quota," but instead sought a flexible "critical mass" of underrepresented minorities. The Court accepted this claim at face value. In so doing, it ignored a number of troublesome facts—all noted by the dissenters—that make the distinction between a "quota" and a "critical mass" problematic. If a critical mass is the somewhat flexible number of students needed to prevent members of an underrepresented group from feeling isolated, and to allow them to contribute to the diversity of the law school class, one would expect that the size of the critical mass would be roughly the same for each of the three minority groups. It was not. During the six-year period examined by the Court, the "critical mass" varied considerably among racial groups: For Native Americans the critical mass was fewer than 20 students, for Hispanics it was about 50, and for African Americans it was around 100. Does it take twice as many African Americans as Hispanics (and five times the number of Native Americans) to form a critical mass? The law school never explained its numbers.[5]

And these differing sizes reflected two other inconvenient facts. First, for each group, the percentage of admitted applicants was, for every year, within a point of the percentage of applicants of that race. It was within *half* a point (five-tenths of one percent) in all six years for Native Americans, four of the six years for African Americans, and three years for Hispanic Americans.

This last statistic, moreover, illustrates a second difficulty: Hispanic Americans were disfavored among the three groups. In documenting that it defined "diversity" to include more than simple racial diversity, the law school pointed out that it had, over the six-year period, rejected sixty-nine minority applicants with academic credentials lower than some whites and Asians admitted. Of those sixty-nine, however, fifty-six were Hispanic. Put together, the data strongly suggest that the law school in fact had a firm target for each group, with narrow variations from year to year depending on the number of applicants in each group. The target for Hispanics was lower than for African Americans, apparently leading to a cap on the number of less-credentialed Hispanics who could be admitted and thus to both a higher rejection rate and a greater disparity between their application rates and their admission rates than was the case for African Americans or Native Americans.[6]

Finally, the law school admissions director admitted to consulting daily on the percentage of minority applicants admitted during the months-long admissions process. This procedure, of course, allowed the admissions personnel to monitor whether they were achieving their numerical goals and to vary their consideration of files accordingly. That admissions officers "testified without contradiction that they never gave race any more or less weight based on the information contained in these reports" should not be sufficient—as the majority found that it was—to rebut the inference that the information helped guide the admissions process. If not, it seems odd that the admissions director would be receiving daily information about an irrelevant statistic. Under strict scrutiny, this testimony about subjective intent should not have been enough to establish that race was merely being used as one factor to increase the diversity of perspectives and experiences in the class rather than being given a dominant role where necessary to achieve targets. Given the secrecy in which all admissions decisions are shrouded, it is hardly surprising that no witness could contradict the admissions officers' testimony. The admissions officers may in fact have been operating in good faith during this particular time period at this particular law school—but it seems dubious that in a case involving strict scrutiny, much weight should be given to testimony about a person's state of mind rather than inferences to be drawn from the actual operation of the program.[7]

There were other indications in *Grutter* that the scrutiny the Court applied was less than searching. In upholding the affirmative action program, the Court deferred to the law school's own statements of the benefits of a racially diverse student body, the lack of alternative methods for obtaining a racially diverse student body, the detrimental effect proposed alternatives might have on the law school, and the temporary nature of the program. This kind of deference to government decision makers is inconsistent with the whole idea of strict scrutiny, which is to subject government actions to searching examination. The point of strict scrutiny, as the name suggests, is to look very hard at the justifications that the government has given for a program, rather than simply taking the government's word that the program is needed to achieve an extraordinarily important government interest.[8]

We recount these problematic aspects of *Grutter* not to suggest that the Court was necessarily wrong to uphold the law school's affirmative action program, but to show that the Court failed to provide a tenable argument for doing so while striking down the undergraduate admissions program. Perhaps the Court should have upheld the program in *Grutter*, but it would have had to use some test other than strict scrutiny. Using strict scrutiny, which the Court claimed to apply, the Court had not upheld a racial classification (except as a remedy for prior discrimination by the particular defendant) since 1944, when it shamefully found constitutional the relocation of Japanese Americans during World War II. The Court has never before suggested that racial classifications are due any sort of deference, and has always subjected them to the most searching examination. Indeed, its record on racial classifications had previously led one commentator to conclude that the scrutiny is "'strict' in theory but fatal in fact." The sorts of inconsistencies between the claims and the data in *Grutter* should, under ordinary strict scrutiny, have led the Court to invalidate the program. In other words, this is not your father's strict scrutiny; rather, it is a form of strict scrutiny lite that bears little resemblance to what the Court has applied in other race cases.[9]

The Court's opinion in *Gratz*, the undergraduate admission case, is also troubling because the system there was arguably no more quotalike in its operation than the law school admission program that the Court upheld. The big difference between the two was that the significance of race in admissions was explicit in *Gratz* but concealed in *Grutter*; the implicit message to institutions was to avoid transparency. There was no real difference between the programs in terms of whether a candidate received individual treatment. In the undergraduate program, the treatment of race was standardized, but the rest of the file of a minority applicant was treated just like the file of a white applicant. In the law school program, a minority applicant's chance of admission might depend on how many other minority applicants had already been admitted (and therefore how close the school was to the critical mass). A minority applicant whose GPA and Law School Admission Test (LSAT) might be too low if there were many minority admittances would have good enough credentials for admission if the school was short on minority candidates. It is hard to see how either system has a clear-cut advantage over the other in terms of treating people as individuals rather than simply as representatives of a minority group.

As the dissenters in *Gratz* argued, if the Court was open to the idea of affirmative action, it should have upheld both programs; otherwise, it should have rejected both. If it was going to accept affirmative action, it should have made it clear that the standard was something other than conventional strict scrutiny.

The consequences of this lack of candor (or more charitably, lack of clear thinking) will likely emerge over the next decade. There is, first, the damage to the Court's legitimacy and reputation. At least one scholar has already accused the Court of catering to elite opinion in fashioning its unpersuasive analysis; and while scholars are likely to criticize any result they disagree with, the Court should not give them ammunition in the form of weak reasoning. More important, however, is the potential for future litigation created by the Court's opinion in *Grutter*. Twenty-five years of unsettled law and unpredictable decisions followed the nondecision in *Bakke*. By purporting to apply strict scrutiny but actually brushing over the facts and deferring to the law school's arguments, the Court in *Grutter* provided a similar lack of guidance for lower courts.

One commentator's astute description of the twenty-five years following *Bakke* is an equally apt description of what is likely to follow *Grutter*. As he said, "What has been consistent since *Bakke* throughout the world of legal education is a code of silence on preferential policies. Schools have been loath to disclose the degree to which they depend on numerical indicators and have been even more secretive about the extent to which they take racial factors into account." Indeed, he observed, when "law school deans, in various contexts, have been asked point-blank about the extent of racial preferences, they have suggested that such preferences were either minimal or nonexistent."[10]

The weakness of the decision will also be exploited by future litigants. They will set out to prove that unlike the University of Michigan Law School, their school of choice actually set quotas—and they will use the same sorts of statistical and circumstantial evidence ignored by the *Grutter* majority. What should a lower court conclude (applying strict scrutiny as it must) when plaintiffs present persuasive evidence that racial targets play a determinative role in admissions, but defendants point out that similar evidence was not enough to invalidate the program in *Grutter*? Should the judge do as the Court says or as the Court does? And to the extent that the Court's dissembling drives the universities themselves to hide their own decision-making process behind a smokescreen of "individualized consideration," the discovery process in future litigation will be a nasty battle of plaintiffs' attempts to uncover illicit motivation and defendants' insistence on keeping the process as secret as possible. A clean win or loss for affirmative action would have avoided these consequences.[11]

A more forthright opinion would also have avoided the risk of watering down the standard for strict scrutiny in cases in which minorities are the disfavored group. Recall that the Court's decision is premised on the view that equal scrutiny applies in both directions. Thus, if a college adopted a system limiting Asian admissions in certain technical fields in order to retain a "critical mass" of whites, the Court is seemingly committed to upholding that decision without probing the program seriously. We view this as unfortunate.

But, we hear you say, the Court had no choice. Had the challenged programs in both *Gratz* and *Grutter* been invalidated, it would have set back the cause of racial equality, cost the Court dearly in lost legitimacy, and simply led universities to engage in ever more opaque and devious methods of ensuring racial diversity while insulating themselves from constitutional review. Assuming for a moment that invalidating both programs *was* the Court's only alternative, even that argument is a weak counter to the demands of transparency and fidelity to the rule of law. The argument against the transparent course of action (invalidation) breaks into three parts corresponding to the three identified consequences: (1) that racial equality is a moral imperative justifying the lack of transparency and the manipulation of precedent; (2) that the Court is not required to be transparent if doing so would cost it the legitimacy it needs to fulfill its constitutional role; and (3) that any other result would simply transfer the lack of transparency from the Court to the universities.

The first argument has been made before, but it ends up undermining the rule of law. For if a perceived moral imperative is sufficient to justify deceit by the very institution charged with enforcing the law, then we can hardly expect others—such as executive branch officials—to give much weight to the value of following the law. And while the argument is often illustrated with such stark examples as antebellum Northern judges required to enforce the fugitive slave acts, in fact the moral imperatives are rarely—if ever—so clear without the benefit of hindsight. In any event, a justice who found the moral pull of affirmative action that overwhelming should have openly discussed how this moral principle related to the Constitution, rather than hiding behind implausible factual assertions.

As for the damage to the Court's legitimacy, we would suggest that it is at best speculative to assume that more damage would be done by an honest invalidation than by a manipulative approval. Certainly many pundits and scholars have inveighed against the inconsistency of what Justice Scalia called a "split double header." To the extent that the programs in *Gratz* and *Grutter* are constitutionally indistinguishable and the application of strict scrutiny variable, the Court becomes vulnerable to charges that it is making ad hoc decisions, implementing its own values, or catering to elite opinion. Dividing the baby may be Solomonic, but it is unlikely to please anyone, and thus no one has much incentive to defend the Court against the inevitable critics. Add to this the damage to the other values served by transparency, as well as the mitigating possibility that a truly unpopular decision might be reversed by constitutional amendment or by subsequent judicial appointments, and the legitimacy argument becomes almost trivial.[12]

It is also not clear how effective the decision was in terms of supporting affirmative action: After all, Michigan voters promptly adopted a constitutional amendment banning affirmative action. Thus the Court's decision was not successful in maintaining Michigan's affirmative action program. If anything, the publicity given to the decision may have helped make voters more aware of the operation of the affirmative action program, prompting their rejection of the concept.

Finally, there is the realist concern that a decision invalidating affirmative action would ultimately have been ignored by universities. But the *actual* decisions in *Gratz* and *Grutter* lead to the same result. Universities that previously used point systems, quotas, or other now-forbidden shortcuts will simply individualize their admissions program (or claim to do so) and still manage, as the University of Michigan Law School did, to achieve an almost perfect correlation between the percentage of minority applicants and the percentage of minorities admitted. Indeed, several of the justices on both sides of the issue suggested that the only difference between the undergraduate program and the law school program was that the latter gave the appearance of achieving racial balance "through winks, nods, and disguises." A Court that not only disguises its own reasoning, but effectively advises other governmental actors to disguise theirs, is doubly problematic.[13]

The preceding arguments, of course, proceed from an assumption that the Court's only alternative to dissembling was to invalidate the law school program and, consequently, put an end to the legality of affirmative action. But the Court had other, much better choices.

One option would have been to revise its general approach to affirmative action cases. It could have forthrightly confronted the precedent on strict scrutiny, overruling the relatively recent—and controversial—cases requiring the application of strict scrutiny to racial classifications that facially discriminate against whites. Instead, as a plurality held in 1990 in *Metro Broadcasting, Inc. v. FCC*, and as three justices urged in *Grutter*, the Court could have held that intermediate scrutiny applies in such cases. Intermediate scrutiny, which is applied in gender discrimination cases and requires that the classification be "substantially related" to an "important" state interest, is much more supple and nuanced than strict scrutiny. Importantly, however, applying intermediate scrutiny would have required deeper and more careful analysis, increasing the transparency of the opinions. The very nature of intermediate scrutiny forces the Court to engage in candid balancing: Is the goal of diversity in education sufficient to justify the means? In essence, the Court could have conceded the dissenters' factual points, but openly admitted that a racially driven admissions process was an appropriate way (even if not the only or best way) to achieve racial diversity. It was the straitjacket of strict scrutiny that forced the majority to sweep inconvenient facts under the rug. Or, under either strict or intermediate scrutiny, the Court might have invalidated both programs as insufficiently narrowly tailored, while still holding that a well-designed affirmative action program would be constitutional.[14]

That intermediate scrutiny does not lead to clear-cut results, but instead requires a closer investigation of the facts, should be neither surprising nor troubling. First, of course, the application of the supposedly more categorical strict scrutiny did not lead to determinate results, as demonstrated by the vehement dissents in *Grutter*, the surprise with which the case was greeted, and the ease with which it can be shown to be inconsistent with precedent. More fundamentally, however, the gist of our argument in this book is that the best adjudication does not always rest on determinacy, but produces results that are generally consistent with the role of the judiciary in a constitutional democracy *and* enables the American public to evaluate those results on the merits. The Court's approach in *Grutter* serves none of these goals, even if it reaches the same bottom-line result that our approach might. Finally, affirmative action is one of those rare instances where the underlying value conflicts make it especially difficult to specify the most persuasive lines of argument: Any reasoning, and any result, will be unsatisfying to a large portion of the population. It does not help public perception of constitutional adjudication when the Court's opinions in such controversial cases are weakly reasoned or less than fully candid.

Closing Words

Our prescription for judges is perhaps deceptively simple: Respect precedent, exercise good judgment, provide reasoned explanations, deliberate with your colleagues, and keep in mind the possible responses of critics. In our view, the first virtue of judges is prudence, and while individual judges may lack such prudence, the system as a whole tends to outperform its weakest members. Prudence is not a monopoly of either Left or Right: In his day, the arch-liberal William O. Douglas was just as lacking in prudence as the arch-conservative Clarence Thomas is today. It is no coincidence that neither of them became leaders on the Court.

Prudence should not be equated with passivity or timidity. "Look before you leap" is important advice, but so is "He who hesitates is lost." Precedents certainly do not control every case, nor is their meaning always clear, and sometimes they are out of tune with deeper constitutional values and must be discarded. Prudence distinguishes the good judge from the bad judge, but it is not enough to make a great judge. For that, vision is also required—not in the sense of a comprehensive roadmap, but in an ability to sense the deep constitutional values underlying a hard issue.

Not every judge has prudence, let alone constitutional vision. It is inevitable that constitutional law will stumble now and then, sometimes badly. It is important not to romanticize the role of the Supreme Court, any more than we should romanticize the president, Congress, or state governments—or for that matter, the movements of public opinion. But judicial review is as American as apple pie, and unless we mean to leave our basic rights entirely up to the political process, judicial review is the only game in town. Constitutionalism is a quest to temper politics with law. As we have tried to show in this book, that quest is not quixotic. At the end of the day, with all of its flaws, the Supreme Court's contribution to our system of government has been crucial and undeniable.

We envision a Court that respects precedent, seeks to articulate constitutional values and reconcile them when they conflict, and explains the reasons for its decisions clearly and honestly. We do not believe that this is a utopian vision, though it *is* utopian to expect it to be satisfied every day in every case. We also reject the view, expressed by some who have read our manuscript, that this is an inherently ideological vision suitable only for the politically wishy-washy.

Judicial review is not without its risks. Judges are as imperfect as the rest of us, and perhaps more prone than the rest of us to bask in the dignity of their positions. Their views may be outmoded, particularly in times of rapid social change. Yet, judicial review on balance has made a strong contribution to our society. We would be poorer as a society—and less democratic and free—without judicial rulings upholding free speech, the rights of religious and racial minorities, equal voting rights, gender equality, and the right of criminal defendants to a fair hearing. Few of these decisions were dictated by clear-cut constitutional language, nor by unambiguous historical evidence. It is hard to believe that our society would be freer or more democratic if these decisions had never existed. Society cannot empower the Court to make good decisions without taking the risk of bad ones, but in our view, the risk is worth taking.

Like others, we are often dissatisfied with the Court's rulings. Many of the justices do not share our political views; some may not be paragons of judicial temperament. We do not wish to be understood as apologists for the current bench, nor do we ignore the flaws of their predecessors. But the imperfections of the institution of judicial review should not blind us to the real contribution it has made to our democratic society. It is in the nature of human institutions to disappoint idealists, but without those institutions, our ideals would have no traction on reality.

Notes

Preface

1. Benjamin Cardozo, The Nature of the Judicial Process 66 (1921).
2. Aharon Barak, *Foreword: A Judge on Judging: The Role of a Supreme Court in a Democracy*, 116 Harv. L. Rev. 16, 29–30 (2002).

Chapter 1

1. The "heavens or abyss" language is borrowed from Martha Nussbaum, *Skepticism About Political Reason in Literature and the Law*, 107 Harv. L. Rev. 714, 730 (1994). For a discussion (and rejection) of the popular, nonacademic version of this stark dichotomy, see Kermit Roosevelt III, *Constitutional Calcification: How the Law Becomes What the Court Does*, 91 Va. L. Rev. 1649, 1650 & n.2 (2005).

Chapter 2

1. *Marbury v. Madison*, 5 U.S. (1 Cranch) 137 (1803).
2. Dr. Bonham's case, 8 Coke Rep. 107a, 118a, 77 Eng. Rep. 638, 652 (1610); William Blackstone, Commentaries, I, at 91 (1st ed., 1765–69).

3. Quoted in G. Edward White, THE MARSHALL COURT AND CULTURAL CHANGE, 1815–1835, at 936–39 (1988).

4. Steven G. Calabresi, *Caesarism, Departmentalism, and Professor Paulsen,* 83 MINN. L. REV. 1421, 1433 (1999) ("elective Caesarism").

5. See *Bolling v. Sharpe,* 347 U.S. 497 (1954); *Youngstown Sheet & Tube Co. v. Sawyer* (The Steel Seizure Case), 343 U.S. 579 (1952); *Clinton v. City of New York,* 524 U.S. 471 (1998); *Flast v. Cohen,* 392 U.S. 83 (1968) (allowing taxpayers to challenge federal expenditures on Establishment Clause grounds); *Tilton v. Richardson,* 403 U.S. 672 (1971) (invalidating part of a federal statute providing federal funds to religious schools); *Mitchell v. Helms,* 530 U.S. 793 (2000) (reviewing federal funding for religious schools and upholding it as constitutional).

6. *Cohens v. Virginia,* 19 U.S. (6 Wheat.) 264, 377 (1821).

7. *Martin v. Hunter's Lessee,* 14 U.S. (1 Wheat.) 304, 332 (1816); *Cohens,* 19 U.S. at 413–14.

8. John C. Calhoun, *A Discourse on Constitution and Government,* in Ross M. Lence, ed., UNION AND LIBERTY: THE POLITICAL PHILOSOPHY OF JOHN C. CALHOUN 82, 95 (1992).

9. In order, the sources for the quotations in this paragraph are James Madison to Spencer Roane, June 29, 1821, in James Madison, WRITINGS 778 (1999); James Madison to Thomas Jefferson, June 27, 1823, in *id.* at 801–2; James Madison to Edward Everett, Aug. 28, 1830, in *id.* at 847. Madison's overall views are well described in Drew R. McCoy, THE LAST OF THE FATHERS: JAMES MADISON AND THE REPUBLICAN LEGACY 134–36 (1989).

10. *Brown v. Board of Education,* 347 U.S. 483 (1954).

Chapter 3

1. See Alexander M. Bickel, THE LEAST DANGEROUS BRANCH: THE SUPREME COURT AT THE BAR OF POLITICS 65–72 (1962).

2. The use of "academic obsession" to describe the countermajoritarian difficulty is borrowed from Barry Friedman, *The Birth of an Academic Obsession: The History of the Countermajoritarian Difficulty, Part Five,* 112 YALE L.J. 153, 159 (2002).

3. Terri Peretti, *An Empirical Analysis of Alexander Bickel's* The Least Dangerous Branch, in Kenneth D. Ward & Cecilia Castillo, eds., THE JUDICIARY AND AMERICAN DEMOCRACY: ALEXANDER BICKEL, THE COUNTERMAJORITARIAN DIFFICULTY, AND CONTEMPORARY CONSTITUTIONAL THEORY 123, 137 (2005) ("I must admit").

4. For the specific voting percentages in this paragraph, see Richard M. Scammon, Alice V. McGillivray, & Rhodes Cook, AMERICA VOTES 24: A HANDBOOK OF CONTEMPORARY AMERICAN ELECTION STATISTICS 1 (2000) (51.2% of the voting age population, and 66.3% of registered voters, voted in the 2000 presidential election); Alice V. McGillivray, Richard M. Scammon, & Rhodes Cook, AMERICA AT THE POLLS 1960–2000, JOHN F. KENNEDY TO GEORGE W. BUSH: A HANDBOOK OF AMERICAN PRESIDENTIAL ELECTION STATISTICS 3 (2001) (47.9% voted for Bush; 48.4% voted for Gore) (thus Bush won 51.2 × 47.9 [= 24.5] percent of the voting-age population and 66.3 × 47.9 [= 31.8] percent of registered voters). For a survey of studies showing the decline in voting rates during the second half of the twentieth century, see Doni Gewirtzman, *Glory Days: Popular Constitutionalism, Nostalgia, and the True Nature of Constitutional Culture*, 93 GEO. L.J. 897, 914–16 (2005).

5. On uncontested seats, see Adam Clymer, *The 2002 Campaign: The House*, New York Times, Nov. 4, 2002, at A6.

6. Cass Sunstein, ONE CASE AT A TIME: JUDICIAL MINIMALISM ON THE SUPREME COURT 30 (1999).

7. Robert H. Jackson, THE SUPREME COURT IN THE AMERICAN SYSTEM OF GOVERNMENT 79 (1955).

Chapter 4

1. On the lack of overlap, see Frederick Schauer, *Foreword: The Court's Agenda— And the Nation's*, 120 HARV. L. REV. 5 (2006).

2. Richard A. Posner, *Foreword: A Political Court*, 119 HARV. L. REV. 31, 41 ("ocean of discretion," "lawless," "about all it is"), 53–54 ("decided differently") (2005).

3. *Citizens to Preserve Overton Park, Inc. v. Volpe*, 401 U.S. 402 (1971).

Chapter 5

1. Sir Edward Coke, FIRST INSTITUTE OF THE LAWS OF ENGLAND, Book I, Chapter 1, at 1 (J. H. Thomas, ed. 1826).

2. Kennedy's change of heart is reported in Linda Greenhouse, *Documents Reveal the Evolution of a Justice*, New York Times, Mar. 4, 2004, at A1 (reporting on the release of Justice Blackmun's papers).

3. *New York Times Co. v. Sullivan*, 376 U.S. 254 (1964).

4. *Griswold v. Connecticut*, 381 U.S. 479 (1965).

5. *Lochner v. New York*, 198 U.S. 45 (1905).

Chapter 6

1. See Philip E. Tetock, Expert Political Judgment: How Good Is It? How Can We Know? 2 (2005), referencing Isaiah Berlin, *The Hedgehog and the Fox*, in The Proper Study of Mankind 436–98 (1997 reissue).

Chapter 7

1. Lewis F. Powell, Jr., *Stare Decisis and Judicial Restraint*, 47 Wash. & Lee L. Rev. 281, 288, 289–90 (1990).

2. *South Carolina v. Gathers*, 490 U.S. 805, 825 (1989) (both quotations).

3. Gary Lawson, *The Constitutional Case Against Precedent*, 17 Harv. J.L. & Pub. Pol'y 23, 27–28 (1994) ("X and Y"); Michael Paulsen, *Captain James T. Kirk and the Enterprise of Constitutional Interpretation: Some Modest Proposals from the Twenty-Third Century*, 59 Alb. L. Rev. 671, 681 (1995) ("no court").

4. Kathleen M. Sullivan, *Foreword: The Justices of Rules and Standards*, 106 Harv. L. Rev. 22, 78 ("the rule"), 87 ("the codifier") (1992); Antonin Scalia, *Assorted Canards of Contemporary Legal Analysis*, 40 Case W. Res. L. Rev. 581, 588 (1989–90) ("the very foundation").

5. Antonin Scalia, *The Rule of Law as a Law of Rules*, 56 U. Chi. L. Rev. 1175, 1177 ("case by case"), 1180–81 ("fact-finding") (1989).

6. Frederick Schauer, Book Review, *Is the Common Law Law?* 77 Cal. L. Rev. 455 (1989); Antonin Scalia, *Common-Law Courts in a Civil-Law System: The Role of United States Federal Courts in Interpreting the Constitution and Laws*, in A Matter of Interpretation 3, 9 (1997).

7. Scalia, *supra* note 5, at 1179–80.

8. Robert H. Bork, The Tempting of America: The Political Seduction of the Law 156–58 (1990).

9. See Randy E. Barnett, *Trumping Precedent with Original Meaning: Not as Radical as It Sounds*, 22 Const. Commentary 257 (2005) (nuanced originalism).

10. Michael Stokes Paulsen, *Abrogating Stare Decisis by Statute: May Congress Remove the Precedential Effect of Roe and Casey?* 109 Yale L.J. 1535, 1545–46 (2000).

11. Richard H. Fallon, Jr., *Stare Decisis and The Constitution: An Essay on Constitutional Methodology*, 76 N.Y.U. L. Rev. 570, 584 (2001). See also *id.* at 593 ("And so the process would continue, literally without surcease, for no question ever could be deemed to have been settled definitively").

12. Frederick Schauer, *Precedent*, 39 Stan. L. Rev. 571, 589 (1987) ("If the future").

13. Henry Paul Monaghan, *Stare Decisis and Constitutional Adjudication*, 88 Colum. L. Rev. 723, 748–749 (1988).

14. The quotation is from Charles J. Cooper, *Stare Decisis: Precedent and Principle in Constitutional Adjudication*, 73 CORNELL L. REV. 401, 410 (1988). Cooper was the assistant attorney general heading the Office of Legal Counsel at the time. Interestingly, the article does not contain the customary disclaimer of nonofficial status ("the views expressed here are solely those of the author," etc.). The case reference is to *Legal Tender Cases*, 79 U.S. (12 Wall.) 457 (1870).

Chapter 8

1. *Youngstown Sheet & Tube Co. v. Sawyer*, 343 U.S. 579, 634–35 (1952) (Jackson, J., concurring). The history of course is controversial, and the debate is far too complex to enter into here. Our own views are close to those in Martin Flaherty, *The Most Dangerous Branch*, 105 YALE L.J. 1725 (1996).

2. James Madison, Alexander Hamilton, & John Jay, *The Federalist Papers* 244–45 (Isaac Kramnick, ed. 1987).

3. Edwin W. Patterson, JURISPRUDENCE: MEN AND IDEAS OF THE LAW 300 (1st printed ed. 1953) ("Yet when one asks").

4. Henry Paul Monaghan, *Stare Decisis and Constitutional Adjudication*, 88 COLUM. L. REV. 723, 763 (1988).

5. *Lujan v. Defenders of Wildlife*, 504 U.S. 555 (1992); *Friends of the Earth, Inc. v. Laidlaw Environmental Services, Inc.*, 528 U.S. 167 (2000); *Massachusetts v. EPA*, 549 U.S. ___, 127 S.Ct. 1438 (2007); *Penn Central Transportation Co. v. City of New York*, 438 U.S. 104 (1978); *Tahoe-Sierra Preservation Council, Inc. v. Tahoe Regional Planning Agency*, 535 U.S. 302 (2002).

6. *Miranda v. Arizona*, 384 U.S. 436 (1966); *Dickerson v. United States*, 530 U.S. 428 (2000). For Rehnquist's earlier views on *Miranda*, see *New York v. Quarles*, 467 U.S. 649 (1984); *Michigan v. Tucker*, 417 U.S. 433 (1974); see also Geoffrey R. Stone, *The* Miranda *Doctrine in the Burger Court*, 1977 SUP. CT. REV. 99, 118 ("Mr. Justice Rehnquist's conclusion that there is a violation of the Self-Incrimination Clause only if a confession is involuntary... is an outright rejection of the core premises of *Miranda*"). As Justice Scalia's dissent in *Dickerson* demonstrates, both the chief justice and some other members of the majority had previously disavowed the idea that *Miranda* was required as an interpretation of the constitutional right against self-incrimination.

7. *Buckley v. Valeo*, 424 U.S. 1 (1976); *Randall v. Sorrell*, 548 U.S. 230 (2006).

8. *Randall*, 548 U.S. at 244 (Roberts); *id.* at 265 n.1 (Thomas). Chief Justice Roberts also refused to overrule in a later case the major post-*Buckley* decision restricting campaign expenditures by corporations and unions, although he took a position that was at least inconsistent with the spirit of the earlier decision if not its letter. See *Federal Election Comm'n v. Wisconsin Right to Life*, 551 U.S. ___, 127 S.Ct. 2652 (2007).

9. Thomas G. Hansford & James F. Spriggs II, THE POLITICS OF PRECEDENT ON THE U.S. SUPREME COURT 129–30 (2006). For another study reaching similar conclusions, see Mark J. Richards & Herbert M. Kritzer, *Jurisprudential Regimes in Supreme Court Decision Making*, 96 AM. POLIT. SCI. ASS'N 305 (2002).

Chapter 9

1. Donald R. Songer et al., CONTINUITY AND CHANGE ON THE UNITED STATES COURTS OF APPEALS 105 (2000) (Courts of Appeals unanimity); Stephen Breyer, ACTIVE LIBERTY: INTERPRETING OUR DEMOCRATIC CONSTITUTION 110 (2005) (Supreme Court unanimous in about 40% of cases); see also issue 1 of the HARVARD LAW REVIEW each year (statistical summary) (between 1996 and 2005 terms, unanimity ranged from 30% to 44%).

2. Alex Kozinski, *What I Ate for Breakfast and Other Mysteries of Judicial Decision Making*, reprinted in David M. O'Brien, ed., JUDGES ON JUDGING: VIEWS FROM THE BENCH 71, 72 (1997).

3. *McGrath v. Kristensen*, 340 U.S. 162, 178 (1950) (Jackson, J., concurring) (citations and some ellipses omitted).

Chapter 10

1. David Shapiro, *In Defense of Judicial Candor*, 100 HARV. L. REV. 731, 737 (1987) (both quotations).

2. *New York v. United States*, 505 U.S. 144 (1992); *Printz v. United States*, 521 U.S. 898 (1997).

3. *New York*, 505 U.S. at 157.

4. *Lawrence v. Texas*, 539 U.S. 558 (2003); *Bowers v. Hardwick*, 478 U.S. 186 (1986).

5. *Bowers*, 478 U.S. at 196 ("majority sentiments"), 190 ("fundamental right") (emphasis added), 188 n.2 (additional plaintiffs).

6. *Lawrence*, 539 U.S. at 578 ("*Bowers* was not correct").

7. Antonin Scalia, *The Rule of Law as a Law of Rules*, 56 U. CHI. L. REV. 1175, 1187 (1989). See also Antonin Scalia, A MATTER OF INTERPRETATION: FEDERAL COURTS AND THE LAW 132 (1997).

8. The description of the French judicial system comes from Mitchel de S.-O.-l'E. Lasser, *Judicial (Self-)Portraits: Judicial Discourse in the French Legal System*, 104 YALE L.J. 1325 (1995). The syllogism appears on p. 1340 and the quotations are on p. 1341 and pp. 1341–42. Lasser has recently elaborated his description, and defended the French system, in a book. Mitchel de S.-O.-l'E. Lasser,

JUDICIAL DELIBERATIONS: A COMPARATIVE ANALYSIS OF JUDICIAL TRANSPARENCY AND LEGITIMACY (2004).

9. Quoted in Lasser, *Judicial (Self-)Portraits*, 104 YALE L.J. at 1380.

10. Ruth Bader Ginsburg, *Remarks on Writing Separately*, 65 WASH. L. REV. 133, 133 (1990).

Chapter 11

1. *Brown v. Board of Education*, 347 U.S. 483 (1954) (*Brown I*). The incremental cases leading up to *Brown* include *McLaurin v. Okla. State Regents for Higher Educ.*, 339 U.S. 637 (1950); *Sweatt v. Painter*, 339 U.S. 629 (1950); *Missouri ex rel. Gaines v. Canada*, 305 U.S. 337 (1938). The quotation and the percentages are from Michael J. Klarman, FROM JIM CROW TO CIVIL RIGHTS: THE SUPREME COURT AND THE STRUGGLE FOR RACIAL EQUALITY 309 (73%), 310 (more than half, quotation) (2004).

2. The "all deliberate speed" case is *Brown v. Board of Education*, 349 U.S. 294 (1955) (*Brown II*). Cases desegregating other public facilities include *New Orleans City Park Improvement Ass'n v. Detiege*, 358 U.S. 54 (1958) (parks); *Gayle v. Browder*, 352 U.S. 903 (1956) (buses); *Holmes v. Atlanta*, 350 U.S. 879 (1955) (golf courses); *Baltimore City v. Dawson*, 350 U.S. 877 (1955) (beaches). For a discussion of how *Brown I* spurred the civil rights movement, see, e.g., David J. Garrow, *Hopelessly Hollow History: Revisionist Devaluing of* Brown v. Board of Education, 80 VA. L. REV. 151 (1994).

3. The 1938 case is *Missouri ex rel. Gaines v. Canada*, 305 U.S. 337 (1938), which held that it was unconstitutional for Missouri to maintain a state law school for whites but none for blacks. The 1939 poll is documented in Eugene L. Horowitz, *"Race" Attitudes*, in Otto Klineberg, ed., CHARACTERISTICS OF THE AMERICAN NEGRO 203–4 (1944). The Detroit poll, as well as a brief discussion (with further citations) of the race problems in Detroit and the other cities as blacks moved into white neighborhoods, is described in Thomas J. Sugrue, *Crabgrass-Roots Politics: Race, Rights, and the Reaction against Liberalism in the Urban North, 1940–1964*, 82 J. AM. HIST. 551 (1995).

4. For one account of Chief Justice Warren's influence on his more impatient brethren, see Charles A. Reich, *Deciding the Fate of Brown: The Populist Voices of Earl Warren and Hugo Black*, 7 GREEN BAG 2D 137 (2004).

5. *Patterson v. Colorado*, 205 U.S. 454, 462 (1907); *Schenck v. United States*, 249 U.S. 47, 52 (1919); see also *Frohwerk v. United States*, 249 U.S. 204 (1919); *Debs v. United States*, 249 U.S. 211 (1919).

6. *Abrams v. United States*, 250 U.S. 616, 630 (1919) (Holmes, J., dissenting).

7. *West Virginia State Bd. of Educ. v. Barnette*, 319 U.S. 624, 642 (1943).

8. *Brandenburg v. Ohio*, 395 U.S. 444, 447 (1969) ("directed at inciting"); *Texas v. Johnson*, 491 U.S. 397, 416 (1989) ("enduring lesson").

9. Daniel A. Farber & Suzanna Sherry, *The Pariah Principle*, 13 Const. Commentary 257 (1996) (defending a predecessor case, *Romer v. Evans*, 517 U.S. 620 (1996)).

10. *Bush v. Gore*, 531 U.S. 98 (2000).

Chapter 12

1. Nathan Lewin, *Judge Arnold and the Golem of Prague*, 58 Ark. L. Rev. 513, 513 (2005).

2. The statute is 18 U.S.C. 3553(b)(1) (Supp. 2004). For further information on the rest of this paragraph, see Rob Hotakainen & Pam Louwagie, *State's Chief U.S. Judge Might Face Subpoena*, Star Tribune, Mar. 13, 2003, at 1A; Edward Walsh & Dan Eggen, *Ashcroft Orders Tally of Lighter Sentences*, Washington Post, Aug. 7, 2003, at A1.

3. Michael C. Dorf, *Does Federal Executive Branch Experience Explain Why Some Republican Supreme Court Justices "Evolve" and Others Don't?* 1 Harv. L. & Pol'y Rev. 457 (2007). See also Lawrence Baum, Judges and Their Audiences: A Perspective on Judicial Behavior 144 (2006) (Justices appointed from outside Washington changed more than those who spent careers in Washington).

4. See Zogby International Poll results reported at http://www.zogby.com/news/ReadNews.dbm?ID=955 (Jan. 26, 2005). One recent study concludes that politicized confirmation hearings have exactly the result we suggest. James L. Gibson & Gregory Caldeira, *Supreme Court Nominations, Legitimacy Theory, and the American Public: A Dynamic Test of the Theory of Positivity Bias*, available at SSRN, http://ssrn.com/abstract=998283 (July 4, 2007).

5. Anthony Lewis, *Abroad at Home: Question of Judgment*, New York Times, Sept. 27, 1987, at D23.

6. Learned Hand, *The Spirit of Liberty*, in The Spirit of Liberty: Papers and Addresses of Learned Hand 189, 190 (Irving Dilliard, ed., 3d ed. 1960).

7. On the Court's shrinking docket, see Lee Epstein et al., The Supreme Court Compendium: Data, Decisions, and Developments 240–41 (4th ed. 2007).

Chapter 13

1. Anthony T. Kronman, *Alexander Bickel's Philosophy of Prudence*, 94 Yale L.J. 1567, 1598 (1985) ("Bickel"); John Henry Schlegel, *An Endangered Species?* 36 J. Legal Educ. 18, 19 (1986) ("law must be separated").

2. Dean Alfange, Jr., Marbury v. Madison *and Original Understanding of Judicial Review: In Defense of Traditional Wisdom*, 1993 Sup. Ct. Rev. 329, 445.

3. Morris B. Hoffman, *Populist Pablum*, 2 Green Bag 2d 97, 98 (1998).

4. Antonin Scalia, *The Dissenting Opinion*, 19 J. Sup. Ct. Hist. 33, 42 (1994).

5. The incidents in this paragraph are described (and criticized) in Suzanna Sherry, *Too Clever by Half: The Problem with Novelty in Constitutional Law*, 95 Nw. U. L. Rev. 921, 930 (2001); Ward Farnsworth, *Talking Out of School: Notes on the Transmission of Intellectual Capital from the Legal Academy to Public Tribunals*, 81 B.U. L. Rev. 13 (2001); Neal Devins, *Bearing False Witness: The Clinton Impeachment and the Future of Academic Freedom*, 148 U. Pa. L. Rev. 165 (1999).

6. Alexis de Tocqueville, Democracy in America 270 (J. P. Mayer, ed., George Lawrence, trans., 1969).

7. Paul Carrington, *Of Law and the River*, 34 J. Legal Educ. 222 (1984).

Chapter 14

1. *Hamdi v. Rumsfeld*, 542 U.S. 507 (2004).

2. Authorization for Use of Military Force, Pub. L. No. 107–40, 115 Stat. 224, 107th Cong. (2001) (AUMF); Detention, Treatment, and Trial of Certain Non-Citizens in the War Against Terrorism, 66 Fed. Reg. 57833 (Nov. 16, 2001) (Nov. 13 order); *Memorandum from President Bush to the Vice-President and Other Officials*, Feb. 7, 2002, in Karen J. Greenberg & Joshua L. Dratel, eds., The Torture Papers: The Road to Abu Ghraib 134–35 (2005) (supplemental order).

3. Nov. 13 Order, *supra* note 2, 66 Fed. Reg. at 57833–35.

4. Memorandum for the President, from Alberto R. Gonzales, "Decision re Application of the Geneva Convention on Prisoners of War to the Conflict with al Qaeda and the Taliban," Jan. 25, 2002; Memorandum to Counsel to the President, from William H. Taft VI, "Comments on Your Paper on the Geneva Convention," Feb. 2, 2002. Both are in Greenberg & Dratel, *supra* note 2, at 118, 119 (Gonzales), 129 (Taft).

5. *Hamdi*, 542 U.S. at 532.

6. See Daniel A. Farber, Lincoln's Constitution (2003).

7. *Hamdan v. Rumsfeld*, 548 U.S. 557 (2006).

8. *Boumediene v. Bush*, 553 U.S. ___, 128 S.Ct. 2229, 2277 (2008).

Chapter 15

1. *Roe v. Wade*, 410 U.S. 113 (1973); *Planned Parenthood of Southeastern Pennsylvania v. Casey*, 505 U.S. 833 (1992).

2. *Doe v. Bolton*, 410 U.S. 179 (1973).

3. *Id.* at 191.

4. *Id.* at 191 ("all attendant circumstances," "farther afield"), 192 ("professional judgment," "all factors"); *Roe*, 410 U.S. at 166 ("abuses the privilege").

5. *Doe*, 410 U.S. at 221 (White, J., dissenting, joined by Rehnquist, J.), 208 (Burger, C.J., concurring).

6. *Roe*, 410 U.S. at 143 (AMA resolution).

7. *Id.* at 153 ("[t]his right of privacy").

8. *Id.* at 152–53.

9. See Bob Woodward, *The Abortion Papers*, Washington Post, Jan. 22, 1989, at D1; Linda Greenhouse, BECOMING JUSTICE BLACKMUN: HARRY BLACKMUN'S SUPREME COURT JOURNEY 97 (2005).

10. Daniel Farber & John Nowak, *Beyond the Roe Debate: Judicial Experience with the 1980's "Reasonableness" Test*, 76 VA. L. REV. 519 (1990) (erosion); *Planned Parenthood of Southeastern Pennsylvania v. Casey*, 505 U.S. 833 (1992) (replacing the trimester system with an "undue burden" test).

11. *Planned Parenthood v. Danforth*, 428 U.S. 52 (1976) (invalidating requirements); *Akron v. Akron Center for Reproductive Health*, 462 U.S. 416 (1983) (same); *Colautti v. Franklin*, 439 U.S. 379 (1979) (same); *Maher v. Roe*, 432 U.S. 464 (1977) (upholding funding restrictions); *Harris v. McRae*, 448 U.S. 297 (1980) (same); *Planned Parenthood Ass'n v. Ashcroft*, 462 U.S. 476 (1983) (upholding parental consent); *H.L. v. Matheson*, 450 U.S. 398 (1981) (upholding parental notification).

12. *Akron v. Akron Center for Reproductive Health*, 462 U.S. 416 (1983); Walter Dellinger & Gene Sperling, *Abortion and the Supreme Court: The Retreat from Roe v. Wade*, 138 U. PA. L. REV. 83 (1989) (predicting overruling).

13. *Webster v. Reproductive Health Services*, 492 U.S. 490, 520 (both quotations) (1989).

14. *Hodgson v. Minnesota*, 497 U.S. 417 (1990).

15. Michael J. Gerhardt, *The Pressure of Precedent: A Critique of the Conservative Approaches to Stare Decisis in Abortion Cases*, 10 CONST. COMMENTARY 67, 67 (1993).

16. *Casey*, 505 U.S. at 847 ("it is tempting," "inconsistent," "promise of the Constitution"); 848 (quoting *Poe v. Ullman*, 367 U.S. 497, 543 (1961) (Harlan, J., dissenting)) ("isolated points," "rational continuum," "certain interests").

17. *Id.* at 851–52.

18. *Id.* at 849.

19. *Id.* at 860 ("central holding"), 858 ("state interest").

20. *Id.* at 865–66 ("Court must take care"), 866 ("Court's legitimacy").

21. *Id.* at 866–67 ("intensely divisive controversy"), 867 ("surrender").

22. Henry Monaghan, *Stare Decisis and Constitutional Adjudication*, 88 COLUM. L. REV. 723, 751 ("ready example," "departure from precedent"), 752 ("adherence to precedent"), 753 ("institutional position"), 762 ("judicial self-protection"), 763 (affirmative answer) (1988).

23. Michael Stokes Paulsen, *Abrogating Stare Decisis by Statute: May Congress Remove the Precedential Effect of* Roe *and* Casey? 109 YALE L.J. 1535, 1551 (2000).

24. *Casey*, 505 U.S. at 955 ("our constitutional watch"), 959–60 ("Court should not respond"), 998 ("appalled," "stand firm").

25. *Stenberg v. Carhart*, 530 U.S. 914, 921 (2000) (quoting *Casey*, which in turn was quoting *Roe*).

26. *Gonzales v. Carhart*, 550 U.S. ___, 127 S.Ct. 1610 (2007).

27. *Id.* 127 S.Ct. at 1637 ("medical uncertainty").

28. *Planned Parenthood Federation of America v. Ashcroft*, 320 F. Supp. 2d 957, 1019 (N.D. Cal. 2004), aff'd, 435 F.3d 1163 (9th Cir. 2006) ("none of the six physicians"); *Carhart v. Ashcroft*, 331 F. Supp. 2d 805, 1011 (D. Neb. 2004), aff'd, 413 F.3d 791 (8th Cir. 2005) ("Congress arbitrarily relied").

29. *Gonzales*, 127 S.Ct. at 1644 (Ginsburg, J., dissenting). As Justice Ginsburg pointed out, the Court also relied on statements in amicus briefs suggesting that women who have abortions later regret their choices. This "antiabortion shibboleth" has been thoroughly disproved in study after study, *id.* at 1648 n.7. See also Chris Guthrie, Carhart, *Constitutional Rights, and the Psychology of Regret*, ___ S. CAL. L. REV. ___ (forthcoming 2008) (using research on the psychology of regret to argue that the majority fundamentally misunderstands how regret operates). The majority's reliance on it—while not crucial to the holding—is further evidence of a lack of candor.

30. 127 S.Ct. 1639 (Thomas, J., concurring).

Chapter 16

1. *Regents of Univ. of California v. Bakke*, 438 U.S. 265 (1978); *Gratz v. Bollinger*, 539 U.S. 244 (2003); *Grutter v. Bollinger*, 539 U.S. 306 (2003).

2. On quotas and individualized consideration, see *Grutter*, 539 U.S. at 334, 336–37; *Gratz*, 539 U.S. at 271; on strict scrutiny, see *Grutter*, 539 U.S. at 326; *Gratz*, 539 U.S. at 270; on the need for a "searching" inquiry, see *Grutter*, 539 U.S. at 326 (quoting *Richmond v. J.A. Croson Co.*, 488 U.S. 469, 493 (1989)); *Gratz*, 539 U.S. at 270 (quoting *Adarand Constructors, Inc. v. Pena*, 515 U.S. 200, 223 (1995)).

3. On the point system generally and awarding of points to underrepresented minorities, see *Gratz*, 539 U.S. at 255; on points for residency, legacy status, and essays, see *id.* at 277–78 (O'Connor, J., concurring). On the points for perfect SAT scores, see Abigail Thernstrom & Stephan Thernstrom, *Secrecy and Dishonesty: The Supreme Court, Racial Preferences, and Higher Education*, 21 CONST. COMMENTARY 251, 258 (2004).

4. *Grutter*, 539 U.S. at 315 ("diversity"), 316 ("critical mass"), 319 ("spokespersons").

5. The figures are from Chief Justice Rehnquist's dissent in *Grutter*, 539 U.S. at 381.

6. For the percentages, see Justice Rehnquist's dissent in *Grutter*, 539 U.S. at 384 (table); for the information on rejected minorities, see *id.* at 382.

7. On the daily reports, see *Grutter*, 539 U.S. at 318; *id.* at 391–92 (Kennedy, J., dissenting). The quotation is from the majority opinion, *id.* at 336.

8. For deference to the law school's statements on the benefits of diversity, see *Grutter*, 539 U.S. at 328; deference on the lack of alternatives and the detrimental effect on the law school, *id.* at 340; deference on the temporary nature of the program, *id.* at 343.

9. See *Korematsu v. United States*, 323 U.S. 214 (1944) (approving Japanese relocation); Gerald Gunther, *In Search of Evolving Doctrine on a Changing Court: A Model for a Newer Equal Protection*, 86 HARV. L. REV. 1, 8 (1972) ("strict in theory"). The Court has upheld racial preferences as a remedy for past discrimination against particular plaintiffs.

10. Richard Sander, *A Systematic Analysis of Affirmative Action in American Law Schools*, 57 STAN. L. REV. 367, 385 (2004). On the Court catering to elite opinion, see Neal Devins, *Explaining* Grutter v. Bollinger, 152 U. PA. L. REV. 347 (2003).

11. Chief Justice Roberts's unconvincing efforts to distinguish *Grutter* from a pupil reassignment plan used by public schools will only add to the confusion. See *Parents Involved in Community Schools v. Seattle School Dist. No. 1*, 551 U.S. ___, 127 S.Ct. 2738 (2007).

12. *Grutter*, 539 U.S. at 348 (Scalia, J., dissenting) ("split double header").

13. *Gratz*, 539 U.S. at 305 (Ginsburg, J., dissenting) ("winks and nods"). A similar sentiment is expressed in Chief Justice Rehnquist's dissent in *Grutter*: "[T]he ostensibly flexible nature of the Law School's admission program... appears to be, in practice, a carefully managed program designed to ensure proportionate representation of applicants from selected minority groups," 539 U.S. at 385–86. See also *Gratz*, 539 U.S. at 298 (Souter, J., dissenting) ("Equal protection cannot become an exercise in which the winners are the ones who hide the ball"); Susan Welch & John Gruhl, AFFIRMATIVE ACTION AND MINORITY ENROLLMENTS IN MEDICAL AND LAW SCHOOLS 63 (1998) (quoting an Association of American Law Schools [AALS] lawyer who called the difference between a quota and a "plus factor" "nothing more than a smirk and a wink").

14. *Metro Broadcasting, Inc. v. FCC*, 497 U.S. 547 (1990). For justices urging intermediate scrutiny, see *Gratz*, 539 U.S. at 298–302 (Ginsburg J., dissenting, joined by Souter and Breyer, JJ.); *Adarand v. Pena*, 515 U.S. 200, 245–46 (1995) (Stevens, J., dissenting). For the application of intermediate scrutiny to gender discrimination, see *Craig v. Boren*, 429 U.S. 190 (1976).

Bibliographic Essay

We have tried to keep endnotes to a minimum. We hope, however, that some readers will want to explore further the subjects we discuss. In this extended bibliography, we try to provide more information about the scholars who have influenced us and the individual topics and arguments in the body of the book. These sources should serve as an entry into the literature for anyone wishing to go deeper.

Part I: The "Problem" of Judicial Review

There is a vast literature on the history discussed in chapter 1. For discussions of judicial review before *Marbury*, see, e.g., Sylvia Snowiss, JUDICIAL REVIEW AND THE LAW OF THE CONSTITUTION (1990); Suzanna Sherry, *The Founders' Unwritten Constitution*, 54 U. CHI. L. REV. 1127 (1987); William Michael Treanor, *Judicial Review Before* Marbury, 58 STAN. L. REV. 455 (2005). For a discussion of the American preference for Lord Coke over Blackstone, see, e.g., Julius Goebel, Jr., HISTORY OF THE SUPREME COURT OF THE UNITED STATES: ANTECEDENTS AND BEGINNINGS TO 1801, at 89–95 (1971); Robert Middlekauff, THE GLORIOUS CAUSE: THE AMERICAN REVOLUTION, 1763–1789, at 12–21 (1982);

Thomas C. Grey, *Origins of the Unwritten Constitution: Fundamental Law in American Revolutionary Thought*, 30 STAN. L. REV. 843, 849–50 (1978). Robert A. Ferguson, THE AMERICAN ENLIGHTENMENT 1750–1820 (1997) explores the American faith in the written word, and Drew R. McCoy, THE ELUSIVE REPUBLIC 32–40 (1980) describes the early American fears of the inevitable decay of republican forms of government. For more on the colonial and early republican experience with executive power, see Daniel A. Farber & Suzanna Sherry, A HISTORY OF THE AMERICAN CONSTITUTION 107–10 (2d ed. 2005). For additional relevant historical information, readers might also want to consult R. Kent Newmyer, JOHN MARSHALL AND THE HEROIC AGE OF THE SUPREME COURT (2001).

For a discussion of judicial review of presidential action, see Daniel A. Farber, *Judicial Review and Its Alternatives: An American Tale*, 38 WAKE FOREST L. REV. 415, 446–48 (2003). For an example of the trend toward judicial review of executive action, compare Andrew Jackson's reputed statement that "John Marshall has made his decision; now let him enforce it" with Earl Warren's twentieth-century response to a law clerk who wondered how the Court was going to make the Army abide by a Supreme Court ruling: "Look,...you don't have to worry. If they don't do this, they've destroyed the whole republic, and they aren't going to do that. So you don't even have to worry about whether they are going to do it or not—*they're going to do it!*" H. W. Brands, ANDREW JACKSON: HIS LIFE AND TIMES 493 (2005) (noting that while Jackson probably never said the words, they "captured his attitude"); Bernard Schwartz, SUPER CHIEF: EARL WARREN AND HIS SUPREME COURT—A JUDICIAL BIOGRAPHY 759 (1983). Along similar lines, although President Richard Nixon briefly threatened to defy the Supreme Court's order that he turn over certain incriminating tape recordings to the special prosecutor, he ultimately complied (and resigned in consequence). See J. Anthony Lukas, NIGHTMARE: THE UNDERSIDE OF THE NIXON YEARS 518–22 (1976).

Three good sources for the federalism debates we discuss are James M. McPherson, ABRAHAM LINCOLN AND THE SECOND AMERICAN REVOLUTION (1991); Jack N. Rakove, ORIGINAL MEANINGS: POLITICS AND IDEAS IN THE MAKING OF THE CONSTITUTION 161–202 (1996); and Richard E. Ellis, *The Persistence of Antifederalism After 1789*, in Richard Beeman et al., eds., BEYOND CONFEDERATION: ORIGINS OF THE CONSTITUTION AND AMERICAN NATIONAL IDENTITY 307 (1987).

On the founders and natural law, see, e.g., Suzanna Sherry, *The Founders' Unwritten Constitution*, 54 U. CHI. L. REV. 1127 (1987). On the founders and political parties, see, e.g., Bruce Ackerman, THE FAILURE OF THE FOUNDING FATHERS: JEFFERSON, MARSHALL, AND THE RISE OF PRESIDENTIAL DEMOCRACY (2005).

The literature on judicial review and the countermajoritarian difficulty is also extensive. We have cited only a small portion that seems most relevant to the particular claims that we make in the text. But we have also found helpful the (joint and several) scholarship of Larry Alexander and Fred Schauer, including Larry Alexander

& Frederick Schauer, *Defending Judicial Supremacy: A Reply*, 17 CONST. COMMENTARY 455 (2000); Larry Alexander & Frederick Schauer, *On Extrajudicial Constitutional Interpretation*, 110 HARV. L. REV. 1359 (1997); Larry Alexander, *Constitutional Rules, Constitutional Standards, and Constitutional Settlement: Marbury v. Madison and the Case for Judicial Supremacy*, 20 CONST. COMMENTARY 369 (2003); Frederick Schauer, *Judicial Supremacy and the Modest Constitution*, 92 CAL. L. REV. 1045 (2004). In addition to the scholarship that we cite in this section, Ted White provides insightful views of some of the issues we discuss in G. Edward White, *The Constitutional Journey of Marbury v. Madison*, 89 VA. L. REV. 1463 (2003); G. Edward White, *The Arrival of History in Constitutional Scholarship*, 88 VA. L. REV. 485 (2002). Barry Friedman has exhaustively examined the history of the countermajoritarian difficulty in a series of articles; we have found his articles helpful, although we disagree with some of the conclusions. His work includes Barry Friedman, *The History of the Countermajoritarian Difficulty, Part One: The Road to Judicial Supremacy*, 73 N.Y.U. L. REV. 333 (1998); Barry Friedman, *The History of the Countermajoritarian Difficulty, Part II: Reconstruction's Political Court*, 91 GEO. L.J. 1 (2002); Barry Friedman, *The History of the Countermajoritarian Difficulty, Part Three: The Lesson of Lochner*, 76 N.Y.U. L. REV. 1383 (2001); Barry Friedman, *The History of the Countermajoritarian Difficulty, Part Four: Law's Politics*, 148 U. PA. L. REV. 971 (2000); Barry Friedman, *The Birth of an Academic Obsession: The History of the Countermajoritarian Difficulty, Part Five*, 112 YALE L.J. 153 (2002).

Alexander Bickel's scholarship has itself spawned much discussion. One edited volume is worth reading in its entirety, although we cite only some of the essays in it: Kenneth D. Ward & Cecilia Castillo, eds., THE JUDICIARY AND AMERICAN DEMOCRACY: ALEXANDER BICKEL, THE COUNTERMAJORITARIAN DIFFICULTY, AND CONTEMPORARY CONSTITUTIONAL THEORY (2005). While Bickel was not reticent in criticizing particular Supreme Court decisions (or series of decisions), he did not—as so many modern critics do—endorse unqualified popular or legislative sovereignty; he refused to sacrifice principle to consent. In addition to THE LEAST DANGEROUS BRANCH: THE SUPREME COURT AT THE BAR OF POLITICS (1962), see generally Alexander M. Bickel, *Constitutionalism and the Political Process*, in THE MORALITY OF CONSENT 3 (1975). Jonathan T. Molot, *Principled Minimalism: Restriking the Balance Between Judicial Minimalism and Neutral Principles*, 90 VA. L. REV. 1753 (2004), makes this point about both Bickel and Herbert Wechsler.

Much has been written about both the majoritarian aspects of the judiciary and the nonmajoritarian aspects of the other branches. For a general sampling, see Edward Rubin, *The Myth of Accountability and the Anti-Administrative Impulse*, 103 MICH. L. REV. 2073 (2005); Terri Peretti, *An Empirical Analysis of Alexander Bickel's* The Least Dangerous Branch, in Kenneth D. Ward & Cecilia Castillo, eds., THE JUDICIARY AND AMERICAN DEMOCRACY: ALEXANDER BICKEL, THE COUNTERMAJORITARIAN DIFFICULTY, AND CONTEMPORARY CONSTITUTIONAL THEORY 123 (2005) and sources cited therein.

On the specifics of House apportionment, see Paul H. Edelman & Suzanna Sherry, *Pick a Number, Any Number: State Representation in Congress After the 2000 Census*, 90 CAL. L. REV. 211 (2002). On the fact that Congress does not always reflect majority preferences, see, e.g., Peretti, *supra*; Doni Gewirtzman, *Glory Days: Popular Constitutionalism, Nostalgia, and the True Nature of Constitutional Culture*, 93 GEO. L.J. 897 (2005); Ilya Somin, *Political Ignorance and the Countermajoritarian Difficulty: A New Perspective on the Central Obsession of Constitutional Theory*, 89 IOWA L. REV. 1287 (2004). On uncontested seats, see generally, Gary C. Jacobson, The POLITICS OF CONGRESSIONAL ELECTIONS 22–23 (5th ed. 2001). On the legislature's reliance on judicial review, see J. Mitchell Pickerill, CONSTITUTIONAL DELIBERATION IN CONGRESS: THE IMPACT OF JUDICIAL REVIEW IN A SEPARATED SYSTEM (2004); Mark A. Graber, *The Nonmajoritarian Difficulty: Legislative Deference to the Judiciary*, 7 STUD. AM. POL. DEV. 35 (1993); Keith E. Whittington, *"Interpose Your Friendly Hand": Political Supports for the Exercise of Judicial Review by the United States Supreme Court*, 99 AM. POL. SCI. REV. 583 (2005). For a diatribe on the general unwillingness of Congress to consider constitutional or other abstract issues when it is considering legislation, see Suzanna Sherry, *Irresponsibility Breeds Contempt*, 6 GREEN BAG 2D 47 (2002).

The grand theories we critique have spawned their own literature, and we provide here only a basic entry into that scholarship. On originalism, see, e.g., Robert H. Bork, THE TEMPTING OF AMERICA: THE POLITICAL SEDUCTION OF THE LAW (1990); Keith E. Whittington, CONSTITUTIONAL INTERPRETATION: TEXTUAL MEANING, ORIGINAL INTENT, AND JUDICIAL REVIEW (1999); Randy Barnett, *An Originalism for Nonoriginalists*, 45 LOY. L. REV. 611 (1999); Frank H. Easterbrook, *Abstraction and Authority*, 59 U. CHI. L. REV. 349 (1992); John Harrison, *Forms of Originalism and the Study of History*, 26 HARV. J.L. & PUB. POL'Y 83 (2003); Richard S. Kay, *Adherence to the Original Intentions in Constitutional Adjudication: Three Objections and Responses*, 82 NW. U. L. REV. 226 (1988); Gary Lawson, *On Reading Recipes...and Constitutions*, 85 GEO L.J. 1823 (1997). One recent critique of originalism is Mitchell N. Berman, *Originalism is Bunk*, 84 NYU L. Rev. __ (2009). On textualism, see, e.g., Akhil Reed Amar, AMERICA'S CONSTITUTION: A BIOGRAPHY (2005); Steven G. Calabresi, *Textualism and the Countermajoritarian Difficulty*, 66 GEO. WASH. L. REV. 1373 (1998). On intratextualism, see Akhil Reed Amar, *Foreword: The Document and the Doctrine*, 114 HARV. L. REV. 26 (2000); Akhil Reed Amar, *Intratextualism*, 112 Harv. L. Rev. 747 (1999). A recent critique of textualism is William Michael Treanor, *Modern Textualism, Original Meaning, and the Case of Amar's Bill of Rights*, 106 MICH. L. REV. 487 (2007). On constitutional dualism, see Bruce Ackerman, WE THE PEOPLE: FOUNDATIONS (1991); Bruce Ackerman, WE THE PEOPLE: TRANSFORMATIONS (1998). On translation theory, see Lawrence Lessig, *Fidelity in Translation*, 71 TEX. L. REV. 1165 (1993). On minimalism, see James Bradley Thayer, *The Origin and Scope of the American Doctrine of Constitutional Law*, 7 HARV. L. REV. 129 (1893); Cass

R. Sunstein, ONE CASE AT A TIME: JUDICIAL MINIMALISM ON THE SUPREME COURT (1999). For the view that Thayer was trying to resurrect a failed approach to judicial power, see G. Edward White, *Historicizing Judicial Scrutiny*, 57 S.C. L. REV. 1, 46–50 (2005). Advocates of departmentalism include Gary Lawson & Christopher D. Moore, *The Executive Power of Constitutional Interpretation*, 81 IOWA L. REV. 1267 (1996); Michael Stokes Paulsen, *The Most Dangerous Branch: Executive Power to Say What the Law Is*, 83 GEO. L.J. 217 (1994); David E. Engdahl, *John Marshall's "Jeffersonian" Concept of Judicial Review*, 42 DUKE L.J. 279 (1992); John Harrison, *The Role of the Legislative and Executive Branches in Interpreting the Constitution*, 73 CORNELL L. REV. 371 (1988). Although the strong form of departmentalism is historically untenable, a more sophisticated version of departmentalism, described as "departmental discretion," has a stronger historical basis. There is evidence that the early Supreme Court drew a distinction between issues that were appropriate for judicial resolution and issues that were left to the discretion of other departments. See White, *Historicizing Judicial Scrutiny, supra*. As White notes, however, the theory of departmental discretion foundered in practice: Although the departmental discretion principle assumes that the line between judicial and nonjudicial questions is both clear and self-evident, in fact most cases that raise nonjudicial questions *also* raise judicial questions, such as the impact of executive decisions on individual rights. For a similar discussion of the inability to draw lines between departments, see Larry Alexander & Lawrence B. Solum, *Popular? Constitutionalism?* 118 HARV. L. REV. 1594, 1610–11 (2005).

For works explicitly claiming a connection between law and politics, see, e.g., Jeffrey Rosen, THE MOST DEMOCRATIC BRANCH: HOW THE COURTS SERVE AMERICA (2006); Michael J. Klarman, FROM JIM CROW TO CIVIL RIGHTS: THE SUPREME COURT AND THE STRUGGLE FOR RACIAL EQUALITY (2004); Gerald N. Rosenberg, THE HOLLOW HOPE: CAN COURTS BRING ABOUT SOCIAL CHANGE? (1991); Neal Devins, *Better Lucky Than Good*, 8 GREEN BAG 2D 33 (2004); Barry Friedman, *The Importance of Being Positive: The Nature and Function of Judicial Review*, 72 U. CIN. L. REV. 1257 (2004); Robert Post, *Foreword: Fashioning the Legal Constitution: Culture, Courts, and Law*, 117 HARV. L. REV. 4 (2003). Both Klarman and Rosenberg have been extensively criticized. See, e.g., David J. Garrow, *"Happy" Birthday, Brown v. Board of Education? Brown's Fiftieth Anniversary and the New Critics of Supreme Court Muscularity*, 90 VA. L. REV. 693 (2004) (critiquing Klarman); Kevin J. McMahon & Michael Paris, *The Politics of Rights Revisited: Rosenberg, McCann, and the New Institutionalism*, in David A. Schultz, ed., LEVERAGING THE LAW: USING THE COURTS TO ACHIEVE SOCIAL CHANGE 63 (1998) (critiquing Rosenberg).

For discussions and critiques of popular constitutionalism implemented by referendums and ballot initiatives, see, e.g., M. Dane Waters, ed., THE BATTLE OVER CITIZEN LAWMAKING: A COLLECTION OF ESSAYS (2001); Thad Kousser & Mathew D. McCubbins, *Social Choice, Crypto-Initiatives, and Policymaking by Direct Democracy*, 78 S. CAL.

L. Rev. 949 (2005); Elizabeth Garrett, *Money, Agenda-Setting, and Direct Democracy*, 77 Tex. L. Rev. 1845 (1999).

Our own prior critique of grand theory, Desperately Seeking Certainty: The Misguided Quest for Constitutional Foundations (2002), contains many citations to other scholarship on judicial review, the countermajoritarian difficulty, and theories of constitutional interpretation.

Part II: Discretion and Judgment

We have spent many years thinking and talking about the issues discussed in this part, and a full accounting of our intellectual debts would be difficult if not impossible. A vast amount has been written about constitutional theory in the past twenty-five years. Jurisprudentially inclined readers will also note that at points we are implicitly critical of other thinkers without specifically identifying them (such as our rejection or at least refinement of the idea of gap-filling discretion typically identified with H. L. A. Hart). We have previously identified ourselves as legal pragmatists. We continue to find the writings of Richard Posner, such as Law, Pragmatism, and Democracy (2003), insightful and provocative, but we have also learned from Tom Grey's more measured vision of pragmatism in writings such as *Holmes and Legal Pragmatism*, 41 Stan. L. Rev. 787 (1989). David Strauss's writings about common law decision making in constitutional law are another obvious influence, though we discuss what we see as some limitations of that approach. See, e.g., David A. Strauss, *Common Law, Common Ground, and Jefferson's Principle*, 112 Yale L.J. 1717 (2003). Finally, the classic article on "muddling through" captures some of what we are trying to do: Charles E. Lindblom, *The Science of "Muddling Through,"* 19 Pub. Admin. Rev. 79 (1959). And just as this book was going to press, Richard Posner, How Judges Think (2008), was released. Although it did not have any direct influence, it resonates with some of what we say here.

Among those in the pragmatist tradition, our view of judicial decision making is probably closest to Karl Llewellyn's. But we have also been influenced by other writers outside of the pragmatist school, some of whom identify themselves as enemies of pragmatism. Someone seeking to pigeon-hole our approach might well consider it a blend (or bastardization, perhaps) of legal pragmatism with the legal process school. In some respects, our views run in parallel with Richard H. Fallon, Jr.'s in Implementing the Constitution (2001), though he is probably closer to the legal process thinkers than we are. Our views are also somewhat consistent with those expressed by Justice Stephen Breyer in Active Liberty: Interpreting Our Democratic Constitution (2005), especially the emphasis on transparency (considered in a later section) and on the inevitability of discretion, although we emphasize process more than outcomes. As evidence that there is nothing new under the sun, some of our ideas resonate with those of Justice Cardozo's 1921 Storrs lectures (Benjamin N. Cardozo, *The Nature of the Judicial Process*

(1921)). Finally, despite political and philosophical differences, we would be delighted if someone would like to compare us with the late Alexander Bickel. In short, we believe that quite a number of disparate writers have had useful insights about constitutional law, and we have tried to learn from all of them.

The reader who is interested in the administrative law issues discussed in part II should see Thomas McGarity, *Some Thoughts on "Deossifying" the Rulemaking Process*, 41 DUKE L.J. 1385 (1992); Robert Glicksman & Christopher Schroeder, *EPA and the Courts: Twenty Years of Law and Politics*, 54 LAW & CONTEMP. PROBS. 249 (Autumn 1991). A good discussion of judicial review as a constraint on agency decision making, in some ways analogous to our analysis of constraints on judges, is Mark Seidenfeld, *Cognitive Loafing, Social Conformity, and Judicial Review of Agency Rulemaking*, 87 CORNELL L. REV. 486 (2002). For more background on *Overton Park*, see Peter Strauss, *Revisiting* Overton Park: *Political and Judicial Controls Over Administrative Actions Affecting the Community*, 39 UCLA L. REV. 1251 (1992). The *Overton Park* test was strongly reconfirmed in *Motor Vehicle Mfrs. Ass'n v. State Farm Mutual Automobile Ins. Co.*, 463 U.S. 29 (1983) (overturning the rescission of an automobile airbag requirement as arbitrary and capricious).

We also suggest some further reading on the various other issues discussed in these chapters. For a good account of "coherence" in the philosophical sense, see Joseph Raz, *The Relevance of Coherence*, 72 B.U. L. REV. 273 (1992). A more legally focused discussion of what counts as a valid public reason for a judicial decision is Lawrence B. Solum, *Procedural Justice*, 78 S. CAL. L. REV. 181, 229–34 (2004). For more on opinions that "won't write," see, e.g., Frederick Schauer, *Giving Reasons*, 47 STAN. L. REV. 633, 652 (1995); Paul A. Freund, *An Analysis of Judicial Reasoning*, in Sidney Hook, ed., LAW AND PHILOSOPHY 282, 288 (1964); Roger J. Traynor, *Some Open Questions on the Work of State Appellate Courts*, 24 U. CHI. L. REV. 211, 218 (1957). For an interesting discussion of Justice Kennedy as a judge who sees and tries to implement "clean, simple, shared American values," see Louis D. Bilionis, *Grand Centrism and the Centrist Judicial Personam*, 83 N.C. L. REV. 1353, 1354 (2005). Another interesting view of how judges should identify and implement fundamental values is found in Aharon Barak, THE JUDGE IN A DEMOCRACY (2006). For a modern defense of *Lochner*, see Howard Gillman, THE CONSTITUTION BESIEGED: THE RISE AND DEMISE OF LOCHNER ERA POLICE POWERS JURISPRUDENCE (1993). For a political science perspective linking constitutional and common law adjudication and finding structure in both, see James R. Stoner, Jr., COMMON-LAW LIBERTY: RETHINKING AMERICAN CONSTITUTIONALISM (2003).

For more on expert judgment, see Philip Tetlock's excellent EXPERT POLITICAL JUDGMENT: HOW GOOD IS IT? HOW CAN WE KNOW? (2005). We also found two articles particularly useful: Keith E. Stanovich & Richard F. West, *Reasoning Independently of Prior Belief and Individual Differences in Actively Open-Minded Thinking*, 89 J. ED. PSYCH. 342 (1997); and Jennifer Lerner & Philip E. Tetlock, *Accounting for the Effects of Accountability*, 125 PSYCHOLOGICAL BULLETIN 255 (1999). A good source on active open-minded thinking is Jonathan Baron, THINKING AND DECIDING 191–218 (3d ed. 2000). Cass Sunstein has written extensively about the tendency of homogeneous groups to self-reinforce. See, e.g., Cass Sunstein, *Deliberative Trouble? Why Groups Go to Extremes*, 110 YALE L.J. 71 (2000). An earlier discussion of the psychological literature by one of us, drawing the analogy to Llewellyn's jurisprudential views, is Daniel A. Farber, *The Inevitability of Practical Reason: Statutes, Formalism, and the Rule of Law*, 45 VAND. L. REV. 533 (1992). We would be remiss if we did not mention that there is a substantial body of literature suggesting that judges suffer from the same cognitive biases as most people, and are therefore no better at making sound decisions. This literature is surveyed and (we think) persuasively critiqued in Gregory Mitchell, *Why Law and Economics' Perfect Rationality Should Not Be Traded for Behavioral Law and Economics' Equal Incompetence*, 91 GEO. L.J. 67 (2002).

An interesting book on personality types, including support for the correlation between dogmatism (adherence to a closed belief system) and poor decision making, is Bob Altemeyer, THE AUTHORITARIAN SPECTER (1996). Altemeyer's book also provides intriguing evidence that dogmatism, lapses in rationality, and other indicators of poor decision making correlate with conservative politics. Tetlock's earlier work also finds less complex reasoning processes among political conservatives than moderates or liberals, but only for the U.S. Senate and U.S. Supreme Court, not for British politicians. Philip E. Tetlock, *Cognitive Style and Political Ideology*, 45 J. PERSONALITY & SOCIAL PSYCH. 118 (1983) (Senate); Philip E. Tetlock et al., *Supreme Court Decision Making: Cognitive Style as a Predictor of Ideological Consistency of Voting*, 48 J. PERSONALITY & SOCIAL PSYCH. 1227 (1985) (Supreme Court); Philip E. Tetlock, *Cognitive Style and Political Belief Systems in the British House of Commons*, 46 J. PERSONALITY & SOCIAL PSYCH. 365 (1984) (Parliament). He later concludes that it is not ideology, but the individual's degree of value pluralism that makes the difference. Philip E. Tetlock, *A Value Pluralism Model of Ideological Reasoning*, 50 J. PERSONALITY & SOCIAL PSYCH. 819 (1986). For a review of the literature linking psychological personality traits with political views, see John T. Jost et al., *Political Conservatism as Motivated Social Cognition*, 129 PSYCH. BULL. 339 (2003).

Part III: Precedent as a Safeguard

For useful overviews, see Michael J. Gerhardt, THE POWER OF PRECEDENT (2008) (especially useful on nonjudicial precedent and on empirical research on judicial behavior); Richard H. Fallon, Jr., *Stare Decisis and the Constitution: An Essay on Constitutional Methodology*, 76 N.Y.U. L. REV. 570 (2001); Earl Maltz, *The Nature of Precedent*, 66 N.C. L. REV. 367 (1988); Henry Paul Monaghan, *Stare Decisis and Constitutional Adjudication*, 88 COLUM. L. REV. 723 (1988); Frederick Schauer, *Precedent*, 39 STAN. L. REV. 571 (1987); Larry Alexander, *Constrained by Precedent*, 63 S. CAL. L. REV. 1 (1989). For insights into how precedent functions in other legal systems, see D. Neil MacCormick & Robert S. Summers, INTERPRETING PRECEDENTS: A COMPARATIVE STUDY (1997).

A good discussion of the relationship between precedent and legitimacy is found in Richard H. Fallon, Jr., *Legitimacy and the Constitution*, 118 HARV. L. REV. 1787 (2005). Those looking for empirical support for the proposition that precedent acts as a constraint, and a nuanced explanation of how it does so, should read Jack Knight & Lee Epstein, *The Norm of Stare Decisis*, 40 AM. J. POL. SCI. 1018 (1996). For a more recent empirical study of precedent in the courts of appeals, see Stefanie A. Lindquist & Frank B. Cross, *Empirically Testing Dworkin's Chain Novel Theory: Studying the Path of Precedent*, 80 N.Y.U. L. REV. 1156, 1205 (2005). An argument that adherence to precedent—in the form of reasoning by analogy—produces better results than an approach that looks for independently correct answers is made in Emily Sherwin, *A Defense of Analogical Reasoning in Law*, 66 U. CHI. L. REV. 1179 (1999).

For an early dissent from the conventional acceptance of stare decisis, arguing that stare decisis is contrary to progressive thinking, see Boyd Winchester, *The Doctrine of Stare Decisis*, 8 GREEN BAG 257 (1896). An even earlier example is Chief Justice Taney's opinion in *The Passenger Cases*, 48 U.S. (7 How.) 283, 470 (1849) (Taney, C.J., dissenting). Even earlier, stare decisis was mocked by Jonathan Swift as an effort to preserve "all the decisions formerly made against common justice and the general reason of mankind." See Geoffrey R. Stone, *Precedent, the Amendment Process, and Evolution in Constitutional Doctrine*, 11 HARV. J.L. & PUB. POL'Y 67 (1988). For an interesting historical description of the relationship between the constraint of precedent and the development of reliable reports of written opinions, see chapter 2 of John V. Orth, HOW MANY JUDGES DOES IT TAKE TO MAKE A SUPREME COURT? (2006).

Readers interested in the differences between rules and standards, and their relationship to precedent, might begin with Kathleen M. Sullivan, *Foreword: The Justices of Rules and Standards*, 106 HARV. L. REV. 22 (1992); Louis Kaplow, *Rules Versus Standards: An Economic Analysis*, 42 DUKE L.J. 557 (1992).

Part IV: Process Safeguards

As with several previous chapters, our core thinking in this section was influenced by the work of Karl Llewellyn and Alexander Bickel, and, more recently, David Strauss. This particular section obviously owes a further debt to Herbert Wechsler. See Herbert Wechsler, *Toward Neutral Principles of Constitutional Law*, 73 HARV. L. REV. 1 (1959). We found illuminating the discussion of Wechsler's ideas in Frank I. Michelman, *Anastasoff and Remembrance*, 58 ARK. L. REV. 555, 580 (2005), which suggests that Wechsler's insistence on neutral principles derived from a need for judicial "accountability to the future." We also learned from Lon Fuller's work, including THE MORALITY OF LAW (1964), LEGAL FICTIONS (1967), and the posthumously published *The Forms and Limits of Adjudication*, 92 HARV. L. REV. 353 (1978). David Shapiro has written excellent articles on a number of the topics we discuss in this section. See, e.g., David Shapiro, *In*

Defense of Judicial Candor, 100 HARV. L. REV. 731 (1987); David Shapiro, *Courts, Legislatures, and Paternalism*, 74 VA. L. REV. 519 (1988). Another useful source for this section is Bruce Ackerman on the judicial role. See, e.g., Bruce Ackerman, WE THE PEOPLE: FOUNDATIONS (1991). Fred Schauer has written insightfully on the idea of reasoned elaboration. Frederick Schauer, *Giving Reasons*, 47 STAN. L. REV. 633 (1995). For political and philosophical defenses of transparency as a condition of democratic legitimacy, see, e.g., John Rawls, POLITICAL LIBERALISM (1996); Lawrence B. Solum, *Constructing an Ideal of Public Reason*, 30 SAN DIEGO L. REV. 729 (1993).

There is a large literature on collegial decision making. Suggested further reading includes Frank M. Coffin, ON APPEAL: COURTS, LAWYERS, AND JUDGING 213–24 (1994); Harry T. Edwards, *The Effects of Collegiality on Judicial Decision Making*, 151 U. PA. L. REV. 1639 (2003); Lewis A. Kornhauser & Lawrence Sager, *The One and the Many: Adjudication in Collegial Courts*, 81 CAL. L. REV. 1 (1993). For some examples of judicial deliberation leading judges to change their minds, see, e.g., Theodore W. Ruger, *Justice Harry Blackmun and the Phenomenon of Judicial Preference Change*, 70 Mo. L. Rev. 1209 (2005). Our suggestion that judges care about how their opinions are received, and thus that the public nature of reasoned elaboration makes a difference, is supported by Lawrence Baum, JUDGES AND THEIR AUDIENCES: A PERSPECTIVE ON JUDICIAL BEHAVIOR (2006).

Readers interested in general arguments against judicial candor will find them cited (and criticized) in Shapiro, *In Defense of Judicial Candor, supra*. More specific arguments include Meir Dan-Cohen, HARMFUL THOUGHTS: ESSAYS ON LAW, SELF, AND MORALITY 28–32 (2002) (public compliance) and Scott Idleman, *A Prudential Theory of Judicial Candor*, 73 TEX. L. REV. 1307 (1995) (legitimacy). For an argument that particularly defends the Court's lack of candor in the affirmative action context, see Daniel Sabbagh, *Judicial Uses of Subterfuge: Affirmative Action Reconsidered*, 118 POL. SCI. Q. 411 (2003). Given the opacity of the French judicial regime discussed in the text, it is intriguing that Mr. Sabbagh is described as "a research fellow at the Centre d'études et de recherches internationales." He has elaborated on the need for "dissimulation" in the affirmative action context in a recent book, Daniel Sabbagh, EQUALITY AND TRANSPARENCY: A STRATEGIC PERSPECTIVE ON AFFIRMATIVE ACTION IN AMERICAN LAW (2007). At least one scholar has suggested that almost all Supreme Court opinions lack candor insofar as they attempt to use formalism to show that there is only one right answer. Erwin Chemerinsky, *The Rhetoric of Constitutional Law*, 100 MICH. L. REV. 2008, 2010–15 (2002). As should be apparent from the text, we disagree with Chemerinsky about the prevalence of this form of lack of candor.

In our discussion of transparency, we touch on cases dealing with historical evidence of federal power. Historical scholarship supporting at least some congressional power to act on states includes Evan Caminker, *State Sovereignty and Subordinacy: May Congress Commandeer State Officers to Implement Federal Law?* 95 COLUM. L. REV. 1001

(1995); Erik M. Jensen & Jonathan L. Entin, *Commandeering, the Tenth Amendment, and the Federal Requisition Power:* New York v. United States *Revisited,* 15 CONST. COM-MENTARY 355 (1998); Gene R. Nichol, *Justice Scalia and the* Printz *Case: The Trials of an Occasional Originalist,* 70 U. COLO. L. REV. 953 (1999); Saikrishna Prakash, *Field Office Federalism,* 79 VA. L. REV. 1957 (1993).

The classic—and still the best—account of the litigation leading up to *Brown v. Board of Education* is Richard Kluger, SIMPLE JUSTICE (1976) (recently reissued for the 50th anniversary of *Brown*). A contemporaneous overview of segregation during the pre-*Brown* period may be found in Charles S. Johnson, PATTERNS OF NEGRO SEGREGA-TION (1943). Northern residential patterns and the resulting de facto school segrega-tion is discussed in many sources, including Arnold R. Hirsch, MAKING THE SECOND GHETTO: RACE AND HOUSING IN CHICAGO, 1940–1960 (1983) and Will Maslow, *De Facto Public School Segregation,* 6 VILL. L. REV. 353 (1961). For information and further sources on occupational segregation, see, e.g., William A. Sundstrom, *The Color Line: Racial Norms and Discrimination in Urban Labor Markets, 1910–1950,* 54 J. ECON. HIST. 382 (1994).

For a sampling of the voluminous criticism of *Bush v. Gore,* see, e.g., Alan M. Dershowitz, SUPREME INJUSTICE: HOW THE HIGH COURT HIJACKED ELECTION 2000 (2001); Howard Gillman, THE VOTES THAT COUNTED: HOW THE COURT DECIDED THE 2000 PRESIDENTIAL ELECTION (2001); Erwin Chemerinsky, Bush v. Gore *Was not Justiciable,* 76 NOTRE DAME L. REV. 1093 (2001). For lukewarm support, mostly for the outcome rather than the reasoning, see Richard A. Posner, BREAKING THE DEADLOCK: THE 2000 ELECTION, THE CONSTITUTION, AND THE COURTS 4 (2001) (calling it "rough justice"); Michael W. McConnell, *Two-and-a-Half Cheers for* Bush v. Gore, 68 U. CHI. L. REV. 657 (2001).

Part V: Internalized Safeguards

This section takes an approach to judges and judging that is similar to that of the "new institutionalist" movement in political science scholarship. That movement rejects the attitudinalist credo that judicial behavior is purely a matter of personal and political preferences; the new institutionalists suggest that other factors—including legal prin-ciples and institutional and professional norms—play a dominant role in influencing judges' decisions. We found a pair of edited volumes particularly helpful: Cornell W. Clayton & Howard Gillman, eds., SUPREME COURT DECISION-MAKING: NEW INSTITU-TIONALIST APPROACHES (1999) and Howard Gillman & Cornell Clayton, THE SUPREME COURT IN AMERICAN POLITICS: NEW INSTITUTIONALIST INTERPRETATIONS (1999). Other sources, not strictly "new institutionalist" but similar in focus, include Ronald Kahn, THE SUPREME COURT AND CONSTITUTIONAL THEORY, 1953–1993 (1994); Tracey E. George & Lee Epstein, *On the Nature of Supreme Court Decision Making,* 86 AM.

POL. SCI. REV. 323 (1992); C. K. Rowland & Robert A. Carp, POLITICS AND JUDGMENT IN FEDERAL DISTRICT COURTS (1996); Frank Cross, *Appellate Court Adherence to Precedent*, 2 J. EMPIRICAL LEG. STUD. 369 (2005); Stephen Skowronek, *Order and Change*, 28 POLITY 91 (1995).

On the description and role of the legal culture, we are particularly indebted to Anthony T. Kronman, THE LOST LAWYER: FAILING IDEALS OF THE LEGAL PROFESSION (1993). The idea of professionalism and experience as aspects of good judgment has a long history, stretching at least as far back as Lord Coke's idea of the "artificial reason" of the law. Two good sources to begin an exploration of this aspect of Anglo-American legal reason are Allen D. Boyer, ed., LAW, LIBERTY, AND PARLIAMENT: SELECTED ESSAYS ON THE WRITINGS OF SIR EDWARD COKE (2004) and John V. Orth, HOW MANY JUDGES DOES IT TAKE TO MAKE A SUPREME COURT? (2006) (especially the title essay). For a survey of studies suggesting that confronting opposing arguments reduces cognitive biases and increases active, open-minded thinking, see Gregory Mitchell, *Mapping Evidence Law*, 2003 MICH. ST. L. REV. 1065, 1118 & n.108.

Readers interested in the Rehnquist Court's moderation of its initial positions on federalism and other issues might want to compare, for example, *Kimel v. Florida Bd. of Regents*, 528 U.S. 62 (2000) (invalidating federal statute on federalism grounds) and *Bd. of Trustees of the University of Alabama v. Garrett*, 531 U.S. 356 (2001) (same) with *Nevada Department of Human Resources v. Hibbs*, 538 U.S. 721 (2003) (upholding similar statute) and *Tennessee v. Lane*, 541 U.S. 509 (2004) (same). On the inconsistency between *Kimel* and *Garrett* on the one hand and *Hibbs* on the other, see Suzanna Sherry, *The Unmaking of a Precedent*, 2003 SUP. CT. REV. 231. Two Commerce Clause cases that appeared to signal imminent cutbacks on federal authority bore no fruit. See *United States v. Lopez*, 514 U.S. 549 (1995); *Morrison v. United States* 529 U.S. 598 (2000). The Court also changed its mind on antisodomy laws, as we discussed in chapter 10.

There is a large body of literature describing problems with the current selection process for federal judges, and suggesting various solutions. A good sampling includes Michael Comiskey, SEEKING JUSTICES: THE JUDGING OF SUPREME COURT NOMINEES (2004); Mark Tushnet, A COURT DIVIDED: THE REHNQUIST COURT AND THE FUTURE OF CONSTITUTIONAL LAW 329–33 (2005); Nancy Scherer, SCORING POINTS: POLITICIANS, ACTIVISTS, AND THE LOWER FEDERAL COURT APPOINTMENT PROCESS (2005); Charles Gardner Geyh, WHEN COURTS & CONGRESS COLLIDE: THE STRUGGLE FOR CONTROL OF AMERICA'S JUDICIAL SYSTEM (2006); Christopher L. Eisgruber, THE NEXT JUSTICE: REPAIRING THE SUPREME COURT APPOINTMENTS PROCESS (2007); Michael J. Gerhardt, *Prelude to Armageddon*, 8 GREEN BAG 2D 399 (2005); William P. Marshall, *Constitutional Law as Political Spoils*, 26 CARDOZO L. REV. 525 (2005); Lawrence B. Solum, *Judicial Selection: Ideology Versus Character*, 26 CARDOZO L. REV. 659 (2005).

For more on judicial character, see, e.g., Steven J. Burton, JUDGING IN GOOD FAITH (1992); Suzanna Sherry, *Judges of Character*, 38 WAKE FOREST L. REV. 793 (2003);

Lawrence B. Solum, *Virtue Jurisprudence: A Virtue-Centred Theory of Judging*, 34 METAPHILOSOPHY 178 (2003); Mark Tushnet, *Constitutional Interpretation, Character, and Experience*, 72 B.U. L. REV. 747 (1992); Lawrence B. Solum, *The Virtues and Vices of a Judge: An Aristotelian Guide to Judicial Selection*, 61 S. CAL. L. REV. 1735 (1988); John T. Noonan, Jr., *Education, Intelligence, and Character in Judges*, 71 MINN. L. REV. 1119 (1987).

Since one of the authors first suggested reinstating circuit riding, in a speech in early 2005, others have independently made the same suggestion. See Suzanna Sherry, *Politics and Judgment*, 70 MO. L. REV. 973, 986 (2005); Steven G. Calabresi & David C. Presser, *Reintroducing Circuit Riding: A Timely Proposal*, 90 MINN. L. REV. 1386 (2005); David R. Stras & Ryan W. Scott, *Retaining Life Tenure: The Case for a "Golden Parachute,"* 83 WASH. U. L.Q. 1397, 1415–18 (2005).

For studies of public perceptions of the Supreme Court, see, e.g., James L. Gibson et al., *Measuring Attitudes Toward the United States Supreme Court*, 47 AM. J. POL. SCI. 354 (2003); John M. Scheb II & William Lyons, *The Myth of Legality and Public Evaluation of the Supreme Court*, 81 SOC. SCI. Q. 928 (2000); Tom R. Tyler, *The Psychology of Public Dissatisfaction with Government*, in John R. Hibbing & Elizabeth Theiss-Morse, eds., WHAT IS IT ABOUT GOVERNMENT THAT AMERICANS DISLIKE? 227 (2001).

There is extensive political science literature adopting the attitudinalist view that a judge's politics determine his or her decisions. The seminal work is Jeffrey A. Segal & Harold J. Spaeth, THE SUPREME COURT AND THE ATTITUDINAL MODEL (1993); see also Jeffrey A. Segal et al., *Ideological Values and the Votes of U.S. Supreme Court Justices Revisited*, 57 J. POLITICS 812 (1995). One emerging caveat in the attitudinalist literature is that ideology matters less in cases with less political salience (which should come as no surprise, regardless of how large a role it plays in either type of case). See Isaac Unah & Ange-Marie Hancock, *U.S. Supreme Court Decision Making, Case Salience, and the Attitudinal Model*, 28 L. & POL'Y 295 (2006). An excellent recent critique of attitudinalism is Mark Graber, *Looking Off the Ball: Constitutional Law and American Politics*, OXFORD HANDBOOK ON PUBLIC LAW (forthcoming), available at SSRN, http://ssrn.com/abstract=1006032.

Legal scholars advocating popular constitutionalism include Larry D. Kramer, THE PEOPLE THEMSELVES: POPULAR CONSTITUTIONALISM AND JUDICIAL REVIEW (2004); Richard D. Parker, "HERE, THE PEOPLE RULE": A CONSTITUTIONAL POPULIST MANIFESTO (1994); Mark Tushnet, TAKING THE CONSTITUTION AWAY FROM THE COURTS (1999); Jeremy Waldron, THE DIGNITY OF LEGISLATION (1999); Scott E. Gant, *Judicial Supremacy and Nonjudicial Interpretation of the Constitution*, 24 HASTINGS CONST. L.Q. 359 (1997). For a critique of popular constitutionalism based on political scientists' empirical findings about popular constitutional culture, see Doni Gewirtzman, *Glory Days: Popular Constitutionalism, Nostalgia, and the True Nature of Constitutional Culture*, 93 GEO. L.J. 897 (2005); see also Erwin Chemerinsky, *Losing Faith: America*

Without Judicial Review? 98 MICH. L. REV. 1416 (2000) (critiquing Tushnet); Laurence H. Tribe, *The People's Court*, New York Times Book Review, Oct. 24, 2004, at 32 (critiquing Kramer).

For a description and critique of social constructionism, see Daniel A. Farber & Suzanna Sherry, BEYOND ALL REASON: THE RADICAL ASSAULT ON TRUTH IN AMERICAN LAW (1997). For descriptions of legal realism, see *id.*; Neil Duxbury, PATTERNS OF AMERICAN JURISPRUDENCE (1995); Laura Kalman, LEGAL REALISM AT YALE, 1927–1960 (1986); Laura Kalman, THE STRANGE CAREER OF LEGAL LIBERALISM (1996); G. Edward White, PATTERNS OF AMERICAN LEGAL THOUGHT (1978). John Henry Schlegel, AMERICAN LEGAL REALISM AND EMPIRICAL SOCIAL SCIENCE (1995) describes in particular the legal realist reliance on expertise and empirical data.

We are not alone in our view of law professors as making poor judges. For an article describing similar differences between scholars and judges, see Charles Fried, *Scholars and Judges: Reason and Power*, 23 HARV. J.L. & PUB. POL'Y 807 (1999). Empirical support for the proposition that law professors who become judges are likely to have the poor judicial temperament we describe is found in Tracey E. George, *Court Fixing*, 43 ARIZ. L. REV. 9 (2001). The lack of collaboration among law professors is documented in Tracey E. George & Chris Guthrie, *Joining Forces: The Role of Collaboration in the Development of Legal Thought*, 52 J. LEGAL EDUC. 559 (2002). A brief but pithy critique of the changes in the legal academy over the past quarter century or so is Richard Posner's memorial tribute to Bernard Meltzer, a wonderful teacher, scholar, and human being, 74 U. CHI. L. REV. 435 (2007).

Part VI: Case Studies

There has already been a great deal written about the constitutional aspects of the "war on terror." Some good starting places are Richard H. Fallon, Jr. & Daniel J. Meltzer, *Habeas Corpus Jurisdiction, Substantive Rights, and the War on Terror*, 120 HARV. L. REV. 2031 (2007); Oren Gross, *Chaos and Rules: Should Responses to Violent Crises Always be Constitutional?* 112 YALE L.J. 1011 (2003); Bruce Ackerman, *The Emergency Constitution*, 113 YALE L.J. 1029 (2004); Aharon Barak, *The Role of a Supreme Court in a Democracy, and the Fight Against Terrorism*, 58 U. MIAMI L. REV. 125 (2003); Noah Feldman, *Choices of Law, Choices of War*, 25 HARV. J.L. & PUB. POL'Y 457 (2002); Harold Hongju Koh, *The Spirit of the Laws*, 43 HARV. INT'L L.J. 23 (2002); David Luban, *The War on Terrorism and the End of Human Rights*, 22 PHIL. & PUB. POL'Y Q. 9 (Summer 2002). A detailed critique of the president's position and its legal rationale can be found in Derek Jinks & David Sloss, *Is the President Bound by the Geneva Conventions?* 90 CORNELL L. REV. 97 (2004).

For a sampling of views on abortion, see David A. Strauss, *Abortion, Toleration, and Moral Uncertainty*, 1992 SUP. CT. REV. 1; Ruth Bader Ginsburg, *Some Thoughts on*

Autonomy and Equality in Relation to Roe v. Wade, 63 N.C. L. REV. 375 (1985); John T. Noonan, Jr., *The Root and Branch of* Roe v. Wade, 63 NEB. L. REV. 668 (1984); Daniel Farber, *Legal Pragmatism and the Constitution*, 72 MINN. L. REV. 1331 (1988); Reva Siegel, *Reasoning from the Body: A Historical Perspective on Abortion Regulation and Questions of Equal Protection*, 44 STAN. L. REV. 261 (1992). For other discussions of stare decisis and the abortion issue, see Dawn Johnson, *Abortion: A Mixed and Unsettled Legacy*, in Craig M. Bradley, ed., THE REHNQUIST LEGACY 301 (2006); William S. Consovoy, *The Rehnquist Court and the End of Constitutional Stare Decisis:* Casey, Dickerson, *and the Consequences of Pragmatic Adjudication*, 2002 UTAH L. REV. 53. On Rehnquist's own view of stare decisis, see Earl M. Maltz, *No Rules in a Knife Fight: Chief Justice Rehnquist and the Doctrine of Stare Decisis*, 25 RUTGERS L.J. 669 (1994).

There is voluminous literature on the Supreme Court's affirmative action jurisprudence. Readers might want to start with Kent Greenawalt, DISCRIMINATION AND REVERSE DISCRIMINATION (1983); Herman Belz, EQUALITY TRANSFORMED: A QUARTER-CENTURY OF AFFIRMATIVE ACTION (1990); John Hart Ely, *The Constitutionality of Reverse Racial Discrimination*, 41 U. CHI. L. REV. 723 (1974); T. Alexander Aleinikoff, *A Case for Race-Consciousness*, 91 COLUM. L. REV. 1060 (1991); Paul Carrington, *Diversity!* 1992 UTAH L. REV. 1105; Elizabeth S. Anderson, *Integration, Affirmative Action, and Strict Scrutiny*, 77 N.Y.U. L. REV. 1195 (2002); Richard Sander, *A Systematic Analysis of Affirmative Action in American Law Schools*, 57 STAN. L. REV. 367 (2004); David L. Chambers et al., *The Real Impact of Eliminating Affirmative Action in American Law Schools: An Empirical Critique of Richard Sander's Study*, 57 STAN. L. REV. 1855 (2005); Richard Sander, *A Reply to Critics*, 57 STAN. L. REV. 1963 (2005); Neil S. Siegel, *Race-Conscious Student Assignment Plans: Balkanization, Integration, and Individualized Consideration*, 56 DUKE L.J. 781 (2006); Ian Ayres & Sydney Foster, *Don't Tell, Don't Ask: Narrow Tailoring After* Grutter *and* Gratz, 85 TEX. L. REV. 517 (2007).

Index

abortion, 6, 30, 80, 130, 141–55. *See also*
   Roe v. Wade
accountability, democratic, 23, 24–26, 98.
   See also countermajoritarian
   difficulty
administrative law
   as analogy, 40–43, 45, 54, 145, 154
   and discretion, 40–43
   doctrines of, 40–41
adversary system, 92, 93
affirmative action, 6, 30, 115, 130,
   157–66
Alito, Samuel, 152–54
arbitrary and capricious. *See* administrative
   law, doctrines of
Articles of Confederation, 100
attitudinalism. *See* legal academy,
   attitudinalism in

Berlin, Isaiah, 58
biases, cognitive, 72–73. *See also* decision
   making, expert
Bickel, Alexander, 23–24, 124, 127. *See also*
   countermajoritarian difficulty
Blackmun, Harry, 44, 116, 144
Blackstone, William, 13–14
Bolling v. Sharpe, 16
Bork, Robert, 51, 68, 118
Boumediene v. Bush, 138
Bowers v. Hardwick, 101–2
Brandeis, Louis, 70
Brennan, William, 109
Breyer, Stephen, 137
Brown v. Board of Education, 19, 47, 68, 73,
   106–8, 109
Buckley v. Valeo, 83
bumblebees, judges analogous to, 53

Burger, Warren, 116, 145
Bush, George H. W., 147
Bush, George W., 25, 54, 134–35
Bush v. Gore, 54, 110

Calhoun, John, 17, 18–19. *See also*
    interposition and nullification
Cardozo, Benjamin, 54, 56
Carrington, Paul, 130
character of judges. *See* constraints on
    judging, judicial character
Civil War, 12, 17, 19, 49
clerks, judicial. *See* judiciary, structure of
Clinton, William Jefferson, 129
Clinton v. New York, 16
cognitive biases. *See* biases, cognitive
Cohens v. Virginia, 17, 18
Coke, Lord Edward, 13–14, 43
common law, 54, 65–66, 69, 113–14
Congress. *See* legislature, federal
Constitution, 49
    amendments to, 23, 164
    drafting and ratification of, 23
    Due Process Clause of, 93
    Establishment Clause of, 16, 23, 44, 46
    interpretation of (*see* constitutional
        interpretation)
    tensions in, 23
constitutional interpretation
    difficulty of, 22–23
    theories of, 3–4, 26–29, 31, 36, 39, 46,
        65–69, 99–101
constraints on judging, 4–5, 6, 27
    deliberation, 6, 71, 90–92, 114
    feedback loop, 115
    incrementalism, 55, 61, 96, 98,
        105–10, 114
    judicial character, 58, 91, 118–19
    judicial structure, 44, 56, 67, 87–96,
        119–21
    precedent (*see* precedent[s])
    professional norms, 6, 113–16, 128–29 (*see
        also* lawyers)
    public scrutiny, 94–96, 98, 128–29 (*see
        also* media)
    reasoned elaboration, 6, 43–45, 51–52, 98
    transparency, 6, 96–104, 109, 114–15, 157,
        162–65

contraception, 64, 67
countermajoritarian difficulty, 23–26, 87,
    124–25. *See also* Bickel, Alexander;
    judicial review, and democracy
courts. *See* judging; judiciary, structure of;
    Supreme Court
Critical Legal Studies, 38, 130. *See also*
    postmodernism

de Tocqueville, Alexis, 128
decision making
    expert, 56–58, 71, 73–75, 134–36,
        141–42, 144
    judicial, 58, 71–72, 74, 125, 143 (*see also*
        constraints on judging; discretion;
        judges; judgment; opinions,
        judicial)
democracy, 142–43, 154
    and judicial review (*see* judicial
        review, and democracy; *see also*
        countermajoritarian difficulty;
        Supreme Court, accountability of)
departmentalism, 15–16, 30
Dewey, John, 47
Dickerson v. United States, 83
discretion, 3–6, 27, 35, 37, 99, 103–4,
    114, 116
    constraints on (*see* constraints on
        judging)
    inevitability of, 22–23, 28–29
    legislative, 38–39
    See also administrative law, and
        discretion; judgment; judging,
        theories of; uncertainty
Doe v. Bolton, 141–42
Douglas, William O., 64, 145
dualism, constitutional. *See* constitutional
    interpretation, theories of
Due Process Clause. *See* Constitution, Due
    Process Clause of

Eisenhower, Dwight, 116
electoral college, 25
Ely, John, 127
Environmental Protection Agency, 39
Establishment Clause. *See* Constitution,
    Establishment Clause of
executive branch. *See* president

Federal Communications Commission, 25, 41, 145
Federal Reserve, 25, 41, 117
federalism, 16–17, 18, 21, 53, 115. *See also* nationalism
Federalist Papers, 76, 78
First Amendment. *See* speech, freedom of
foreign affairs, 16
formalism, 52, 81, 97, 99, 103–4
foundationalism. *See* constitutional interpretation, theories of
foxes (vs. hedgehogs), 27, 58, 117, 118
Friends of the Earth, Inc. v. Laidlaw Environmental Services, Inc., 80

gay rights, 30, 101–2, 110, 115
Geneva Conventions, 150–51, 153, 154
Ginsburg, Ruth Bader, 103–4
Giuliani, Rudy, 117
Gonzalez, Alberto, 134
Gonzalez v. Carhart, 153
Greenhouse, Linda, 119
Gratz v. Bollinger, 157–59, 162–64
Griswold v. Connecticut, 49
Grutter v. Bollinger, 157–65

H.L. v. Matheson, 146
Hamdan v. Rumsfeld, 138
Hamdi v. Rumsfeld, 135–38
Hamilton, Alexander, 67, 76
Hand, Learned, 54, 118
Harlan, John Marshall, 164
hedgehogs. *See* foxes
Hodgson v. Minnesota, 147
Holmes, Oliver Wendell, Jr., 6, 54, 70, 108–9, 113
homosexuality. *See* gay rights
Humphrey, Hubert, 116

incrementalism. *See* constraints on judging
interposition and nullification, 18, 19
intratextualism. *See* constitutional interpretation, theories of

Jackson, Michael, 129
Jackson, Robert, 31, 77–78, 91, 109
James, William, 47, 63
Jay, John, 76

Jefferson, Thomas, 18
Johnson, Lyndon, 106
journalists. *See* media
judges
    appointment of, 5, 26, 87, 116–19, 125
    character of (*see* constraints on judging)
    constraints on (*see* constraints on judging)
    French, 103–4
    as generalists, 93
    See also discretion; judging; opinions, judicial; Supreme Court
judgment, 6, 29, 31, 53–59, 118–19. *See also* constraints on judging; decision making; discretion; judging
judging
    activist, 24, 29, 96, 124
    constraints on (*see* constraints on judging; precedent[s])
    institutional context of, 44, 56, 67, 105, 115–16 (*see also* judiciary, structure of)
    norms of (*see* constraints on judging)
    politics as influencing (*see* politics, as an influence on judges)
    theories of, 31, 123 (*see also* pragmatism)
    values (*see* opinions, judicial, values in)
    See also constraints on judging; discretion; judgment; judges; opinions, judicial
judicial review
    critiques of, 3–4
    and democracy, 5, 7, 11, 13, 19, 21–31, 98, 124, 165–66 (*see also* countermajoritarian difficulty; popular constitutionalism)
    history of, 12–13
    as inevitable, 11–19, 25
    in other countries, 3, 11–12, 51, 95
judiciary, structure of
    as constraint (*see* constraints on judging)
    description of, 5, 88–89, 119–20

Kalven, Harry, 127, 140
Katzenbach, Nicholas, 118
Kennedy, Anthony, 44, 83, 89, 102, 138, 149, 153–54

law school. *See* lawyers, education of; legal
    academy
Lawrence v. Texas, 101–2, 109–10
lawyers, 92, 93
    education of, 5, 113–14, 128–29
    professional norms of, 74, 113–16
legal academy, 123–30
    attitudinalism in, 124–25
    novelty in, 126–28
    popular constitutionalism in (*see* popular
        constitutionalism)
    postmodernism in (*see* postmodernism)
    as preparation for judging, 53, 113–14,
        127–28
    role of, 37, 96
    suggested improvements, 129–30
legal education. *See* lawyers, education of;
    legal academy
legal realism, 42, 126, 130
Legal Tender Cases, 73
legislature
    state, 14
    federal, 13–14, 24, 30, 73, 78, 100
    House of Representatives, 26
    Senate, 14, 25, 26
liberty. *See* rights
Llewellyn, Karl, 54, 57
Lochner v. New York, 50–52
Lujan v. Defenders of Wildlife, 80

Madison, James, 17, 18–19, 67, 76–77
majority rule. *See* judicial review, and
    democracy
Marbury v. Madison, 12, 38, 73
Marshall, John, 12, 17–19, 22, 70
Marshall, Thurgood, 106
Martin v. Hunter's Lessee, 17
Massachusetts v. EPA, 80
media, 94–95, 119
Metro Broadcasting v. FCC, 165
minimalism. *See* constitutional
    interpretation, theories of
Miranda v. Arizona, 79, 82–83
Mobbs, Michael, 151–52

NAACP, 106
nationalism, 17–18. *See also* federalism
New Deal, 27, 40

New York v. United States, 99–100
nullification. *See* interposition and
    nullification

Occupational Safety and Health
    Administration, 39, 55
O'Connor, Sandra Day, 83, 89, 100, 101–2,
    117, 136, 146, 149
opinions, judicial
    constraints on (*see* constraints on
        judging)
    and precedent (*see* precedent[s])
    reasoned elaboration in (*see* constraints
        on judging)
    relevant factors, 46–48, 87
    values in, 46–50, 136, 152
originalism. *See* constitutional
    interpretation, theories of

Parliament, 13–14
*Penn Central Transportation Co. v. City of
    New York*, 80
Planned Parenthood Ass'n v. Ashcroft,
    146–47
Planned Parenthood v. Casey, 80, 141
politics, as an influence on judges, 3–5, 27,
    29, 44–48, 56, 96, 117–18, 123–25, 130,
    134–36, 139–43, 145–46, 154
popular constitutionalism, 21, 24, 26–27,
    29–30, 124–26
populism. *See* popular constitutionalism
Posner, Richard, 38–39, 55
postmodernism, 38, 125–26
Powell, Lewis, 64, 158
pragmatism, 36, 47, 80
precedent(s), 5, 99, 101–2
    in abortion cases, 80, 147–55
    arguments for adherence to, 68, 70–74,
        150–51
    bedrock, 68–70
    as constraint, 6, 7, 67, 81–84, 87,
        89, 98
    following, 78–84, 97, 138, 159–60
    and originalism, 65–69
    and rule of law, 36, 64–69, 80
    sources of, 75–78
    and stability, 69, 71–74
    and textualism, 85

president, 13, 14–15, 25
  power of, 77–78, 134–38
  precedents of, 77 (*see also* precedent[s], sources of)
  See also electoral college
Printz v. United States, 99–100
professionalism of judges. *See* constraints on judging

Randall v. Sorrell, 83, 99–100
Reagan, Ronald, 116, 117
realism, legal. *See* legal realism
reasoning, judicial. *See* common law; constraints on judging
Reconstruction, 19, 27, 50
referenda, 30
Regents of the University of California v. Bakke, 157–58, 162
Rehnquist, William, 83, 89, 102, 115, 117, 146–47
rights, 11, 14, 22–25, 30, 41, 43, 46, 63, 65, 67, 80, 150
Roane, Spencer, 8
Roberts, John, 83–84, 154
Roe v. Wade, 80, 108, 109, 141–45, 147–50
rules and standards. *See* standards, rules and
rule of law, 4, 64–69, 71, 89, 98–99, 110, 114, 130, 163–64. *See also* precedent(s), and rule of law; stability

Scalia, Antonin, 64–67, 71, 80, 83, 100, 102–3, 127–28, 137–38, 164
Schiavo, Terri, 129, 145
Securities and Exchange Commission, 25, 39, 41, 55
segregation, racial, 12, 24, 45, 47, 72, 106–8. *See also* affirmative action; *Brown v. Board of Education*
Selective Service Act, 91
Simpson, O. J., 129
speech, freedom of, 13, 46–47, 49, 99–100, 108–9
Souter, David, 137, 149
sovereignty, popular. *See* popular constitutionalism

stability, 5, 16, 19, 36–37, 69, 71–74, 84. *See also* precedent(s); rule of law
standards, rules and, 47, 65, 78–80
stare decisis. *See* precedent(s)
states, as constitutional arbiters, 14, 16–19. *See also* federalism
Steel Seizure Case. See Youngstown Sheet & Tube Co. v. Sawyer
Stenberg v. Carhart, 154
Stevens, John Paul, 137–38
Stewart, Potter, 144
Story, Joseph, 17
Sunstein, Cass, 28, 79
Supreme Court, 88–92, 96, 98, 102
  accountability of, 24, 56–57
  role of, 5–6
  selection of justices (*see* judges, appointment of)
  suggested changes in, 92, 119–21
  See also judging; judicial review

Taft, William H., IV, 134
terrorism, war on, 6, 100, 130, 133–40
textualism. *See* constitutional interpretation, theories of
Thayer, James Bradley, 28
thinking, critical, 51, 73–74, 114. *See also* decision making, expert
Thomas, Clarence, 66, 83, 102, 137–38
translation theory. *See* constitutional interpretation, theories of
transparency. *See* constraints on judging
Truman, Harry, 48, 107

uncertainty, 22–23, 27–29, 32, 38, 40–43, 45, 55, 86, 88, 119, 165–66, 170
United States v. Booker, 116

values, in judging. *See* opinions, judicial, values in

Warren, Earl, 12
Webster v. Reproductive Health Services, 146–47
Wechsler, Herbert, 45, 127

Youngstown Sheet & Tube Co. v. Sawyer, 16

Printed in the USA/Agawam, MA
February 1, 2023

805235.010